The *New* Dudley Genealogies

THE DESCENDANTS OF FRANCIS OF CONCORD [MASSACHUSETTS]

COMPILED BY

Reverend Gary P. Dudley

HERITAGE BOOKS
2012

HERITAGE BOOKS

AN IMPRINT OF HERITAGE BOOKS, INC.

Books, CDs, and more—Worldwide

For our listing of thousands of titles see our website
at
www.HeritageBooks.com

Published 2012 by
HERITAGE BOOKS, INC.
Publishing Division
100 Railroad Ave. #104
Westminster, Maryland 21157

International Standard Book Numbers
Paperbound: 978-0-7884-1655-2
Clothbound: 978-0-7884-9231-0

Dedication

To my wonderful wife of 29 years

BONNIE JO (EDWARDS) DUDLEY
May 24, 1951–October 23, 1999

"The soul takes flight into the world that is invisible, and there arriving she is sure of bliss, and forever dwells in paradise."
–Plato, as read by Queen Jane Grey Dudley

Contents

Preface

This is the second number of the New Genealogies. The first (on the Descendants of William of Guilford, Ct.) met with great response. I had no idea (and neither did the publisher), that the first printing would sell so fast! For those who do not have a copy of that tome, this should help explain these new books.

I readily admit that this will be taken as an attempt to "improve" or "replace" Dean Dudley's monumental "*History of the Dudley Family*", the acknowledged classic genealogy of our great and historical family, (and has become a "bible" of our family) but it is not. Since this humble attempt at compiling a number of resources has fallen into your hands, it should be taken as an attempt to centralize all that is currently known of the families. This was done for a number of reasons:

1. There are now a more books that have listed various Dudley lines, some complementing Dean Dudley's work, some augmenting it, and some disputing. These HAD to be reconciled to *The History*.....someone had to do it.

2. Many have stated that Dean Dudley had many, many errors in his work. This was both true and false. The problem has usually been the *way* he published his work, and the scope of it. *The History of the Dudley Family* was published during the years 1886-1894, with a supplement being published in 1898. It consisted of 11 volumes (12, with the supplement), usually published one year apart. Add to this that he published at least two volumes entitled "Dudley Genealogies" and the picture becomes foggier. To which volume of *The History* are we referring? What made Dean Dudley's work so complicated is that when people saw The Concord Dudley's listed in Volume 5, they assumed that was all the work he did on them. It was *not*! There were corrections and additions in subsequent volumes, and one had to dig through all 11 volumes to find the completed line. The problem is worse for those of Gov. Thomas' line. It was time someone compiled them all together in ONE place.

3. Genealogy has become an art and science. It has also become a popular pastime. Because of all this, many new reference books and materials have become available to the genealogist. New names, dates, and research places are available that Dean Dudley could only have dreamed of. The most obvious improvement is that Vital Records (Town Record books containing the birth, marriage, and death dates that occurred within the town), once only available by going directly to the town in question and reading them (as Dean Dudley did), are now available by going to one of the many, many, libraries that have a genealogy department. All of this has borne fruit, many of the things that Dean Dudley left out are now able to be put back in. Many of his REAL errors can be eliminated, his guesses either substantiated or corrected. This is the purpose of these new genealogies.

Dean Dudley's work will NEVER be replaced. It is a monument to our Family Name, and to the efforts of that great antiquarian.

The scope of this work

These genealogies will be done in volumes. Each volume will initially contain ONE line, this second being the Concord, Massachusetts branch. I plan to put out a separate volume for the Gov. Thomas line. A future volume will contain the various Virginia Branches, another on the newly found Bedfordshire branch, and another the smaller Dudley lines. I expect approximately seven volumes when done.

I do NOT plan on many biographies—IF I include any at all, I may include a biography of the founder of the line. Dean Dudley has the rest in his work, simply look them up. The reason is very simple—this is NOT a history of the family, but only compiled genealogies. I will have many small sketches with the names of the people, mostly notes. This really should suffice.

I have only followed female lines out to their marriage and children. I have not gone farther because this is a genealogy of the DUDLEY's. There is enough information for those of other families to find their connections here.

I have not included sources in this volume, for to list the number of sources and other records used would almost take up another volume. There is an extensive Bibliography in the back of this volume which will show you the main sources used. If you desperately need to know the actual source of a given entry, please write or email me, and I will send it to you.

The genealogies follow the Register format most familiar to genealogists. I have divided them into generations for ease of use, and everything is numbered and should be quite easy to follow. Of course, an index is in the back of each volume.

Upon completion, all volumes will be updated with any corrections and additions, and bound together. They will still adhere to the "Line", or "Branch" format for ease of research, and each line will have their own index—again, for ease of use.

I would hope that if anyone finds any errors, or have any additions or suggestions, please send them to me either email at garydud@juno.com, or to my home address:

102 Saddlebrook
San Antonio, Tx 78245.

Rev. Gary P. Dudley

Introduction
The Concord Branch

While so closely located to the Governor Thomas Dudley line, this branch of the family is as different from the other branch as night is from day. In a sense, so it must be. Every family has something different to offer, and usually has its own personality....and so it is with the Concord branch.

This is a completely different line from the Guilford branch of the Dudley's in more ways than one. First, there is almost nothing known of the founder of the line, Francis. Secondly, this branch of the family did NOT stay in place. They spread out with the country, populating California, Wisconsin, Ohio, Washington State—just everywhere! One of its sons was an actual participant in the writing of the California Constitution!

In addition, this family had more than its share of its men serving in the Civil War. One family, Gen. Peter Dudley's, had 12 of its sons serve. There was even a DIVORCE in this family over the war! Of note, so far it seems that all the Dudley's in all the different branches of the family served with the Union.

The Concord branch also had more farmers than the others, and, for the most part, had less scholars. This line, then, is more middle class than some of the other branches.

There will be no biography of its founder. As I have already stated, almost nothing is known of him—not even his birth place. Dean Dudley postulates that his father may have been named John. He writes:

> "There was a John Dudley living at Charlestown, Mass., 1655-71. Their ages and social status were favorable to this supposition. I find in Middlesex Court Files the following items about John and Francis Dudley: File No. 4, package 69, A.D. 1665, John Dudley was a witness in an action against Mr. Wall. In a case concerning a John Cromwell's debts, John Dudley was a witness, Oct 6, 1661. The estate of Cromwell owed him for wood. John Dudley had a suit Dec 16, 1669, for his services in 1662. "John Dudley of Charlestown, aged 55 years," was a witness in a case March 30, 1671. He conveyed 14 acres of land "on Mystic side" to W. Stilson, June 10, 1671. "Francis Dudley, aged about 26 years" was a witness "2mo.8d., 1666;" and again 8 mo. 4d, 1670, Francis Dudley of Concord was a witness."[1]

_____

[1]"Dudley, Dean History of the Dudley Family, Vol 5, pg 558.

However, Dean Dudley stops short of saying that John WAS the father. In light of that, and lack of other evidence, so will I. So again we are stuck, like the Gov Thomas and Guilford branches, with a line without verifiable roots. Add to that The History of the town of Concord, Middlesex County, Massachusetts, by Lemuel Shattuck (1835), which says: "Francis Dudley of Concord, Mass., was the ancestor of the Sutton Dudleys (supposed to have been a relative of Gov. Thomas Dudley), and was born in England, and immigrating to his country settled at Concord, Mass., about 1663." Now there is *no* evidence for any of that, but does go to show the confusion over the branches of the family.

I will also question Dean Dudley that Francis seemed to be of high social status, and respected in the community. I believe that it would be fair to say that Francis *married* into a prominent family. His sons seemed to have been apprenticed, which explains why there are so many blacksmiths and housewrights. Had he been noble upon arrival in America, or had, at least, a noble upbringing, this probably would not have happened, and the family would have far more politicians like (for instance) Gov. Thomas' line did.. The questions posed here, however, may finally be answered when other documents, such as will probates and other court records, are found. This family did, however, maintain literacy throughout its generations—especially among its women. This is a rarity in pioneer families.

As the 1600's were not noted for their record keeping, it is not surprising that roots to England were lost. I also had that problem with my own branch—even in the days of the telephone and computers—until a lucky phone call helped out after five years! America, at the time of Francis, was just being formed. Someday, perhaps we will know even more.

A note on the records

Dean Dudley stated that the records of Concord and adjoining areas were confusing. He was a master of understatement. Justine B. Gengras, whom volunteered to assist me in the research for this book, and I almost (actually, we did) get migraine headaches with the records (the printed Vital Records, to be exact). They really were in a mess. Untold hours went into figuring out who went with whom, and trying to figure out *why* Dean Dudley placed a few of the people. In Dean Dudley's work, we found multiple marriages to the same people, duplicate children, children out of order with no indication of which wife they went with, and even a *sex change*!!! (obviously the result of a misreading of original records) What lies within, then, is very different from Dean Dudley's original work. Ms. Gengras and myself spent hundreds of hours not only pouring over the records (now available in print), but also contacted descendants, and re-verifying *everything* multiple times to ensure the accuracy of this work. While we both totally admire Mr. Dudley for accomplishing what he did, with what he had, there were so many errors that we can say without hesitation, THIS is the most accurate presentation of this branch ever to have been in print. Even so, we are *still* not completely comfortable with the Sudbury/Wayland/Westford Dudley's. The records were *so* confusing that you may wish to double check these before adding them to your lines.

Note that where I differ with Dean Dudley, and other sources, I readily state what the Vital Record., church or town records, and Dean Dudley, had to say, and the reason I chose the specific data. In many cases, you will see the conflicting records, and the problem researching what certain aspects of this branch entailed. Overall, I believe my decisions were logical. Be aware, however, that though I had assistance with the compiling and checking of the data, that the ultimate decision to resolve any problems was *mine* alone, and therefore any errors that are made were mine only. Note also, that many times I state the source for differing dates and places so that you know the vital record I based my decision on

Please note: for those of you, like me, who are geographically challenged when it comes to Massachusetts towns, you will find numerous references to Sudbury, Acton, etc. Some of these references seem to relate to the same town–and depending on the time, they DO! Here, briefly, is a time line of town name changes:

Concord, original town settled 1635
Acton, granted from Concord 1735
Sudbury, original town settled 1639
East Sudbury came from Sudbury 1780
East Sudbury became Wayland 1835 (new name, same town).

In addition, when some of them migrated to N.Y., please note that CATO became MERIDIAN in the early 1800's. This is only a *partial* list. Massachusetts towns were expanding and merging so much during this period that is was very difficult to keep track. There are extensive listings of the changes available on the Internet, should you be so equipped.

That should help you.

Rev Gary P. Dudley, B.S., M.A.
June, 2000

Acknowledgments

I can say with certainty, that this work would not be as accurate as it is without the help of Justine B. Gengras, a direct descendant of this family. She selflessly poured hundreds of hours into helping me with this work, and in the process taught me more about research than I had known. God Bless you.

In addition, the following folks have provided much information on their ancestors. They are all descendants of this family.

Marilyn Dudley Fogg, Arlene Dudley Parker, Karen Dudley Howard, Rob Fox, Rebecca Anderson, Pam Miles, Barbara Curran Christensen, and Karen Hill-Walker.

I know there are more than these–and that doesn't include all the folks at the San Antonio Central Library, Genealogy Department, and the folks at the Carver Center for Genealogical Research in Houston, Texas–AND the kind people at the San Antonio Historical and Genealogical Society for their help! God bless all of you!

If I have missed anyone, I am truly sorry.

Rev. Gary Dudley

1. **Francis Dudley** b. abt. 1640, England, m. 26 Oct 1665, in Concord, Middlesex, Mass., **Sarah Wheeler**, b. 30 Jan 1639/40, Concord, Middlesex, Mass., (daughter of **George Wheeler**) d. 12 Dec 1713, Concord, Middlesex, Mass. Francis died abt 1705, Concord, Middlesex, Mass. Moved to Concord about 1663. Was a soldier in King Philip's Indian war, and got 1 pound, 12 shillings for his participation on 29 Feb 1675.

        Children:

2.   i   **Mary Dudley** b. 7 Feb 1666/67.
3.   ii   **Joseph Dudley** b. 1666.
       iii   **Benjamin Dudley** b. abt 1677, d. 6 Jan 1681/82, Concord, Middlesex, Mass.
       iv   **Sarah Dudley** d. 4 Aug 1701, Concord, Middlesex, Mass.
4.   v   **John Dudley** b. 10 Mar 1674/75.
5.   vi   **Francis Dudley**.
6.   vii   **Samuel Dudley** b. 27 Apr 1682.

2. **Mary Dudley** (1.Francis[1]) b. 7 Feb 1666/67, Concord, Middlesex, Mass., m. 7 Jun 1688,
   in Concord, Middlesex, Mass., **Joseph Fletcher**, (son of **Francis Fletcher** and
   Elizabeth Wheeler). Mary died 28 Apr 1705, Concord, Middlesex, Mass. All children
   verified by Concord V.R.

   Children:
   - i **Joseph Fletcher** b. 7 June 1689, Concord, Middlesex, Mass.
   - ii **Benjamin Fletcher** b. 1 Jan 1690, Concord, Middlesex, Mass.
   - iii **Samuel Fletcher** b. 20 Nov 1692, Concord, Middlesex, Mass.
   - iv **Ebenezer Fletcher** b. 23 Mar 1693/94, Concord, Middlesex, Mass., d. 7 Jan
     1705/06, Concord, Middlesex, Mass.
   - v **Mary Fletcher** b. 17 Dec 1695, Concord, Middlesex, Mass.
   - vi **Francis Fletcher** b. 12 Nov 1698, Concord, Middlesex, Mass.
   - vii **Jane Fletcher** b. 29 Nov 1700, Concord, Middlesex, Mass.

3. **Joseph Dudley** (1.Francis[1]) b. 1666, Concord, Middlesex, Mass., occupation: Blacksmith
   and farmer, m. 25 Feb 1690/91, in Concord, Middlesex, Mass., **Abigail Goble**, b. 19 Jan
   1668/69, Concord, Middlesex, Mass., (daughter of **Thomas Goble** and **Mary**) d. 19 Dec
   1705, Concord, Middlesex, Mass. Joseph died 3 Nov 1702, Concord, Middlesex, Mass. His
   father helped to settle his estate, which was valued at 72 pounds--his house and land at Concord
   being worth 34 pounds, and land at Sudbury worth 32 pounds. Abigail was the administratrix,
   and his father and Thomas Goble signed her bond. John Wheeler was appointed guardian for
   the children. Joseph was the oldest son, so had a double portion of the estate which was given
   him in 1718 and was worth 84 pounds.

   Children:
   - 7. i **Abigail Dudley** b. 11 Jun 1692.
   - 8. ii **Sarah Dudley** b. 11 Jun 1692.
   - 9. iii **Jane Dudley** b. 9 Mar 1693/94.
   - 10. iv **Joseph Dudley** b. 20 Apr 1697.
   - 11. v **Benjamin Dudley** b. 20 Mar 1698/99.
   - 12. vi **Mary Dudley** b. 8 Feb 1701.
   - 13. vii **Sibillah Dudley** b. 22 Sep 1702.

4. **John Dudley** (1.Francis[1]) b. 10 Mar 1674/75, Concord, Middlesex, Mass., m. 19 May
   1697, in Concord, Middlesex, Mass., **Hannah Poulter**, b. 4 Mar 1674/75, Billerica,
   Middlesex, Mass., (daughter of **John Poulter** and **Rachel Eliot**) d. 20 Dec 1707,
   Concord, Middlesex, Mass.

   Hannah: It appears that Hannah may have died trying to bear the son that died on the same
   date. Her sister, Rachel, had a son (Jonathan Brown) who married Sibillah Dudley, daughter of
   Joseph and Abigail. Note that Dean Dudley lists her surname as "POULTIER". It was found

more frequently as listed here.

Children:

14.   i   **John Dudley** b. 16 Aug 1699.

         ii   **Hannah Dudley** b. 9 Mar 1702/03, Concord, Middlesex, Mass., d. 18 Oct 1716, Concord, Middlesex, Mass.

         iii   **Sarah Dudley** b. 16 Feb 1705/06.

         iv   **Son** b. 20 Dec 1707, Concord, Middlesex, Mass., d. 20 Dec 1707, Concord, Middlesex, Mass.

5. **Francis Dudley** (1.Francis[1]) m. (1) **Sarah**, m. (2) **Abigail**. There is no confirmation from Vital or Church records for this child. He comes from Dean Dudley only.

         Children by Sarah:

         i   **Samuel Dudley** b. 1 Aug 1700, Concord, Middlesex, Mass.

         Children by Abigail:

         ii   **Francis Dudley** b. 10 Dec 1706. This child is doubtful. Dean Dudley has another Francis born on the same date to Samuel Dudley and Abigail King.

6. **Samuel Dudley** (1.Francis[1]) b. 27 Apr 1682, Concord, Middlesex, Mass., occupation: Town Clerk, m. (1) 1 Nov 1704, in Concord, Middlesex, Mass., **Abigail King**, d. 9 Aug 1720, Littleton, Middlesex, Mass., m. (2) ABT. 1721, in Littleton, Middlesex, Mass., **Lydia Weatherbee**, b. abt 1693, Stow, Middlesex, Mass., d. 27 Mar 1742, Douglas, Worcester, Mass., m. (3) 25 Nov 1747, in Uxbridge, Worcester, Mass., **Sarah Shepherd**, b. ABT. 1726, d. 29 Apr 1797, Douglas, Worcester, Mass. Samuel died 27 May 1777, Douglas, Worcester, Mass. Samuel moved to Littleton in 1714/15, and was town clerk in 1716/17, and moved from there to Sutton about 1728, and thence to Douglas about 1745. Note that children David, Jonathan, and Abigail are TRIPLETS (the only set in this branch) and are noted so in the V.R.

   Abigail: She may have also have been named Abigail Rogers.

Sarah: Douglas V.R. 173 states: she died "in her 71st yr."

         Children by Abigail King:

15.   i   **Samuel Dudley** b. 28 Jul 1705.

16.   ii   **Francis Dudley** b. 10 Dec 1706.

17.   iii   **David Dudley** b. 4 Nov 1709.

18.   iv   **Jonathan Dudley** b. 4 Nov 1709.

         v   **Abigail Dudley** b. 4 Nov 1709, Concord, Middlesex, Mass. Died young.

19.   vi   **Mary Dudley** b. 24 Aug 1711.

         vii   **Sarah Dudley** b. 28 Jul 1713, Concord, Middlesex, Mass.

         viii   **Abigail Dudley** b. 28 Oct 1714, Littleton, Middlesex, Mass., m. 25 May 1735, in Sutton, Worcester, Mass., **Benjamin Morse**.

         ix   **Mercy Dudley** b. 22 Feb 1715/16, Littleton, Middlesex, Mass., d. 12 Feb 1789, Cornish, Sullivan, N.H. Dean Dudley has her listed as Mary, but the Littleton V.R. says "Marcy", and the NEHGR has an article listing her as "Mercy."

I accepted Mercy as it was a common name at the time. In addition, IF Dean Dudley were right, he had her marrying Samuel Chase at age 11! Her sister Mary, born 1711 made much more sense.

20. x **Peter Dudley** b. 13 Sep 1718.

21. xi **Rogers Dudley** b. 9 Aug 1720.

22. xii **Prudence Dudley**.

    Children by Lydia Weatherbee:

   xiii **Paul Dudley** b. 24 Sep 1721, Littleton, Middlesex, Mass., d. 24 Jun 1726, Littleton, Middlesex, Mass.

   xiv **Charles Dudley** b. 10 Dec 1722, Littleton, Middlesex, Mass.

23. xv **William Dudley** b. 28 May 1726.

24. xvi **Lydia Dudley** b. abt 1729.

    Children by Sarah Shepherd:

25. xvii **Douglassa Dudley** b. 9 Sep 1748.

Third Generation

7. **Abigail Dudley** (3.Joseph[2], 1.Francis[1]) b. 11 Jun 1692, m. 17 Dec 1713, in Concord,
Middlesex, Mass., **John Davis**, occupation: Doctor, d. abt 1762, Acton, Middlesex, Mass.
There's no confirmed birth date for Abigail in Concord V.R. Dean Dudley is the only source.
However, since records for the 6 children he stated that she had were confirmed, I have
included her. She may have either been born elsewhere, or her birth was simply not recorded.
> *Children:*
> i **John Davis** b. 15 Jul 1714, Concord, Middlesex, Mass.
> ii **Ezekiel Davis** b. 8 Jun 1717, Concord, Middlesex, Mass.
> iii **Micah Davis** (details excluded).
> iv **Isaac Davis** b. 24 Oct 1723, Concord, Middlesex, Mass., d. 28 Feb 1740,
> Acton, Middlesex, Mass.
> v **Abigail Davis** b. 22 Mar 1726/27, Concord, Middlesex, Mass.
> vi **Samuel Davis** b. 23 Apr 1730, Concord, Middlesex, Mass.

8. **Sarah Dudley** (3.Joseph[2], 1.Francis[1]) b. 11 Jun 1692, m. 31 Oct 1716, in Concord,
Middlesex, Mass., **Jonathan Marble**. Sarah is the supposed twin to Abigail, was alive 14
Jan 1750. No record of her birth in Concord V.R. Her marriage is confirmed. Her name IS in
the Middlesex Probate file #6474, so she DID exist and no birth seems to have been recorded
for whatever reason. Sarah and Jonathan relocated to Marlborough, as all children were born
there, confirmed through the Marlborough V.R.
Jonathan: Name also spelled "Marable."
> *Children:*
> i **Mary Marble** b. 10 Sep 1717, Marlborough, Middlesex, Mass.
> ii **Joseph Marble** b. 20 Mar 1719, Marlborough, Middlesex, Mass.
> iii **Jonathan Marble** b. 27 Mar 1721, Marlborough, Middlesex, Mass.
> iv **Jedidiah Marble** b. 7 Oct 1722, Marlborough, Middlesex, Mass.
> v **Elizabeth Marble** b. 28 Sep 1724, Marlborough, Middlesex, Mass.
> vi **Samuel Marble** b. 5 Aug 1726, Marlborough, Middlesex, Mass.
> vii **Child** b. 26 Apr 1727, Marlborough, Middlesex, Mass., d. 26 Apr 1727.
> Stillborn.
> viii **Sibill Marble** b. 26 Jun 1730, Marlborough, Middlesex, Mass.
> ix **Jotham Marble** b. 28 Jul 1732, Marlborough, Middlesex, Mass.
> x **Sarah Marble** b. 17 Apr 1734, Marlborough, Middlesex, Mass.
> xi **Nathan Marble** b. 11 Jul 1735, Marlborough, Middlesex, Mass.

9. **Jane Dudley** (3.Joseph[2], 1.Francis[1]) b. 9 Mar 1693/94, Concord, Middlesex, Mass., m.
23 Mar 1713/14, in Watertown, Middlesex, Mass., **Samuel Wood**.
> *Children:*
> i **Mary Wood** b. 30 Oct 1714, Concord, Middlesex, Mass.

ii   **Samuel Wood** b. 23 Mar 1715/16, Concord, Middlesex, Mass.

iii **Rebekah Wood** b. 26 Jan 1717, Concord, Middlesex, Mass.

10. **Joseph Dudley** (3.Joseph[2], 1.Francis[1]) b. 20 Apr 1697, occupation: blacksmith, m. 2 Oct 1718, in Concord, Middlesex, Mass., **Mary Chandler**, d. abt 1772. Joseph died abt 1746.

Children:

26.   i   **Joseph Dudley** b. 24 Jul 1719.

27.   ii **Elizabeth Dudley** (details excluded).

28.   iii **Mary Dudley** b. 17 Jan 1722/23.

       iv **Samuel Dudley** b. 7 Mar 1724/25, Concord, Middlesex, Mass., occupation: Blacksmith. He was the executor of his father's will.

29.   v **Lucy Dudley** b. 1 Apr 1727.

30.   vi **Huldah Dudley**.

     vii **Rebecca Dudley** b. abt 1732, d. 2 May 1798, Concord, Middlesex, Mass. The Concord V.R. lists her age at death as 66.

31.   viii **James Dudley** b. 21 Nov 1734.

      ix **John Dudley** b. 11 Jan 1736/37, Concord, Middlesex, Mass. According to a nephew (also named John Dudley), he was apparently a rich man and lived in England.

       x **Abigail Dudley** b. abt 1739, Concord, Middlesex, Mass., baptized: 7 Oct 1739, d. 3 Jun 1812, Concord, Middlesex, Mass. Apparently died unmarried. She left a will, and her estate was valued at $870.49. Age on grave stone says 73 yrs.

32.   xi **Benjamin Dudley** b. 25 Nov 1741.

11. **Benjamin Dudley** (3.Joseph[2], 1.Francis[1]) b. 20 Mar 1698/99, Concord, Middlesex, Mass., occupation: Yeoman, m. 17 Nov 1726, in Sudbury, Middlesex, Mass., **Elizabeth Rice**, b. 4 Dec 1705, (daughter of **John Rice** and **Elizabeth Clapp**). Benjamin was raised by Isaac Rice of Sudbury, who left him in 1718 the north half of Indian Head farm in Framingham, which consisted of the Kendall and Bent farms. Benjamin enlisted in 1725 to fight Indians under William Brintnall. He sued a man named Phineas Parmenter in 1742 and won 5.11.4 pounds.

Children:

33.   i **Joseph Dudley** b. abt 1727.

34.   ii **Benjamin Dudley** b. abt 1729.

35.   iii **Abigail Dudley** b. abt 1731.

36.   iv **Ebenezer Dudley** b. abt 1735.

37.   v **William Dudley** b. abt 1740.

12. **Mary Dudley** (3.Joseph[2], 1.Francis[1]) b. 8 Feb 1701, Concord, Middlesex, Mass., m. 16 Jul 1719, in Weston, Middlesex, Mass., **Josiah Blanchard**.

Children:
  i   **Mary Blanchard** (details excluded).
  ii   **Abigail Blanchard** b. 28 Jun 1726, Concord, Middlesex, Mass.
  iii   **Love Blanchard** b. 8 May 1728, Concord, Middlesex, Mass.
  iv   **Josiah Blanchard** b. 2 Jun 1730, Concord, Middlesex, Mass., d. bf 1733.
  v   **Elizabeth Blanchard** b. 8 Feb 1731/32, Concord, Middlesex, Mass.
  vi   **Josiah Blanchard** b. 10 Dec 1733, Concord, Middlesex, Mass.

13. **Sibillah Dudley** (3.Joseph[2], 1.Francis[1]) b. 22 Sep 1702, Concord, Middlesex, Mass.,
    m. 5 Sep 1718, in Concord, Middlesex, Mass., **Jonathan Brown**, b. 30 Jul 1698, Concord,
    Middlesex, Mass., (son of **Thomas Brown** and **Rachel Poulter**). Dean Dudley reports
    the name being spelled Sibylla. They were married by Justice Minot.
    Children:
  i   **Love Brown** b. 14 Aug 1719, Concord, Middlesex, Mass.
38.   ii   **Mary Brown** b. 16 Apr 1721.
  iii   **John Brown** b. 1 Jul 1724, Concord, Middlesex, Mass.
  iv   **Gideon Brown** b. 13 Mar 1725/26, Concord, Middlesex, Mass.
  v   **Thomas Brown** b. 17 Nov 1737, Concord, Middlesex, Mass.
  vi   **Jonathan Brown** b. 3 Apr 1740, Concord, Middlesex, Mass.
  vii   **Lois Brown** b. 15 Dec 1742, Concord, Middlesex, Mass.

14. **John Dudley** (4.John[2], 1.Francis[1]) b. 16 Aug 1699, Concord, Middlesex, Mass.,
    occupation: housewright, m. abt 1728, **Mary**. John died abt 1751. John lived in the
    Section of Concord that became Acton, Mass, in 1735. Dean Dudley lists a son James, born
    1734. That could NOT be proved, and there is another son James born the same date as a son
    of Joseph Dudley, which could be proved. Therefore, I did not list a son James for this family.
    In addition, Dean Dudley lists a son John, born 11 Jan 1738. His birth could not be proved
    either, and as son Ephraim is born Sep 1737, I did not believe a 4 month pregnancy realistic.
    Therefore, John is not listed either.
    Children:
39.   i   **John Dudley** b. 13 Mar 1729/30.
40.   ii   **Peter Dudley** b. 26 Aug 1731.
41.   iii   **Daniel Dudley** b. 22 Jun 1733.
  iv   **Hannah Dudley** b. 24 Aug 1735, Acton, Middlesex, Mass.
42.   v   **Ephraim Dudley** b. 8 Sep 1737.
43.   vi   **Francis Dudley** b. 1 Jan 1739/40.
  vii   **Mary Dudley** b. 3 Jan 1741, Acton, Middlesex, Mass., d. 18 Jan 1741.
  viii   **Charles Dudley** b. 22 May 1744, Acton, Middlesex, Mass.

15. **Samuel Dudley** (6.Samuel[2], 1.Francis[1]) b. 28 Jul 1705, Concord, Middlesex, Mass.,
    occupation: husbandman and gentleman, m. 17 Feb 1728/29, in Oxford, Worcester, Mass.,

Abigail Waters. Samuel died abt 1750, Littleton, Middlesex, Mass. Killed by accidental discharge of a gun. Dean Dudley reports the children born in Sutton, but Vital Records show all born at Littleton.

Children:

44.   i   **Samuel Dudley** b. 14 Jan 1730.

       ii **Abigail Dudley** b. 13 Sep 1733, Littleton, Middlesex, Mass., d. 16 Jun 1740, Littleton, Middlesex, Mass., buried: Old Burying Ground at Littleton Common. Abigail and Timothy's marriage intention was filed 22 Jan 1764 in Littleton.

45.   iii **Stephen Dudley** b. 2 Jul 1735.

       iv **Lois Dudley** b. 12 Jun 1737, Littleton, Middlesex, Mass., m. 1 Mar 1758, in Littleton, Middlesex, Mass., **Oliver Hartwell**.

       v   **Joseph Dudley** b. 12 Aug 1739, Littleton, Middlesex, Mass., d. abt 1757. Killed in the French Indian war in 1757

       vi **Abigail Dudley** b. 29 Oct 1741, Littleton, Middlesex, Mass., m. 22 Jan 1764, in Littleton, Middlesex, Mass., **Timothy Fox**. The marriage date is the intention date.

16. **Francis Dudley** (6.Samuel[2], 1.Francis[1]) b. 10 Dec 1706, Concord, Middlesex, Mass., m. 23 May 1732, in Holliston, Worcester, Mass. **Sibillah Leland**, b. 11 Jul 1708, Sherborn, Worcester, Mass., (daughter of **Ebenezer Leland** and **Patience**) d. 1764.

Children:

       i   **Siballah (Sybella) Dudley** b. 19 Aug 1733, Sutton, Worcester, Mass., m. 18 Oct 1750, in Sutton, Worcester, Mass., **Joseph Mosely**.

       ii **Martha Dudley** b. 27 Jun 1736, Sutton, Worcester, Mass., m. 2 Jun 1764, in Sutton, Worcester, Mass., **Simeon Gleason**.

       iii **Mary Dudley** b. 6 Dec 1740, Sutton, Worcester, Mass., m. 19 Dec 1765, in Sutton, Worcester, Mass., **Joel Wheeler**.

       iv **Sarah Dudley** b. 7 Jun 1744, Sutton, Worcester, Mass.

46.   v   **Francis Dudley** b. 18 Feb 1747/48.

       vi **Mary Dudley** baptized: 28 Jul 1735, Sutton, Worcester, Mass., d. bef. 1740.

       vii **Beulah Dudley** baptized: 15 Jul 1739, Sutton, Worcester, Mass.

17. **David Dudley** (6.Samuel[2], 1.Francis[1]) b. 4 Nov 1709, Concord, Middlesex, Mass., m. **Hannah Sibley**, b. abt 1720, d. 3 Aug 1784, Sutton, Worcester, Mass. David died 10 Jan 1797, Sutton, Worcester, Mass.

Children:

       i   **Betty Dudley** b. 26 Jul 1738, Sutton, Worcester, Mass.

       ii **Hannah Dudley** b. 14 Feb 1743/44, Sutton, Worcester, Mass.

47.   iii **Abel Dudley** b. 21 Oct 1746.

       iv **Timothy Dudley** b. 16 Aug 1751, Sutton, Worcester, Mass.

       v   **Abigail Dudley** b. 15 Jun 1758, Sutton, Worcester, Mass., m. 12 Apr 1774, in

Sutton, Worcester, Mass., **Isaac Gleason**.

    vi **Lucy Dudley** b. 2 Aug 1761, Sutton, Worcester, Mass., m. 22 Nov 1784, in Sutton, Worcester, Mass., **John Totman**.

18. **Jonathan Dudley** (6.Samuel[2], 1.Francis[1]) b. 4 Nov 1709, Concord, Middlesex, Mass., m. 18 Aug 1736, in Sutton, Worcester, Mass., **Hannah Putnam**, b. abt 1718, (daughter of **Elisha Putman**) d. 21 May 1801, Sutton, Worcester, Mass. Jonathan died 23 Nov 1789, Sutton, Worcester, Mass. He left $48.57 to each of his children, but the eldest received a double portion.

          Children:

48.   i **Jonathan Dudley** b. 22 Mar 1738.

      ii **Hannah Dudley** b. 20 Jan 1739/40, Sutton, Worcester, Mass., m. **Mr. Woodbury**. Hannah died 25 Aug 1786.

49.   iii **John Dudley** b. 20 Aug 1743.

     iv **Prudence Dudley** b. 4 May 1747, Sutton, Worcester, Mass., m. 18 Jun 1772, in Sutton, Worcester, Mass., **Henry King**.

      v **Anna Dudley** b. 9 Apr 1753, Sutton, Worcester, Mass., m. 15 Dec 1774, in Sutton, Worcester, Mass., **Alpheus Marble**, b. 7 Aug 1753, d. 21 Jul 1807. **Alpheus**: Alpheus was a Sergeant in the Revolutionary War.

     vi **Samuel Dudley** b. 4 Jan 1755, Sutton, Worcester, Mass., d. 6 Nov 1775, Sutton, Worcester, Mass.

50.   vii **Peter Dudley** b. 10 Jan 1758.

19. **Mary Dudley** (6.Samuel[2], 1.Francis[1]) b. 24 Aug 1711, Littleton, Middlesex, Mass., m. **Samuel Chase**, b. 28 Sep 1707.

          Children:

      i **Samuel Chase** b. 28 Nov 1728, m. 29 May 1751, **Silence Stow**, b. Grafton, Worcester, Mass.

     ii **Dudley Chase** b. 29 Aug 1730, m. 23 Aug 1753, **Alice Corbett**, b. Mendon, Worcester, Mass.

    iii **Elizabeth Chase** b. 23 Nov 1735.

     iv **March Chase** b. 21 Jun 1738, m. (1) **Mary Dodge**, m. (2) 10 Oct 1759, **Beulah Coye**, d. 7 May 1795. March died 26 Sep 1822.

      v **Mary Chase** b. 2 Jul 1740.

     vi **Sarah Chase** b. 2 Jul 1740, m. 9 Mar 1758, **Ebenezer Rawson**.

    vii **Mary Chase II** b. 25 Feb 1743/44, m. **Unknown Bellows**, b. Walpole, NH.

   viii **Abigail Chase** b. 15 Jul 1753.

20. **Peter Dudley** (6.Samuel[2], 1.Francis[1]) b. 13 Sep 1718, Littleton, Middlesex, Mass., m. 12 Nov 1741, in Marlborough, Middlesex, Mass., **Abigail Gleason**. Peter died 20 Jan 1775, Harvard, Worcester, Mass. Dean Dudley lists PATTY vice PETER. He MUST have

misread the record here! The original Littleton record reads "Petter." Also, Please note that HARVARD is spelled "Harford" in many records.

Abigail: She was living in 1790, a widow.

Children:

    i **Abigail Dudley** b. 29 May 1743, Harvard, Worcester, Mass.

    ii **Zacheus Dudley** b. 6 Nov 1745, Harvard, Worcester, Mass., m. 28 Aug 1780, in Bolton, Worcester, Mass., **Mary Conant**. Zacheus died 29 Nov 1819, Harvard, Worcester, Mass.

    iii **Mary Dudley** b. 17 Oct 1749, Harvard, Worcester, Mass., d. 13 Oct 1793, Harvard, Worcester, Mass.

    iv **Mercy Dudley** b. 7 Mar 1753, Harvard, Worcester, Mass., d. 24 Sep 1778, Harvard, Worcester, Mass.

    v **Sarah Dudley** b. 26 Aug 1755, Harvard, Worcester, Mass., d. 28 Oct 1755, Harvard, Worcester, Mass.

    vi **Samuel Dudley** b. 12 Nov 1756, Harvard, Worcester, Mass., d. 27 May 1758, Harvard, Worcester, Mass. According to the church record, he was 18 months old.

    vii **Prudence Dudley** b. 18 Apr 1759, Harvard, Worcester, Mass., m. 10 Sep 1783, in Harvard, Worcester, Mass., **Jacob Phelps**.

    viii **Lydia Dudley** b. 26 May 1761, Harvard, Worcester, Mass., m. 1 May 1783, in Harvard, Worcester, Mass., **Reuben Conant**.

    ix **Oliver Dudley** b. 29 Apr 1764, Harvard, Worcester, Mass., d. 7 Aug 1767, Harvard, Worcester, Mass.

21. **Rogers Dudley** (6.Samuel[2], 1.Francis[1]) b. 9 Aug 1720, Littleton, Middlesex, Mass., m. 31 May 1743, in Sutton, Worcester, Mass., **Mary Sibley**.

    Children:

    i **Nabbe Dudley** b. abt 29 May 1744, Sutton, Worcester, Mass., baptized: 29 May 1748, Sutton, Worcester, Mass., m. 3 Dec 1797, in Sutton, Worcester, Mass., **Simeon Gould**. On the marriage record, her name is "Nabby."

    ii **Mercy Dudley** b. 20 Apr 1746, Sutton, Worcester, Mass.

51.   iii **David Dudley** b. 14 Jan 1749/50.

    iv **Mary Dudley** b. 14 Dec 1751, Sutton, Worcester, Mass., m. 1764, **Jonathan Eliot**. Her marriage is recorded in Dean Dudley, but no marriage record has been found. It was unusual, but not unheard of, for girls to marry at 13 yrs old.

22. **Prudence Dudley** (6.Samuel[2], 1.Francis[1]) m. 25 Mar 1737/38, in Sutton, Worcester, Mass., **Ebenezer Whipple**, b. 14 Sep 1713, (son of **John Whipple** and **Mary W. Fifield**). No birth record on her. Her marriage is confirmed by the Sutton V.R.

    Children:

    i **Samuel Whipple** b. 28 Nov 1737, Sutton, Worcester, Mass.

 ii **Paul Whipple** b. 20 Dec 1737, Sutton, Worcester, Mass.

 iii **Sarah Whipple** b. 8 Dec 1740, Sutton, Worcester, Mass., m. **Shearjashub Spooner**.

 iv **Joseph Whipple** b. 5 Feb 1743, Sutton, Worcester, Mass.

 v **Mary Whipple** b. 23 Feb 1745, Sutton, Worcester, Mass.

 vi **Samuel Whipple** b. 7 Dec 1751, Hardwick, Worcester, Mass.

 vii **John Whipple** b. 6 Jan 1754, Hardwick, Worcester, Mass.

 viii **Prudence Whipple** b. 17 Mar 1756, m. 13 Apr 1775, **George Field**. Prudence died 15 Dec 1838.

23. **William Dudley** (6.Samuel², 1.Francis¹) b. 28 May 1726, Littleton, Middlesex, Mass., occupation: Town clerk/selectman, m. 12 Jan 1747/48, in Douglas, Worcester, Mass., **Ann Shepherd**, b. abt 1732, Stoughton, Norfolk, Mass., d. 22 Jan 1799, Douglas, Worcester, Mass. William died 8 Sep 1786, Douglas, Worcester, Mass. William was also a town constable. On gravestone: "Great God, I own thy sentenc just, And nature must decay; I yield my body to the dust, To dwell with fellow clay." Was on many committees and a surveyor of Lumber. He left an estate worth 410 pounds, and his son Paul ministered it. There is no VR for his death.

    Children:

52. i **Benjamin Dudley** b. 8 Jun 1752.

53. ii **Paul Dudley** b. 21 Aug 1758.

54. iii **Lemuel Dudley** b. 26 Mar 1762.

 iv **David Dudley** b. 29 May 1764, Douglas, Worcester, Mass., d. 1783. Died unmarried.

55. v **Hannah Dudley** b. 19 Aug 1766.

56. vi **Polly Dudley** b. 7 Nov 1768.

 vii **Olive Dudley** b. 15 Dec 1771, Douglas, Worcester, Mass., m. 19 Apr 1789, in Douglas, Worcester, Mass., **Asa Chase**, b. abt 1765, d. 9 Oct 1847, Douglas, Worcester, Mass.

24. **Lydia Dudley** (6.Samuel², 1.Francis¹) b. abt 1729, Sutton, Worcester, Mass., baptized: 26 Oct 1729, Sutton, Worcester, Mass., m. 9 Nov 1747, in Uxbridge, Worcester, Mass., **Benjamin Wallis**, b. 1723, d. 25 Dec 1814, Douglas, Worcester, Mass. Lydia died 28 Oct 1820, Douglas, Worcester, Mass.

    Children:

 i **Lydia Wallis** b. 10 Sep 1748, Douglas, Worcester, Mass., m. 7 Dec 1767, in Douglas, Worcester, Mass., **Josiah Hums**.

57. ii **Benjamin Wallis** b. 4 Mar 1750/51.

 iii **David Wallis** b. 16 Oct 1753, Douglas, Worcester, Mass., m. 2 Nov 1778, in Douglas, Worcester, Mass., **Abial (Biul) Albe**, b. 1756, d. 28 Feb 1831, Douglas, Worcester, Mass. David died 20 May 1827, Douglas, Worcester, Mass.

Abial: The Marriage records has the given name as "BIUL", but the given name was ABIAL as per the Douglas VR.

58.   iv   **Mercy Wallis** b. 12 Feb 1756.

59.   v   **Samuel Wallis** b. 12 Jan 1758.

       vi   **James Wallis** b. 28 Aug 1761, Douglas, Worcester, Mass., m. **Chloe Humes**, b. Douglas, Worcester, Mass.

      vii   **Patty Wallis** b. 8 Apr 1763, Douglas, Worcester, Mass., m. 24 Apr 1788, in Douglas, Worcester, Mass., **Daniel Hunt**.

     viii   **Jonathan Wallis** b. 26 Feb 1765, Douglas, Worcester, Mass., d. 28 Feb 1765, Douglas, Worcester, Mass.

      ix   **Aaron Wallis** b. 12 Sep 1768, Douglas, Worcester, Mass., m. 15 Dec 1788, in Douglas, Worcester, Mass., **Prudence Aldrich**, b. 7 Jul 1769, Douglas, Worcester, Mass., d. 28 Aug 1845, Douglas, Worcester, Mass. Aaron died 9 Aug 1845, Douglas, Worcester, Mass.

       x   **Peter Wallis** b. 22 Jan 1770, Douglas, Worcester, Mass., d. 17 Sep 1775, Douglas, Worcester, Mass.

25. **Douglassa Dudley** (6.Samuel[2], 1.Francis[1]) b. 9 Sep 1748, Douglas, Worcester, Mass., m. 27 Jun 1768, in Douglas, Worcester, Mass., **Elijah Smith**, b. 5 Dec 1746, d. 17 Nov 1839, Douglas, Worcester, Mass. The marriage date is the intention date.

         Children:

       i   **Sarah Smith** b. 1 Jun 1769, Douglas, Worcester, Mass.

      ii   **Lydia Smith** b. 27 Oct 1771, Douglas, Worcester, Mass., m. 14 Dec 1791, in Douglas, Worcester, Mass., **Elijah Baily**.

60.   iii   **Robert Smith** b. 2 May 1774.

      iv   **Susanna Smith** b. 29 Jun 1776, Douglas, Worcester, Mass.

       v   **Rebekkah Smith** b. 8 May 1778, Douglas, Worcester, Mass.

      vi   **Elijah Smith** b. 2 Dec 1780, Douglas, Worcester, Mass., m. 13 Apr 1807, in Douglas, Worcester, Mass., **Sally Balcome**, b. Douglas, Worcester, Mass.

     vii   **Samuel Smith** b. 22 Sep 1783, Douglas, Worcester, Mass.

    viii   **Amasa Smith** b. 18 Apr 1786, Douglas, Worcester, Mass., d. 14 Dec 1805, Douglas, Worcester, Mass.

      ix   **Mercy Smith** b. 8 Aug 1789, Douglas, Worcester, Mass., m. 19 Mar 1809, in Douglas, Worcester, Mass., **Minor Morse**.

       x   **Dudley Smith** b. 12 May 1793, Douglas, Worcester, Mass.

26. **Joseph Dudley** (10.Joseph³, 3.Joseph², 1.Francis¹) b. 24 Jul 1719, Concord,
    Middlesex, Mass., occupation: blacksmith, m. 16 Jan 1740/41, in Concord, Middlesex, Mass.,
    Mary Brown, b. 16 Apr 1721, Concord, Middlesex, Mass., (daughter of **Jonathan
    Brown** and **Sibillah Dudley**). Joseph died 1773, Concord, Middlesex, Mass. Joesph and
    Mary lived in East Sudbury. His estate was settled by Probate Court. He had a few debts at his
    death. His son Samuel settled it. Was called a Lieutenant, but in what we do not know. His
    personal estate was sold at public vendue, and brought 15.19.0 pounds. He also owned 1/2 of
    the dwelling house, and that brought 3.14.8.
    Mary: She was "admitted to the church" 25 Aug 1754.
    Children:
    61.   i   **Joseph Dudley** b. 16 Sep 1743.
    62.   ii **Samuel Dudley** b. 29 Sep 1746.
          iii **Mary Dudley** b. 4 Aug 1749, Concord, Middlesex, Mass., baptized: 6 Aug
              1759, m. 28 May 1768, in Concord, Middlesex, Mass., **John Cole**. Mary died
              27 Feb 1819, Wayland, Middlesex, Mass.
          iv **Hepzibah Dudley** b. 17 Aug 1752, Concord, Middlesex, Mass., baptized: 30
              Aug 1752, Concord, Middlesex, Mass.
    63.   v   **Nathan Dudley** b. 17 Jun 1755.
          vi **Abishai Dudley** b. 24 Jul 1758, Concord, Middlesex, Mass., occupation:
              Blacksmith. Revolutionary War Vet. Was 16 when he enlisted. Capt. Abishai
              Brown's Co, Col John Nixon's 5th Reg, enlisted 25 Apr 1775; served 3 mon 14
              days, Capt Adam Wheeler's 2nd Co., Lt Col Thomas Nixon's 4th Reg 1776, also
              Col Rufus Putnam's 5th Reg. A sad note--he was reported deserted 2 June 1779,
              and was entered on the list of deserters 20 November 1781. According to the
              records, he was 5' 8", dark complexion, black hair. (the "List of Diserters" is made
              after a period of time to ensure he isn't captured or killed).
          vii **Abigail Dudley** b. 13 Jun 1761, Concord, Middlesex, Mass.
          viii **Rebecca Dudley** b. 28 Aug 1763, Concord, Middlesex, Mass.

27. **Elizabeth Dudley** (10.Joseph³, 3.Joseph², 1.Francis¹) (details excluded), m.
    Joseph Stratton, occupation: cordwainer, d. 1755.
          Children:
          i   **Sarah Stratton**.
          ii **Joseph Stratton**.

28. **Mary Dudley** (10.Joseph³, 3.Joseph², 1.Francis¹) b. 17 Jan 1722/23, Concord,
    Middlesex, Mass., m. 5 Dec 1745, in Concord, Middlesex, Mass., **Jonathan Lamson**.
          Children:
          i   **Ephraim Lamson**.

29. **Lucy Dudley** (10.Joseph[3], 3.Joseph[2], 1.Francis[1]) b. 1 Apr 1727, Concord, Middlesex, Mass., m. 6 Dec 1744, in Concord, Middlesex, Mass., **John Perry**. Lucy died abt 1753. She sometimes wrote her name "Loice". She and John were married by Justice Flint.
       Children:
        i **Thomas Perry**.

30. **Huldah Dudley** (10.Joseph[3], 3.Joseph[2], 1.Francis[1]) b. Concord, Middlesex, Mass., m. 8 Mar 1756, in Lincoln, Middlesex, Mass., **Joseph Locke**. No birth record was found on Huldah, but she was listed among the children of her mother in the distribution of dower. The marriage date is the intention date. Dean Dudley says she was never married.
       Children:
        i **Joseph Locke** baptized: 9 Feb 1755, Lincoln, Middlesex, Mass.

31. **James Dudley** (10.Joseph[3], 3.Joseph[2], 1.Francis[1]) b. 21 Nov 1734, Concord, Middlesex, Mass., m. (1) 25 Dec 1755, in Lancaster, Worcester, Mass., **Mehitabel Woodburry**, d. abt 1761, m. (2) 21 Apr 1763, **Mary Raymond**. James died abt 1775. His sister Abigail had a note against his estate for 11 pounds, and Josiah Piper had one for 11.5. His personal real estate was valued at 178.16.8., and was 22 acres of tillage. He also had smiths tools, and another 2 1/2 acres of woodland. When he died, his children had to pick a guardian in 1776. Why they had to do this is unknown, probably because his wife Mary was not able to, or unwilling to, take care of them. His wife gave bond as administratrix in Feb, but could have died before July.
    Mehitabel: Spelling of name is from Court records.
       Children by Mehitabel Woodburry:
        i **James Dudley** b. 31 Mar 1757, Concord, Middlesex, Mass. Died young.
        ii **Lucy Dudley** b. 17 Mar 1759, Concord, Middlesex, Mass., m. 17 Nov 1783, in Royalston, Worcester, Mass., **Amasa Green**.
       Children by Mary Raymond:
64.   iii **Samuel Dudley** b. 1 Jun 1765.
        iv **Molly Dudley** b. 9 May 1767, Acton, Middlesex, Mass.
        v **Sarah Dudley**. Was under 14 in 1776. She is not confirmed by Acton or Concord V.R.'s.
        vi **Levina Dudley** b. 1 Apr 1769, Acton, Middlesex, Mass. Name could be "Levine".
65.   vii **Paul Dudley** b. 6 Mar 1771.

32. **Benjamin Dudley** (10.Joseph[3], 3.Joseph[2], 1.Francis[1]) b. 25 Nov 1741, Concord, Middlesex, Mass., m. 16 Apr 1765, in Weston, Middlesex, Mass., **Mary Stratton**, b. 1745, d. 27 Apr 1813, Lincoln, Middlesex, Mass. Benjamin died 2 Apr 1820, Lincoln, Middlesex, Mass.

Children:

   i **Abigail Dudley** b. Marlborough, Middlesex, Mass., d. Feb 1820, Lincoln, Middlesex, Mass.

66. ii **John Dudley** b. 27 Apr 1770.

67. iii **Samuel Dudley** b. 24 Dec 1773.

33. **Joseph Dudley** (11.Benjamin³, 3.Joseph², 1.Francis¹) b. abt 1727, Sudbury, Middlesex, Mass., m. 27 Feb 1752, in Westborough, Middlesex, Mass., **Mary Warren**. Joseph died 1802, East Sudbury, Middlesex, Mass. Joseph signed his will by mark, and his estate was valued at (total) $1,374.02. As his will was read in East Sudbury, I have added that as the place of death.

Mary: The only record that could fit her is a "Molly" (an accepted nickname for Mary) that died in East Sudbury at age 80, a pauper. IF this is the same, her birth date is abt 1739, her death is 27 Feb 1819.

   Children:

   i **Mary Dudley** b. 17 Jun 1752, Sudbury, Middlesex, Mass. Died "aged", ob. s.p.

   ii **Sarah Dudley** b. 13 Oct 1754, Sudbury, Middlesex, Mass., d. bef Oct 1798. Death approximation based on her not being mentioned in her father's will.

68. iii **Nahum Dudley** b. 4 May 1757.

   iv **Joseph Dudley** b. 20 Mar 1760, Sudbury, Middlesex, Mass.

   v **Daniel Dudley** b. 22 Feb 1763, Sudbury, Middlesex, Mass., d. 24 Apr 1808, Wayland, Middlesex, Mass.

   vi **Submit Dudley** b. 14 Aug 1765, Sudbury, Middlesex, Mass., d. 1783. Died unmarried.

69. vii **Moses Dudley** b. 31 Jan 1769.

70. viii **Luther Dudley** b. 5 May 1772.

   ix **Jonas Dudley** b. abt 1776, d. 5 Oct 1836, Wayland, Middlesex, Mass. Was apparently shuffled from foster home to foster home from 1818-1836. It was due to a mental condition. He did have property, however, that was valued at $544 in 1831. Church record says he died 61 yrs old.

34. **Benjamin Dudley** (11.Benjamin³, 3.Joseph², 1.Francis¹) b. abt 1729, m. 14 Dec 1752, in Weston, Middlesex, Mass., **Mary Walker**, b. abt 1732, (daughter of **John Walker**) d. 21 Jan 1814, Wayland, Middlesex, Mass. Benjamin died 2 Dec 1814, Wayland, Middlesex, Mass. The minister who married Benjamin and Mary was Rev. Samuel Woodward of Weston. Death record says he died of "mortification of the foot and general, age 85." One doctor says that was probably gangrene.

   Children:

   i **Elizabeth Dudley** b. abt 1753, m. 3 Mar 1774, in Sudbury, Middlesex, Mass., **Joseph Bacon**.

71.   ii **Abigail Dudley** b. abt 1755.
       iii **Mary Dudley** b. abt 1756, m. 25 Oct 1775, in Sudbury, Middlesex, Mass., **Joseph Nichols**.
       iv **William Dudley** b. abt 1756, d. abt 1758. Died at 2 yrs old
        v **Lydia Dudley** b. abt 1758, m. 6 Jun 1784, in Wayland, Middlesex, Mass., **David Drury**.
           David: Name may be spelled DREWRY.
72.   vi **Jane Dudley** b. abt 1760.
       vii **Sarah Dudley** b. abt 1762, m. 26 Oct 1794, in East Sudbury, Middlesex, Mass., **Jonas Brown**.
73.   viii **Benjamin Dudley** b. 1766.
74.   ix **John Dudley** b. abt 1768.
        x **Jonathan Dudley** b. abt 1768. Died young.
75.   xi **Jonathan Dudley** b. 18 Apr 1772.
76.   xii **Josiah Dudley** b. abt 1774.

35. **Abigail Dudley** (11.Benjamin[3], 3.Joseph[2], 1.Francis[1]) b. abt 1731, Massachusetts, m. 12 Apr 1750, in Sudbury, Middlesex, Mass., **Samuel Howe**, b. 27 Jun 1727, Framingham, Middlesex, Mass., (son of **Nehemiah How** and **Margaret Willard**) d. 9 Apr 1806, Westmoreland, Cheshire, New Hampshire, buried: Canoe Meadow Cemetery, Westmoreland, NH. Abigail died 13 Feb 1814, Westmoreland, Cheshire, New Hampshire. After her husband died, Abigail went to live her daughter Elizabeth.
   Samuel: His father was captured by Indians and held in Canada where he died. Samuel was noted as "a man of wealth, and possessed so much land that he gave each of his children a farm, besides his homestead, a beautiful estate overlooking the Connecticut River." A Rev. War vet, and was at the Battle of Bunker Hill. The list of children are different from Dean Dudley's. There was another Samuel Howe in Mass, and I believe he copied the wrong list. Those listed here are confirmed.
           Children:
        i **Nehemiah Howe** m. 27 Jun 1775, **Sarah Glenne**. Nehemiah died ABT 1840, Londonderry, Vt. Was one of the first settlers to Londonderry. Seven children.
       ii **Caleb Howe** b. ABT 1751, m. 22 Apr 1783, in Westmoreland, Cheshire, New Hampshire, **Silence Hutchins**. Caleb died 10 Sep 1833, Westmoreland, Cheshire, New Hampshire. Caleb and Silence had 7 children born between 1785-1804 in Westmoreland.
       iii **Elizabeth Howe** b. ABT 1753, m. 28 Jun 1792, in Westmoreland, Cheshire, New Hampshire, **Zebulon Hodges**.
       iv **Samuel Howe** b. ABT 1755, m. 9 Jun 1776, in Middleborough, Plymouth, Mass., **Mehitable Hackett**. Samuel died 10 May 1802, Westmoreland, Cheshire, New Hampshire. He had 4 known children. His father gave him a farm.

77. v **Margaret Howe** b. Apr 1759.

vi **William Howe** b. ABT 1762, d. 28 Nov 1774, Westmoreland, Cheshire, New Hampshire.

vii **Abigail Howe** b. ABT 1764, d. 13 Nov 1774, Westmoreland, Cheshire, New Hampshire.

viii **Benjamin Dudley Howe** b. ABT 1765, d. 24 Nov 1774, Westmoreland, Cheshire, New Hampshire.

36. **Ebenezer Dudley** (11.Benjamin[3], 3.Joseph[2], 1.Francis[1]) b. abt 1735, Sudbury, Middlesex, Mass., occupation: housewright, m. 1757, **Grace Rice**, b. 1734, (daughter of **Israel Rice**) d. 1821, Hebron, Oxford, Maine. Ebenezer died abt 1786. According to "Mass. Soldiers and Sailors of the Rev. War.", he was a private in Capt. Nathaniel Cudworth's Company of Minute Men, and Col. Abijah Pierce's regiment, which was called on April 19, 1775. He served 6 days. He was also a Sergeant in Capt. Samuel Patch's Company, of Col William Prescoat's (Prescott's) reigiment; with a return dated October 7, 1775. Dean Dudley says he was a Captain in the Revolution, but no records exists of that.
>   *Children:*

i **Abigail Dudley** b. 3 Jun 1758, Sudbury, Middlesex, Mass., m. **Jonathan Walker**. Abigail died Petersham, Worcester, Mass. No marriage record was found.

78. ii **Nathan Dudley** b. 20 Mar 1760.

iii **Rachel Dudley** b. 23 Feb 1762, Sudbury, Middlesex, Mass., m. 27 May 1793, in Weston, Middlesex, Mass., **John Roberts**. Rachel died Sudbury, Middlesex, Mass.

79. iv **David Dudley** b. 1 Oct 1763.

v **Eunice Dudley** b. abt 1765, East Sudbury, Middlesex, Mass., m. **Nicholas Manson**. Eunice died Boston, Suffolk, Mass. No records were found on her, Dean Dudley is the only source.

vi **Susan Dudley** b. abt 1767, Sudbury, Middlesex, Mass., m. 29 Jun 1794, in Petersham, Worcester, Mass., **Erasmus Babbitt**. In the marriage records, she is referred to as "Sukey."

80. vii **Ebenezer Dudley** b. 20 Apr 1771.

37. **William Dudley** (11.Benjamin[3], 3.Joseph[2], 1.Francis[1]) b. abt 1740, m. 25 Jul 1762, **Judith Curtis**. Belonged to the 1st Foot Company in Sudbury, 1757, under Capt. Moses Maynard in the Crown Point Expedition. They lived in East Sudbury, "now called Wayland."
>   *Children:*

81. i **William Dudley** b. 25 Jul 1763.

ii **Ephraim Dudley** b. 29 Jan 1766, d. Castleton, Vt.

iii **Nathaniel (Samuel) Dudley**. Drowned in Jonson Pond.

iv **Nancy Dudley** b. abt 1770, m. 3 May 1808, in Wayland, Middlesex, Mass.,

Thomas Piper.

82.   v   **Jason Dudley** b. abt 1772.
       vi   **Son Dudley**. It is not known why his name is not recorded. He was killed by the Captain on board a war ship when he was 20. It could be he was dishonored.
83.   vii   **Abigail Dudley**.
     viii   **Catherine Dudley**. Died young.
       ix   **Elizabeth Dudley** b. abt 1775, m. 29 Jan 1795, in East Sudbury, Middlesex, Mass., **Sherabiah Evans**.
          Sherabiah: He was a Revolutionary war veteran.

38. **Mary Brown** (13.Sibillah³, 3.Joseph², 1.Francis¹) (See marriage to number 26.)

39. **John Dudley** (14.John³, 4.John², 1.Francis¹) b. 13 Mar 1729/30, Concord, Middlesex, Mass., m. 1 Mar 1759, in Groton, Middlesex, Mass., **Sibyl Russell**, b. ABT 1739, (daughter of **Jason Russell and Elizabeth**) d. 13 Jul 1816, Westmoreland, Cheshire, New Hampshire, buried: North Church Cemetery, Westmoreland. John died 8 Oct 1820, Westmoreland, Cheshire, New Hampshire, buried: 9 Oct 1820, North Church Cemetery, Westmoreland. According to the "History of Westmoreland," John was brought up by a minister. He was spoken of as an "upright Christian." At his funeral, Priest Pratt preached from John 1:47. John died suddenly at the home of his daughter, Elizabeth.
Sibyl: Various spellings for first name. Her marriage record says "Sibyl." Had two brothers named Parker Russell born in Harvard, but both died young.

       Children:
        i   **Sibel Dudley** b. 5 Dec 1759, Groton, Middlesex, Mass.
       ii   **John Dudley** b. 11 Oct 1761, Groton, Middlesex, Mass. According to the History of Westmoreland, N.H., John married and had a daughter whom his wife ran away with. He mourned so that he did not live long!
84.   iii   **Elizabeth Dudley** b. 30 Nov 1763.
       iv   **Jason Dudley** b. 8 Jul 1766, Groton, Middlesex, Mass., m. 20 May 1791, in Westmoreland, Cheshire, New Hampshire, **Patty Russell**. The History of Westmoreland says there was no issue from the marriage.
       v   **Hannah Dudley** b. 13 Nov 1768, Groton, Middlesex, Mass.
       vi   **Parker Russell Dudley** b. 27 May 1771, Groton, Middlesex, Mass., d. 19 Jan 1846, Newport, Cheshire, New Hampshire. The History of Westmoreland says "he settled in Newport, NH. Studied to be a doctor, but ill health (fits) prevented him from practicing. Had no children, but adopted 4." He was obviously married, but there is no record or wife mentioned in Westmoreland History.
      vii   **Molly Dudley** b. 29 Aug 1773, Harvard, Worcester, Mass., m. 6 May 1799, **Rufus Kendall**. History of Westmoreland gives first name of "Polly."
          Rufus: Was "of Claremont, N.H."
     viii   **Francis Dudley** b. 31 Dec 1775, Harvard, Worcester, Mass., m. 3 Sep 1797,

Lucy Jackson.

ix   **Lucy Dudley** b. 19 Nov 1781, Harvard, Worcester, Mass., m. 27 Jan 1802, **Samuel Page**.
Samuel: Of Keene, NH.

40. **Peter Dudley** (14.John[3], 4.John[2], 1.Francis[1]) b. 26 Aug 1731, Concord, Middlesex, Mass., m. 12 Dec 1754, in Southborough, Middlesex, Mass., **Experience Newton**. Please notice 14 Oct must have been a riot at this household!! 3 children shared the same birthday!
Children:

    i   **Mary Dudley** b. 14 Oct 1755, Southborough, Middlesex, Mass., m. **Beriah Pratt**.

    ii   **Peter Dudley** b. 14 Oct 1758, Framingham, Middlesex, Mass., m. 8 May 1783, in Hopkinton, Middlesex, Mass., **Elisabeth Hiscock**. He was married in Hopkinton, later moved to New York State.

    iii   **Levina Dudley** b. 7 Dec 1760, Framingham, Middlesex, Mass., m. Jan 1783, in Framingham, Middlesex, Mass., **Thaddeus Hemenway**.

    iv   **Experience Dudley** b. 15 Feb 1764, Framingham, Middlesex, Mass., d. 19 Jun 1789, New York State. Died unmarried.

85.   v   **Nathan Dudley** b. 5 May 1766.

86.   vi   **Abraham Dudley** b. 14 Oct 1768.

    vii   **Sarah Dudley** b. 29 Sep 1772, Framingham, Middlesex, Mass.

    viii   **Charles Dudley** b. 1 Sep 1775, Framingham, Middlesex, Mass.

    ix   **Anne Dudley** b. 12 Sep 1777, Framingham, Middlesex, Mass., m. **David Luke**.

41. **Daniel Dudley** (14.John[3], 4.John[2], 1.Francis[1]) b. 22 Jun 1733, Concord, Middlesex, Mass., m. 28 Jun 1757, in Concord, Middlesex, Mass., **Hannah Farrar**, b. 24 Feb 1736/37, Concord, Middlesex, Mass., (daughter of **Henry Farar** and **Sarah**). Daniel died 25 Feb 1817, Waterville, Kennebec, Maine. Daniel moved to Westford in 1759. He died at the home of his niece, Jane (Dudley) Blanchard, wife of Freeman Blanchard. His marriage was performed by Justice Whiting. Dean Dudley lists another Josiah as a son to this family, but as it is a obvious double entry, I have removed him.
Children:

87.   i   **Daniel Dudley** b. 27 Mar 1758.

    ii   **Josiah Dudley** b. Concord, Middlesex, Mass. This is the 2nd Josiah that Dean Dudley lists as marrying Abigail Brown on 31 Aug 1797. This Josiah is not confirmed in Wesford Vital Records as a son of Daniel and Hannah Farrar, and I do not believe this is the correct line, and therefore did not list Abigail brown as his wife here. The other Josiah is the son of Benjamin Dudley and Mary walker, and the connection makes much more sense. The children Dean Dudley attributes to THIS Josiah are virtually identical to the other, and are entered there.

iii **Ebenezer Dudley** b. 17 Oct 1759, Westford, Middlesex, Mass.
iv **Jesse Dudley** b. 18 Apr 1761, Westford, Middlesex, Mass., baptized: 26 Apr 1761, Chelmsford, Middlesex, Mass., d. ABT 17 May 1778, Army. He was in the Revolution, enlisted for Town of Westford 13 Dec 1766. His death date was a report from "Mass. Soldiers & Sailors in the Revolution."
v **Sarah Dudley** b. 30 Jun 1763, Westford, Middlesex, Mass.
vi **John Dudley** b. 3 Oct 1765, Westford, Middlesex, Mass., m. 11 Nov 1787, in Westford, Middlesex, Mass., **Sarah Dutton**.
vii **Isaac Dudley** b. 4 Jun 1770, Westford, Middlesex, Mass.

42. **Ephraim Dudley** (14.John³, 4.John², 1.Francis¹) b. 8 Sep 1737, Acton, Middlesex, Mass., occupation: farmer, m. 16 May 1764, **Abigail Shepard**, b. 1740, d. 3 Jun 1818, Acton, Middlesex, Mass. Ephraim died 4 Mar 1815, Acton, Middlesex, Mass. Ephraim was in the Revolution for the town of Acton, beginning 14 Aug 1781 and served 6 months. According to the records, he was 5' 6", his hair, eyes and complexion was "dark."
   Children:
   i **Abigail Dudley** b. 26 Jul 1769, Acton, Middlesex, Mass.
   ii **Ephraim Dudley** b. 31 Jul 1771, Acton, Middlesex, Mass.
   iii **Nathan Dudley** b. 27 Jun 1773, Acton, Middlesex, Mass.

43. **Francis Dudley** (14.John³, 4.John², 1.Francis¹) b. 1 Jan 1739/40, Acton, Middlesex, Mass., baptized: 1st Congregational Church, Acton, Mass., occupation: canoemaker, surveyor, m. 6 Nov 1770, in Hallowell, Kennebec, Maine, **Anne Thorn**, d. 2 Mar 1814, Waterville, Kennebec, Maine. Francis died 1 Jan 1804, Winslow, Kennebec, Maine. A Rev. War vet, he is on the list raised on Lincoln Co. to serve with guards over troops of convention, magazines and public stores, under Gen. Heath, as returned by Brig. Gen. Charles Cushing, dated Pownalborough, Aug. 20,177?, enlisted July 23, 1778, from Col. North's (2nd Lincoln Co.) regiment. Francis died intestate. His children are known from probate records for the estate of Francis Dudley and deeds passed to settle his estate.
   Anne: She married 2nd Nov 11 1810, Nehemiah Getchell, his 3rd wife.
   Children:
88. i **James H. Dudley** b. ABT 1775.
89. ii **Ann Williams Dudley** b. ABT 1776.
   iii **Daniel Dudley** b. Winslow, Kennebec, Maine, occupation: lumberman, m. 28 Jun 1812, in Winslow, Kennebec, Maine, **Mary McIntire**. Daniel died AFT 1849. Witnesses present at marriage: Tiley Hayden, Ann Hayden, Jane Dudley, Francis Dudley, Ann McIntire. According to Dean Dudley, he was living in Calais, ME in 1849, but no records has been found to support that information.
90. iv **Rowland Dudley**.
   v **Jane Hunter Dudley** b. ABT 1780, Winslow, Kennebec, Maine, m. 1 Dec 1814, in Winslow, Kennebec, Maine, **Freeman Blanchard**, b. ABT 1777,

occupation: lawyer, d. 3 Oct 1861, Vassalboro, Kennebec, ME. Jane died 16 Feb 1870, Vassalboro, Kennebec, ME.

Freeman: He handled his Dudley brothers-in-law's interests in settling the estate of Francis Dudley. Also, according to Francis' probate, Daniel, Francis' elder brother, resided with the Blanchards, likely after widow Anne Dudley's death or remarriage to Nehemiah Getchell. Apparently Daniel left no estate, as the Blanchards charged the estate of Francis Dudley for their costs related to Daniel, after Daniel's death in 1817.

vi **Francis Dudley** b. Winslow, Kennebec, Maine. Francis was found in probate papers of his father, Francis Dudley. Dean Dudley [p. 843] notes a "Francis Dudley, living on the Kennebec in 1827." He is the only candidate as Francis, his father, died in 1804. He has not been found as head of household is Maine US Census records.

44. **Samuel Dudley** (15.Samuel[3], 6.Samuel[2], 1.Francis[1]) b. 14 Jan 1730, Littleton, Middlesex, Mass., occupation: blacksmith, m. 15 Jan 1756, in Acton, Middlesex, Mass., **Rebecca Hayward**. Samuel died 1803, Waterford, Maine. Samuel and Rebecca's marriage intention was filed in Acton 20 Sep 1755.

Rebecca: She was of Acton, Mass.

Children:
- i **Rebecca Dudley** b. 27 Apr 1757, Littleton, Middlesex, Mass.
- ii **Mary Dudley** b. 29 Feb 1760, Littleton, Middlesex, Mass.
- iii **Samuel Dudley** b. 6 Mar 1762, Littleton, Middlesex, Mass., d. 1834, Harvard, Worcester, Mass.
- 91. iv **Joseph Dudley** b. 11 Jul 1765.
- 92. v **Josiah Dudley** b. 25 Dec 1767.

45. **Stephen Dudley** (15.Samuel[3], 6.Samuel[2], 1.Francis[1]) b. 2 Jul 1735, Littleton, Middlesex, Mass., m. 21 Dec 1758, in Littleton, Middlesex, Mass., **Lydia Harwood**. Stephen died abt 1784, South Carolina. Was a Revolutionary War Soldier. He died while on Business in S. Carolina. Stephen and Lydia were married by Rev. Daniel Rogers.

Children:
- 93. i **Stephen Dudley** b. 14 Nov 1760.
- ii **Lydia Dudley** b. 11 Aug 1762, Littleton, Middlesex, Mass.
- iii **Abigail Dudley** b. 3 Jul 1764, Littleton, Middlesex, Mass.
- 94. iv **Joseph Dudley** b. 30 Sep 1766.
- v **Samuel Dudley** b. 29 Apr 1769, Littleton, Middlesex, Mass., d. 16 Dec 1795.
- vi **Mary Dudley** b. 22 Sep 1771, Littleton, Middlesex, Mass., m. (1) **Mr Barton**, m. (2) **Jesse Heald**.
- 95. vii **Peter Dudley** b. 29 Nov 1773.
- 96. viii **Jonathan Dudley** b. 27 Sep 1778.

ix   **Asa Dudley** b. 30 Jun 1782.

46. **Francis Dudley** (16.Francis[3], 6.Samuel[2], 1.Francis[1]) b. 18 Feb 1747/48, Sutton,
    Worcester, Mass., m. 21 May 1771, in Sutton, Worcester, Mass., **Elizabeth Whipple**, b. abt
    1747, (daughter of **Joseph Whipple**) d. 18 Dec 1836, Petersham, Worcester, Mass.
    Francis died 7 Mar 1825, Petersham, Worcester, Mass. He moved to Petersham about 1800.
        Children:
97.   i   **Mary Dudley** b. 19 Dec 1771.
       ii **Francis Dudley** b. 5 Feb 1774, Sutton, Worcester, Mass., d. 11 May 1783,
           Sutton, Worcester, Mass. Records say "drowned in the River." However, one says
           "age about 5" another "age about 7." This suggests that two little boys drowned.
       iii **Elizabeth Dudley** b. 5 Jan 1776, Sutton, Worcester, Mass., d. 27 Nov 1848,
           Petersham, Worcester, Mass. Died unmarried.
98.   iv **Samuel Dudley** b. 1 Apr 1781.
       v   **Beulah Dudley** b. 2 Apr 1783, Sutton, Worcester, Mass., m. 3 Mar 1808, in
           Petersham, Worcester, Mass., **Joseph Temple**.
99.   vi **Joseph Dudley** b. abt 1785.
100.   vii **Simon Dudley** b. 23 Apr 1787.
101. viii **Lucy Dudley** b. 16 Apr 1791.

47. **Abel Dudley** (17.David[3], 6.Samuel[2], 1.Francis[1]) b. 21 Oct 1746, Sutton, Worcester,
    Mass., m. **Sarah**, b. 1735, d. 10 Feb 1817, Shrewsbury, Worcester, Mass. Abel died 13 Sep
    1813, Sutton, Worcester, Mass. Abel was a soldier in the Revolution
        Children:
       i   **Hannah Dudley** b. 12 Jan 1769, Sutton, Worcester, Mass., m. 11 Oct 1789,
           Archelaus Sibley. Died without children
       ii **David Dudley** b. 1 Jan 1771, Sutton, Worcester, Mass., m. 6 Nov 1791, in
           Sutton, Worcester, Mass., **Rachel Chase**, (daughter of **Caleb Chase**).
           David died 14 Sep 1826, Sutton, Worcester, Mass.
       iii **Unknown Dudley** b. 4 Jun 1773, Sutton, Worcester, Mass., d. 4 Jul 1773,
           Sutton, Worcester, Mass.
       iv **Tabitha Dudley** b. 1 Aug 1774, Sutton, Worcester, Mass., m. 26 May 1791, in
           Sutton, Worcester, Mass., **Daniel Torrey**, (son of **Daniel Torrey**).
       v   **Abigail Dudley** b. 10 Sep 1776.
102.   vi **Abel Dudley** b. 15 Sep 1780.
       vii **Sarah Dudley** b. 15 Apr 1782, m. 28 Feb 1803, in Sutton, Worcester, Mass.,
           Dexter Rawson. Dexter and Sarah lived at Webster, Mass.

48. **Jonathan Dudley** (18.Jonathan[3], 6.Samuel[2], 1.Francis[1]) b. 22 Mar 1738, Sutton,
    Worcester, Mass., m. (1) 1 Feb 1763, in Sutton, Worcester, Mass., **Mary Garfield**, b. abt
    1745, d. 3 Jun 1777, Sutton, Worcester, Mass., m. (2) 22 Jun 1786, in Sutton, Worcester,

Mass., **Jemima Stearns**, b. abt 1753, d. 16 Jul 1840, Sutton, Worcester, Mass. Jonathan died 7 Aug 1795, Sutton, Worcester, Mass. His inheritance was 33.16.6 pounds, but died before the estate was settled. His was a double portion.

Children by Mary Garfield:

103. i **Elijah Dudley** b. 26 Jul 1764.
104. ii **Jonathan Dudley** b. 27 Feb 1766.
    iii **Hannah Dudley** b. 24 Mar 1768, m. **Asa Walker**.
    iv **Samuel Dudley** b. 9 Apr 1771, Sutton, Worcester, Mass., d. 6 Nov 1774, Sutton, Worcester, Mass.
    v **Mary Dudley** b. 24 Mar 1773, m. **Mr. Brigham**.

Children by Jemima Stearns:

    vi **Lucy Dudley** b. 10 May 1787, Sutton, Worcester, Mass., m. 15 Sep 1808, in Sutton, Worcester, Mass., **Reuben Eaton**, b. 27 Oct 1780, Sutton, Worcester, Mass., (son of **Reuben Eaton**) d. 17 Nov 1813, Sutton, Worcester, Mass.
    vii **Jemima Dudley** b. abt 1789, m. 27 Nov 1808, **Warren Hathaway**.
105. viii **Sally Dudley** b. 16 Aug 1790.
    ix **Prudence Dudley** b. abt 1793.

49. **John Dudley** (18.Jonathan³, 6.Samuel², 1.Francis¹) b. 20 Aug 1743, Sutton, Worcester, Mass., m. 13 Oct 1768, in Sutton, Worcester, Mass., **Mary Morse**. John died 25 Aug 1786, Sutton, Worcester, Mass.
Mary: She married Soloman Leland after John's death. She administered John's estate, and was guardian of their children. "Early Massachusetts Marriages," based on court records, records her name as "Morss".

Children:

106. i **John Dudley** b. 19 Oct 1769.
107. ii **Joseph Dudley** b. 18 Sep 1773.
    iii **Sarah Dudley** b. 22 Jan 1779, d. 25 Feb 1795. Birth date may be off by one year. Inscription in Wilkinsonville Cemetery says was 17 years old, and reads: "This blooming youth, the fairest face."
    iv **James Dudley** b. 23 Nov 1783, Sutton, Worcester, Mass., d. 22 Feb 1803, Sutton, Worcester, Mass.

50. **Peter Dudley** (18.Jonathan³, 6.Samuel², 1.Francis¹) b. 10 Jan 1758, Sutton, Worcester, Mass., m. 12 Dec 1781, in Sutton, Worcester, Mass., **Sarah P. Chase**, d. 24 Feb 1836, Sutton, Worcester, Mass. Peter died 8 Sep 1836, Sutton, Worcester, Mass.

Children:

    i **Caleb Dudley** b. 14 Sep 1782, Sutton, Worcester, Mass., d. 15 Sep 1784, Sutton, Worcester, Mass., buried: Wilkinsonville Cemetery, Sutton, Mass.
108. ii **Pheobe Dudley** b. 21 Mar 1784.

51. **David Dudley** (21.Rogers³, 6.Samuel², 1.Francis¹) b. 14 Jan 1749/50, Sutton, Worcester, Mass., m. 16 Dec 1773, in Sutton, Worcester, Mass., **Lois Whitney**, b. ABT 1753, d. 13 Jan 1822, Millbury, Worcester, Mass. David died 8 Aug 1814, Millbury, Worcester, Mass., buried: Country Bridge Cemetery, Millbury. David was a Private in the Revolutionary War.

Lois: Cemetery inscription gives death date of 14 January, but a listing by Reuben Dodge in 1898 says 1 January. Above date by Dean Dudley. Both cemetery lists give age of 69.

> *Children:*
>
> i **Polly Dudley** b. 3 Jul 1775, Auburn, Worcester, Mass., m. 15 Jul 1793, in Sutton, Worcester, Mass., **Samuel Dwinnel**, b. Brooklyn, New York.
>
> ii **Sarah Dudley** b. 27 Jul 1777, Auburn, Worcester, Mass.
>
> 109.   iii **John Dudley** b. 27 Jan 1780.
>
> 110.   iv **David Dudley** b. 5 Jun 1781.
>
> 111.   v **Luther Dudley** b. 12 Jun 1783.
>
> vi **Betsey Dudley** b. 9 Feb 1787, Sutton, Worcester, Mass., m. 18 Aug 1811, in Sutton, Worcester, Mass., **John March**, b. Connecticut.
>
> 112.   vii **Joseph Dudley** b. 14 Mar 1790.
>
> 113.   viii **Amasa Dudley** b. 17 Oct 1792.

52. **Benjamin Dudley** (23.William³, 6.Samuel², 1.Francis¹) b. 8 Jun 1752, Douglas, Worcester, Mass., occupation: Captain, m. 18 Aug 1778, in Douglas, Worcester, Mass., **Mercy Wallis**, b. 12 Feb 1756, Douglas, Worcester, Mass., (daughter of **Benjamin Wallis** and **Lydia Dudley**) d. 24 Oct 1824, Douglas, Worcester, Mass. Benjamin died 24 Oct 1831, Douglas, Worcester, Mass. Was a Revolutionary War Soldier

Mercy: The VR's record her name as MARCY.

> *Children:*
>
> i **Anna Dudley** b. 11 Mar 1779, Douglas, Worcester, Mass., m. 9 Dec 1798, in Douglas, Worcester, Mass., **Reubin Rich**. Anna's name is also spelled ANNE in the VR's.
>
> 114.   ii **Samuel Dudley** b. 21 Dec 1781.
>
> 115.   iii **Benjamin Dudley** b. 25 Feb 1784.
>
> iv **Marcy Dudley** b. 19 Mar 1787, Douglas, Worcester, Mass. Marcy was a deaf mute, as was sister Polly. There is no indication whether this was due to a birth defect.
>
> v **Polly Dudley** b. 21 Nov 1789, Douglas, Worcester, Mass. Polly was a deaf mute.
>
> vi **Lydia Dudley** b. 31 Jun 1792, Douglas, Worcester, Mass., m. 29 Nov 1810, in Douglas, Worcester, Mass., **William Wallis**.
>
> vii **Patty Dudley** b. 4 Sep 1795, Douglas, Worcester, Mass., m. **Asa Putnam**, b. 13 Jun 1795, Sutton, Worcester, Mass.
>
> viii **Phoebe Dudley**. There is no VR record of this child.

ix   **Martha Dudley**. There is no VR record for this child.

53. **Paul Dudley** (23.William[3], 6.Samuel[2], 1.Francis[1]) b. 21 Aug 1758, Douglas, Worcester, Mass., occupation: Major, m. 16 Jul 1782, in Taunton, Bristol, Mass., **Dorothy Reed**, b. ABT 1760, Taunton, Bristol, Mass., (daughter of **John Reed** and **Sarah**) d. 2 Sep 1847, Douglas, Worcester, Mass. Paul died 9 Feb 1837, Douglas, Worcester, Mass. Paul was a soldier in the Revolutionary War. No death VR.
Dorothy: Her surname could be spelled READ. This spelling is from the VR. The VR also records her first name as DORATHA. Dorothy died of "dropsy".
Children:
116.   i   **David Dudley** b. 11 Nov 1787.
117.   ii   **John Dudley** b. 8 Sep 1791.
118.   iii   **William Dudley** b. 29 Oct 1793.
119.   iv   **Willard Dudley** b. 25 Nov 1796.
120.   v   **Dorothy Dudley** b. 29 Mar 1802.
121.   vi   **Harriot Dudley** b. 15 Dec 1804.

54. **Lemuel Dudley** (23.William[3], 6.Samuel[2], 1.Francis[1]) b. 26 Mar 1762, Douglas, Worcester, Mass., m. 15 Sep 1793, in Douglas, Worcester, Mass., **Hannah Cutler**, b. 21 Mar 1771, Thompson, Ct., d. 3 Sep 1853, Douglas, Worcester, Mass. Lemuel died 29 Mar 1835, Douglas, Worcester, Mass.
Hannah: The Douglas VR (26) confirms birth year.
Children:
    i   **Molley Dudley** b. 26 Mar 1796, Douglas, Worcester, Mass., m. 5 Jan 1817, in Douglas, Worcester, Mass., **Jason Bigelow**. Name may have been Mary
122.   ii   **William Dudley** b. 27 Jun 1798.
    iii   **David Dudley** b. 10 Jan 1801, Douglas, Worcester, Mass., d. 30 Mar 1801, Douglas, Worcester, Mass.
123.   iv   **Rueben Dudley** b. abt 1803.
    v   **Warner Dudley**. Died unmarried. There is NO confirmation on this child. Dean Dudley is the only source.
    vi   **Lydia Dudley** m. 21 Nov 1833, in Douglas, Worcester, Mass., **Daniel Buxton**. There is no birth record of Lydia.

55. **Hannah Dudley** (23.William[3], 6.Samuel[2], 1.Francis[1]) b. 19 Aug 1766, Douglas, Worcester, Mass., m. **Samuel Wallis**, b. 12 Jan 1758, Douglas, Worcester, Mass., (son of **Benjamin Wallis** and **Lydia Dudley**) d. 1 Jan 1848, Douglas, Worcester, Mass.
Children:
    i   **Hannah Wallis** b. 10 May 1794.
124.   ii   **Nancy Wallis** b. 17 Feb 1797.
    iii   **Polly Wallis** b. 12 Feb 1800, Douglas, Worcester, Mass.

iv John Wallis b. 29 Mar 1802, Douglas, Worcester, Mass.
v **Dudley Wallis** b. 17 Mar 1806, Douglas, Worcester, Mass., m. **Mary Ann Wallis**.
vi **Salem Wallis** b. 2 Jan 1808, Douglas, Worcester, Mass., m. (1) 29 Oct 1840, in Douglas, Worcester, Mass., **Cynthia Ann Hazelton**, b. ABT. 1817, d. 22 Feb 1845, Douglas, Worcester, Mass., m. (2) 6 May 1846, in Douglas, Worcester, Mass., **Maria L Flagg**.
vii **Lorinda Wallis** b. 21 Jan 1810, Douglas, Worcester, Mass.
viii **Julia Ann Wallis** b. 10 Apr 1814, Douglas, Worcester, Mass., d. 14 Nov 1842, Douglas, Worcester, Mass.

56. **Polly Dudley** (23.William³, 6.Samuel², 1.Francis¹) b. 7 Nov 1768, Douglas, Worcester, Mass., m. 26 Feb 1793, in Douglas, Worcester, Mass., **William Robinson**. One source records her name as "Molley." The marriage intention was filed at Dudley 5 Mar 1792.
    William: There was a town named "Dudley" at this time, and the entry records him as being "of Dudley."
    Children:
    i **William Robinson** b. Douglas, Worcester, Mass., m. **Mrs. Angel**.
    ii **Rugus Robinson** b. Douglas, Worcester, Mass.
    iii **Sylvanus Robinson** b. Douglas, Worcester, Mass.
    iv **Mary Robinson**. Was married twice.
    v **Nancy Robinson** b. Douglas, Worcester, Mass.
    vi **Lucinda Robinson** b. Douglas, Worcester, Mass.
    vii **Phebe Robinson** b. Douglas, Worcester, Mass.

57. **Benjamin Wallis** (24.Lydia³, 6.Samuel², 1.Francis¹) b. 4 Mar 1750/51, Douglas, Worcester, Mass., m. 17 Feb 1777, in Douglas, Worcester, Mass., **Sarah Thayre**, b. 18 Jun 1757, Douglas, Worcester, Mass., d. 25 Feb 1838, Douglas, Worcester, Mass. Benjamin died 11 Jan 1821, Douglas, Worcester, Mass.
    Children:
    i **Lydia Wallis** b. 23 Feb 1778, Douglas, Worcester, Mass.
    ii **Peter Wallis** b. 22 Dec 1779, Douglas, Worcester, Mass., m. 26 Nov 1807, in Douglas, Worcester, Mass., **Polly Elliot**, b. 16 Jan 1784, Sutton, Worcester, Mass. Peter died 29 Oct 1846, Douglas, Worcester, Mass.
    iii **Benjamin Wallis** b. 28 May 1782, Douglas, Worcester, Mass.
125. iv **Sarah Wallis** b. 10 Jul 1785.
    v **Joseph Wallis** b. 24 Sep 1788, Douglas, Worcester, Mass.
    vi **Moses Wallis** b. 17 Mar 1793, Douglas, Worcester, Mass., d. 14 Nov 1842, Douglas, Worcester, Mass.
    vii **Rufus Wallis** b. 26 Feb 1797, Douglas, Worcester, Mass.

58. **Mercy Wallis** (24.Lydia³, 6.Samuel², 1.Francis¹) (See marriage to number 52.)

59. **Samuel Wallis** (24.Lydia³, 6.Samuel², 1.Francis¹) (See marriage to number 55.)

60. **Robert Smith** (25.Douglassa³, 6.Samuel², 1.Francis¹) b. 2 May 1774, Douglas, Worcester, Mass., m. 13 Mar 1801, in Douglas, Worcester, Mass., **Hannah Truman Emerson**.
>   *Children:*
126.   i **Persis Smith** b. 25 May 1802.

61. **Joseph Dudley** (26.Joseph[4], 10.Joseph[3], 3.Joseph[2], 1.Francis[1]) b. 16 Sep 1743, Concord, Middlesex, Mass., baptized: 18 Sep 1743, occupation: Laborer/farmer, m. (1) **Sarah Wesson**, b. 1751, d. 16 Sep 1787, m. (2) 28 Jul 1789, in Concord, Middlesex, Mass., **Eunice Derby**, b. abt 1749, d. 13 Jan 1793, m. (3) 17 Dec 1801, in Concord, Middlesex, Mass., **Mary Handly**. Joseph died 14 May 1807, Concord, Middlesex, Mass. Joseph died intestate, Ephraim Wood was administrator. Estate was worth Armorer from 1781. According to the records: "complexion, light; eyes, blue." He served for the town of Concord.

    Sarah: Died within days of the birth of her last child, Joseph, who was born "with unsound mind." Could she have had a disease? No marriage record found in Concord, but a V.R. death does list "Mrs. Sarah, w. of Joseph, age 36."
Eunice: Joseph and Eunice were married by Ephraim Wood, Esq. Death record lists "Mrs. Eunice, w. of Joseph, age 44." Her surname is "Darby" in the records.
Mary: Her surname is "Handley" in the records.

    Children by Sarah Wesson:
- i **Timothy Dudley** b. 3 Dec 1768, baptized: 6 Feb 1769. died young
- ii **Timothy Dudley** baptized: 24 Feb 1771.
- iii **Sarah Dudley** b. 23 Jul 1772, baptized: 2 Aug 1772, m. 20 Sep 1801, **Timothy Barrett**, d. 18 Jun 1804.
- iv **Molly Dudley** b. 7 Nov 1774. Died young.
- v **Molly Dudley** b. 9 Dec 1775, baptized: 26 Jan 1779, d. 23 Aug 1823, Concord, Middlesex, Mass.
- vi **Eunice Dudley** b. 18 Dec 1778, d. 24 Feb 1779, Concord, Middlesex, Mass.
- vii **Eunice Dudley** b. 7 May 1780, m. 9 Nov 1800, **Amos Baker**.
- viii **Joseph Dudley** b. 2 Sep 1787, baptized: 1 Mar 1788, d. 6 Feb 1866. Was "of unsound mind", and chose Abiel Heywood for his guardian. In 1832 Daniel Clark of Concord was appointed his guardian. He owned a farm of 195 acres, and had personal property of considerable value.

    Children by Eunice Derby:
- ix **Hephzibah Dudley** b. abt 1790. In 1808, Hephzibah was over 14, and her mother had died. She chose a Ephraim Wood (administrator of her father's estate) for her guardian.

62. **Samuel Dudley** (26.Joseph[4], 10.Joseph[3], 3.Joseph[2], 1.Francis[1]) b. 29 Sep 1746, occupation: Blacksmith, m. (1) **Lucy**, b. abt 1756, d. 7 Feb 1816, Concord, Middlesex, Mass., m. (2) **Sarah**. Samuel died 9 May 1806, Concord, Middlesex, Mass.

    Children by Lucy:
- i **Lucy Dudley** b. 3 Jun 1774, Concord, Middlesex, Mass., d. 23 Jun 1801, Concord, Middlesex, Mass.
- ii **Polly Dudley** b. 27 Nov 1776, d. abt 1777, Concord, Middlesex, Mass.

   iii **Polly Dudley** b. 25 May 1778, d. 25 Aug 1823, Concord, Middlesex, Mass.

   iv **Betsy Dudley** b. 2 Apr 1781.

   v **Rebecca Dudley** b. 23 Sep 1784, Concord, Middlesex, Mass., d. Aug 1803, Concord, Middlesex, Mass.

   vi **Sally Dudley** b. 28 Oct 1787.

63. **Nathan Dudley** (26.Joseph[4], 10.Joseph[3], 3.Joseph[2], 1.Francis[1]) b. 17 Jun 1755, Concord, Middlesex, Mass., m. (1) 24 Jan 1786, in Lexington, Middlesex, Mass., **Sarah Monroe**, d. 16 Jan 1801, Lexington, Middlesex, Mass., m. (2) 20 Jan 1804, in Bedford, Middlesex, Mass., **Hannah Lane**, b. abt 1772, d. 26 Jan 1847, Lexington, Middlesex, Mass. Nathan died 17 Jul 1835, Lexington, Middlesex, Mass. Was a Lieutenant in the Lexington artillery, and revolutionary war soldier. Moved to Lexington in 1779, was taxed there 1780. He and Sarah joined the church 27 Jan 1790. His real estate was worth $1,430. Personal property $1,816.71.

     Children by Sarah Monroe:

   i **Sally Dudley** b. 16 Oct 1786, Lexington, Middlesex, Mass., m. 12 Jan 1806, in Lexington, Middlesex, Mass., **John Viles**.

   ii **Nathan Dudley** b. 3 Apr 1789, Lexington, Middlesex, Mass., d. 8 Feb 1795, Lexington, Middlesex, Mass. Dean Dudley has a death date of 3 Feb, most likely a transcription error.

127.   iii **John Dudley** b. 18 Nov 1790.

   iv **Polly Dudley** b. 18 Sep 1792, Lexington, Middlesex, Mass., m. 8 Sep 1811, in Lexington, Middlesex, Mass., **Thomas Johnson**.

   v **Rebecca Dudley** b. 14 Aug 1794, Lexington, Middlesex, Mass., baptized: 27 Aug 1794, Lexington, Middlesex, Mass., d. 12 Apr 1795, Lexington, Middlesex, Mass.

   vi **Betsy Dudley** b. 1 Jun 1798, Lexington, Middlesex, Mass., baptized: 3 Jun 1798, Lexington, Middlesex, Mass., m. 6 Feb 1820, in Lexington, Middlesex, Mass., **Solomon Harrington**.

     Children by Hannah Lane:

   vii **Rebecca Dudley** b. 31 Dec 1808, Lexington, Middlesex, Mass., baptized: 1 Jan 1809, Lexington, Middlesex, Mass., m. 15 Jul 1827, in Lexington, Middlesex, Mass., **William Shaw**.

   viii **Nathan Dudley** b. 29 Jul 1810, Lexington, Middlesex, Mass., baptized: 5 Aug 1810, Lexington, Middlesex, Mass., d. 9 Aug 1813, Lexington, Middlesex, Mass.

64. **Samuel Dudley** (31.James[4], 10.Joseph[3], 3.Joseph[2], 1.Francis[1]) b. 1 Jun 1765, Acton, Middlesex, Mass., m. **Susanna Wentworth**. Settled at Mt. Holly, Vt.

     Children:

128.   i **Samuel R. Dudley** b. 16 Jun 1793.

   ii **Edmund W. Dudley** b. abt 1795.

    iii **Mary Dudley** b. abt 1797, Reading, Windsor Co., Vt.

    iv **Sarah Dudley** b. abt 1798, Reading, Windsor Co., Vt.

    v **Asa W. Dudley** b. abt 1799, Reading, Windsor Co., Vt.

    vi **Luther Dudley** b. abt 1800, Reading, Windsor Co., Vt.

65. **Paul Dudley** (31.James[4], 10.Joseph[3], 3.Joseph[2], 1.Francis[1]) b. 6 Mar 1771, Acton, Middlesex, Mass., m. (1) 30 Aug 1796, in Boston, Suffolk, Mass., **Abigail Durant**, d. 2 Jan 1839, Concord, Middlesex, Mass., m. (2) 18 Nov 1840, in Concord, Middlesex, Mass., **Rebecca Nichols**. Paul died 8 Jun 1843, Acton, Middlesex, Mass. Paul and Abby were married by Rev. James Freeman.

    Children by Abigail Durant:

129.   i **James Dudley** b. 23 Sept 1797.

130.   ii **Paul Dudley** b. 19 Sep 1799.

    iii **Mary Dudley** b. 28 May 1802, Acton, Middlesex, Mass., m. 2 May 1835, in Concord, Middlesex, Mass., **Rudolpho Parker**. The marriage date is the intention date.

        Rudolpho: Was of Brookline, Mass.

131.   iv **John L. Dudley** b. 27 Oct 1805.

132.   v **Josiah P. Dudley** b. 22 May 1808.

133.   vi **Asa P. Dudley** b. 13 Nov 1811.

66. **John Dudley** (32.Benjamin[4], 10.Joseph[3], 3.Joseph[2], 1.Francis[1]) b. 27 Apr 1770, Marlborough, Middlesex, Mass., baptized: 1 Jul 1770, Marlborough, Middlesex, Mass., occupation: Carpenter, m. 1 Sep 1793, in Lincoln, Middlesex, Mass., **Mary Whitney**, d. 30 Apr 1820, Weston, Middlesex, Mass. John died 20 Dec 1848, Weston, Middlesex, Mass. Joseph was "bright and smart and fond of a good joke." He lived at Weston in 1848. His intentions of marriage to a Miss Beula Baker of Concord was published at Lincoln on 1 September 1793, but apparently this did not work out. Was admitted to church fellowship 26 Jun 1796. He died "of old age."

    Children:

    i **John Dudley** b. 3 Sep 1795, Weston, Middlesex, Mass., baptized: 7 Aug 1796, Weston, Middlesex, Mass., occupation: housewright, m. 12 Aug 1820, in Weston, Middlesex, Mass., **Lucinda Maria Blake**. He lived in Cambridgeport, Mass. in 1848. The marriage date is the intention date.

    ii **Mary Dudley** b. 6 Jan 1799, Weston, Middlesex, Mass., baptized: 17 Feb 1799, Weston, Middlesex, Mass.

    iii **Francis Kittredge Dudley** b. 26 Dec 1800, Weston, Middlesex, Mass., baptized: 29 Mar 1801, Weston, Middlesex, Mass., m. 18 May 1823, in Lexington, Middlesex, Mass., **Susan P. Smith**.

        Susan: She was of Lexington

    iv **Susan Norcross Dudley** b. 22 Mar 1803, Weston, Middlesex, Mass., baptized:

27 Mar 1803, Weston, Middlesex, Mass., m. 1824, in Weston, Middlesex, Mass., **Samuel Saunders**. Marriage intentions filed Feb 1824 in Weston. The marriage record was returned to the town certifying that it took place, but no date.

Samuel: Was of Weston, then Cambridgeport.

    v **Harriet Maria Dudley** b. 13 Apr 1806, Weston, Middlesex, Mass., baptized: 20 Apr 1806, Weston, Middlesex, Mass., m. 11 Jun 1835, in Weston, Middlesex, Mass., **Joel Newton**. She and Joel lived in East Boston in 1848

    vi **Jane Dudley** b. 23 Aug 1809, Weston, Middlesex, Mass., baptized: 3 Sep 1809, Weston, Middlesex, Mass., m. **John Lakin**. No marriage record was found.

        John: John was from Durham, N.H.

    vii **Samuel Whitney Dudley** b. 17 Feb 1812, Weston, Middlesex, Mass., baptized: 1 Mar 1812, Weston, Middlesex, Mass., m. 25 Dec 1837, in Cambridge, Middlesex, Mass., **Lucy Pollard**. Lived in Cambridgeport in 1848. No marriage record was found.

67. **Samuel Dudley** (32.Benjamin[4], 10.Joseph[3], 3.Joseph[2], 1.Francis[1]) b. 24 Dec 1773, Weston, Middlesex, Mass., m. 28 Apr 1805, in Lincoln, Middlesex, Mass., **Betsey Heywood**. Samuel died 3 Jan 1812, Lincoln, Middlesex, Mass. Married by Rev Charles Stearns.

Betsey: She asked that Samuel's brother John would be administrator of Samuel's will. She was originally from Concord, and her name may have been spelled Hayward.

    Children:

    i **Caroline Dudley** b. 1 Jul 1805, Lincoln, Middlesex, Mass., m. 1826, in Weston, Middlesex, Mass., **Jonas Parks**. They filed intentions to marry 9 Sep 1826, and were married by Congregational minister Rev Joseph Field, who did not provide a wedding date. Both were of Weston when married.

        Jonas: He and Caroline lived at Watertown and Bremen, Maine.

    ii **Eliza Dudley** b. 1 Jun 1808, Lincoln, Middlesex, Mass., m. 30 May 1829, in Wayland, Middlesex, Mass., **Dexter Moulton**. She and Dexter lived at Natick. The marriage date is the intention date.

        Dexter: Was of Wayland.

134.   iii **James Heywood Dudley** b. 30 Mar 1810.

68. **Nahum Dudley** (33.Joseph[4], 11.Benjamin[3], 3.Joseph[2], 1.Francis[1]) b. 4 May 1757, East Sudbury, Middlesex, Mass., m. **Margaret Howe**, b. Apr 1759, Sudbury, Middlesex, Mass., (daughter of **Samuel Howe** and **Abigail Dudley**) d. 9 Aug 1803, Westmoreland, Cheshire, New Hampshire. Nahum died 15 Oct 1799, Westmoreland, Cheshire, New Hampshire. Soldier in the Revolution, fought at Lexington and Concord, and Bunker Hill. Went to Westmoreland in 1783. Most of his children were raised by their

grandfather Samuel Howe.

> *Children:*
>   i   **Polly (Mary) Dudley.**
>   ii **Samuel Dudley.**
>   iii **Nahum Dudley** d. ABT 1806, Westmoreland, Cheshire, New Hampshire.
135.   iv **Joseph Dudley** b. ABT 1780.
>   v   **Abigail Dudley** b. ABT 1788, Westmoreland, Cheshire, New Hampshire, d.
>   23 Apr 1812, Westmoreland, Cheshire, New Hampshire.
136.   vi **Moses Dudley** b. 18 Oct 1794.
>   vii **Margaret Dudley** b. 1798, Westmoreland, Cheshire, New Hampshire, m. 6
>   Dec 1818, in Westmoreland, Cheshire, New Hampshire, **Calvin Lane**.
>   Margaret died 8 Oct 1858, Westmoreland, Cheshire, New Hampshire.
>   **Calvin:** Was of Norton, Mass.
>   viii **Warren Dudley** b. ABT 1800, Westmoreland, Cheshire, New Hampshire. On
>   30 April 1814, he chose Dr. Moses Dudley as his guardian, as he was over 14.

69. **Moses Dudley** (33.Joseph[4], 11.Benjamin[3], 3.Joseph[2], 1.Francis[1]) b. 31 Jan 1769,
Sudbury, Middlesex, Mass., occupation: Doctor, m. (1) 16 Jan 1798, in Wayland, Middlesex,
Mass., **Abigail Robie**, (daughter of **Eben Robie**) d. 15 Mar 1804, Westmoreland,
Cheshire, New Hampshire, m. (2) **Sarah Carlisle**, b. ABT 1775, d. 24 Jan 1829,
Westmoreland, Cheshire, New Hampshire. Moses died 15 Nov 1817, Westmoreland,
Cheshire, New Hampshire. Moses studied medicine with Dr. Adams of Natick. Moses and
Abigail had children, but there is no record of them. The North Church Cemetery at
Westmoreland had a gravestone a death date of 15 Nov 1817, but states "in his 49th year". It is
probably an addition error.
Sarah: Sarah was found in a cemetery record. However, there is a SALLY, "widow of Dr
Moses" found in another cemetery whom died in 1839. It is probably the same person.

> *Children by Abigail Robie:*
>   i   **Child** d. 29 Aug 1799, Westmoreland, Cheshire, New Hampshire.

70. **Luther Dudley** (33.Joseph[4], 11.Benjamin[3], 3.Joseph[2], 1.Francis[1]) b. 5 May 1772,
East Sudbury, Middlesex, Mass., m. 17 Oct 1791, in Wayland, Middlesex, Mass., **Martha
(Nancy) Willington**. Luther died Paris, Oxford, Maine. Lived near the King place in Paris,
on the road between Paris Hill and the cape. He died two years after moving to Paris.
    Martha: Married William Cobb of Hebron, Maine, after Luther's death. Her name is
listed as "Nancy" in "History of Woodstock."

> *Children:*
137.   i   **Josiah Wellington Dudley** b. 23 Jan 1792.
138.   ii **Moses Dudley** b. 11 Oct 1794.
>   iii **Mary Dudley** b. 3 Mar 1797, Wayland, Middlesex, Mass., m. **Joel B.
>   Thayer.**

Joel: Was from Paris

- iv **Warren Dudley** b. 4 Jul 1800, Wayland, Middlesex, Mass., m. 4 Oct 1822, in Woodstock, Oxford, Maine, **Alvina Barrett**.
- v **Nancy Dudley** b. 26 Jun 1809, m. **Johnson Holt**. There is no VR for this child.

  Johnson: Was from Paris.
- vi **Luther Dudley** b. 10 Dec 1811.
- vii **Martha Dudley** m. **Otis Bicknell**.

  Otis: Was from Buckfield, Maine.

71. **Abigail Dudley** (34.Benjamin⁴, 11.Benjamin³, 3.Joseph², 1.Francis¹) b. abt 1755, m. 16 Jun 1777, in Sudbury, Middlesex, Mass., **Elijah Goodnow**.
    Children:
    - i **David Goodnow** b. 25 Jan 1778, Sudbury, Middlesex, Mass.
    - ii **Nabby Goodnow** b. 25 Jun 1779, Sudbury, Middlesex, Mass. "Nabby" was a nickname for Abigail--so her name may really have been that.
    - iii **Elijah Goodnow** b. 25 Dec 1780, Sudbury, Middlesex, Mass.
    - iv **Adams Goodnow** b. 19 Mar 1782, Sudbury, Middlesex, Mass.
    - v **Elizabeth Goodnow** b. 5 Sep 1784, Sudbury, Middlesex, Mass.
    - vi **Mary W. Goodnow** b. 17 Feb 1787, Sudbury, Middlesex, Mass.
    - vii **George Goodnow** b. 2 Jan 1789, Sudbury, Middlesex, Mass.

72. **Jane Dudley** (34.Benjamin⁴, 11.Benjamin³, 3.Joseph², 1.Francis¹) b. abt 1760, m. 14 Mar 1787, in Wayland, Middlesex, Mass., **Nathan Dudley**, b. 20 Mar 1760, Sudbury, Middlesex, Mass., (son of **Ebenezer Dudley** and **Grace Rice**) d. 19 Feb 1838.
    Nathan: After marriage, moved to Shepardstown, Maine. Info on Children from "Annals of Oxford." He was pensioned in 1819 for service in Mass. Continentals. "Annals of Oxford" has a marriage date of 14 Mar 1779, but I feel it is incorrect due to date of the first born. All the children below were found in the "Annals."
    Children:
    - i **Sarah Dudley** b. 18 Jul 1788, m. 16 Mar 1811, **Bela Chandler**.
    - ii **Mary Dudley** b. 1790, m. 6 Oct 1808, **Shepard Churchill**.
    - iii **Jane Dudley** b. 14 Apr 1792, m. 4 Feb 1816, **Isaac Washburn**.
139. iv **Nathan Dudley** b. 21 May 1795.
140. v **Ebenezer Dudley** b. 19 Jan 1798.
    - vi **Therza Dudley** b. 7 Mar 1802. I hate to admit this, but I am not sure if Therza is male or female!

73. **Benjamin Dudley** (34.Benjamin⁴, 11.Benjamin³, 3.Joseph², 1.Francis¹) b. 1766, m. (1) 7 Sep 1793, **Sybil Stevens**, b. abt 1774, (daughter of **Ephraim Stevens**) d. 17 Sep 1824, Sudbury, Middlesex, Mass., m. (2) 15 Mar 1826, in Framingham, Middlesex, Mass.,

Anna Belcher, b. abt 1781, d. 2 Jan 1838, buried: Sudbury, Middlesex, Mass. Benjamin died 27 Apr 1855, buried: Sudbury, Middlesex, Mass. Death date from gravestone.
Sybil: Dean Dudley reports name as "Sibyl."

Children by Sybil Stevens:

141.   i   **Abijah Dudley**.

      ii   **Silvia Dudley** b. 13 Feb 1795, Framingham, Middlesex, Mass., baptized: 25 Aug 1799, Sudbury, Middlesex, Mass., m. **John Jones**.

     iii   **Phebe Dudley** b. 9 Feb 1797, Framingham, Middlesex, Mass., baptized: 25 Aug 1799, Sudbury, Middlesex, Mass., m. 12 Sep 1819, in Sudbury, Middlesex, Mass., **Benjamin Pattee**.
            Benjamin: "Of Walpole."

142.   iv   **Benjamin Dudley** b. 25 Oct 1799.

      v   **Louisa Dudley** b. 1802, baptized: 10 Oct 1802, Sudbury, Middlesex, Mass., m. 8 Apr 1823, in Sudbury, Middlesex, Mass., **Sabine Ellis**.
            Sabine: "Of Walpole." Name is spelled SABIN in the VR.

      vi   **Loruhama Dudley** b. 13 Sep 1804, Sudbury, Middlesex, Mass., baptized: 18 Nov 1804, Sudbury, Middlesex, Mass., m. (1) 1826, **Fisher Howe**, (son of **Ezekiel Howe**) d. abt 1857, m. (2) 1858, **John Hunt**. Marriage intention filed in Framingham 2 Jul 1826.
            Fisher: He appears as Fisher EAMES on marriage intention. Misspelling? Was "of Sudbury" on the marriage intention, filed in Framingham.
            John: He was 82 at the time of his marriage to Loruhama.

     vii   **Samuel Stevens Dudley** b. 1806, baptized: 31 Aug 1806, occupation: Methodist Minister. Was in New Hampshire in 1848.

    viii   **Sibyl Dudley** baptized: 9 Apr 1808, m. 1830, **Lewis L. Metcalf**. Sibyl died 3 Jan 1835.
            Lewis: "Of Wrentham."

      ix   **Mary Dudley** baptized: 5 Aug 1809, m. 30 Oct 1828, in Sudbury, Middlesex, Mass., **Luman Boyden**, occupation: Methodist Minister.
            Luman: "Of Walpole."

      x   **Moses Dudley** b. 25 Nov 1810, baptized: 7 Jun 1812, Sudbury, Middlesex, Mass., m. 7 Dec 1837, in Marlborough, Middlesex, Mass., **Susan Maria Bliss**.
            Susan: "Of Berlin."

      xi   **Timothy Dudley** b. 1814, baptized: 3 Jul 1814, Sudbury, Middlesex, Mass., d. 15 Aug 1817, Sudbury, Middlesex, Mass. Dean Dudley has conflicting dates. Timothy's date of death MAY be 21 Jul 1817.

     xii   **Keziah Dudley** b. 10 Feb 1816, baptized: 6 Jul 1816, Sudbury, Middlesex, Mass., m. abt 1836, **Lewis Sumner**.

74. **John Dudley** (34.Benjamin[4], 11.Benjamin[3], 3.Joseph[2], 1.Francis[1]) b. abt 1768, m. 31 May 1792, in Framingham, Middlesex, Mass., **Zerviah Rice**, baptized: 12 Jul 1772,

(daughter of **David Rice** and **Hannah Winch**). John died 1814, Petersham, Worcester, Mass. John moved to Petersham in 1802. Upon his death Joel Negus was administrator of John's estate. The children appear to be heirs of their grandfather David Rice...and also of Lydia Gleason of Framingham who specifically mentions her estate going to "the children John, Mary, and Caleb Dudley." Also, Eli Bullard of Framingham was appointed their guardian in 1805.

Zerviah: One record spells her name Serviah.

> *Children:*
> i   **John Dudley** b. 10 May 1793, Framingham, Middlesex, Mass.
> ii **Hannah Dudley** b. 5 Feb 1795, Framingham, Middlesex, Mass., d. Mar 1795, Framingham, Middlesex, Mass. The V.R. does not list the exact day of death.
> iii **Mary Dudley** b. 5 Feb 1795, Framingham, Middlesex, Mass. Twin to Hannah.

143.   iv **Caleb Dudley** b. 11 Feb 1797.

> v   **Nathan Dudley** b. 22 Feb 1799. May have died young.

75. **Jonathan Dudley** (34.Benjamin[4], 11.Benjamin[3], 3.Joseph[2], 1.Francis[1]) b. 18 Apr 1772, East Sudbury, Middlesex, Mass., m. 21 Apr 1795, in Beverly, Essex, Mass., **Hannah Carter**. Jonathan died 10 Jul 1847, Danvers, Essex, Mass. The Danvers V.R. says Jonathan died of consumption, age 75 yrs.

> *Children:*
> i   **Ruth Dudley** b. 29 Nov 1795, Beverly, Essex, Mass., d. 15 Oct 1806, Beverly, Essex, Mass.

144.   ii **John P. Dudley** b. 13 Aug 1797.

145.   iii **Josiah Dudley** b. 7 Dec 1799.

> iv **Elizabeth Dudley** b. 3 Dec 1802, Danvers, Essex, Mass., d. 4 Jul 1805, Beverly, Essex, Mass. Death record says she died of "worms and cancer."

76. **Josiah Dudley** (34.Benjamin[4], 11.Benjamin[3], 3.Joseph[2], 1.Francis[1]) b. abt 1774, East Sudbury, Middlesex, Mass., m. 31 Aug 1797, in Sudbury, Middlesex, Mass., **Abigail Brown**. After much research, I believe this is the correct Josiah for the marriage to Abigail Brown. The marriage and children are all verified by Vital records. Dean Dudley lists another Josiah, a son of Daniel Dudley, also marrying the same Abigail on the same date.

Abigail: She was from Sudbury when she married him.

> *Children:*
> i   **Elizabeth Dudley** b. 25 Mar 1798, Wayland, Middlesex, Mass., m. 29 Jul 1816, in Wayland, Middlesex, Mass., **Martin Hemmingway**. The marriage banns were published in Framingham, where it states she was from East Sudbury. **Martin**: Was from Framingham.
> ii **Josiah Dudley** b. 9 Nov 1799, Wayland, Middlesex, Mass.
> iii **Josiah Dudley** b. 9 Oct 1800, Wayland, Middlesex, Mass. According to Dean Dudley, he "ran off from home."

    iv   **Rebecca Dudley** b. 9 Oct 1801, Wayland, Middlesex, Mass., d. 7 Apr 1809, Wayland, Middlesex, Mass. According to the Wayland Church Record, she died "by scalding, age 8y".

    v   **Joseph Curtis Dudley** b. 25 Sep 1802, Wayland, Middlesex, Mass., m. 17 Jan 1822, in Framingham, Middlesex, Mass., **Olive Winch**. Lived in Westboro' in 1848.

    vi **Abigail Dudley** b. 2 Oct 1803, Wayland, Middlesex, Mass., m. 20 May 1829, in Framingham, Middlesex, Mass., **Moses Frost**.
        Moses: Was from Natick.

146.   vii **Joseph Dudley**.

    viii **Henry Dudley**. Died when he was 7 years old.

    ix **Hannah Dudley** baptized: 18 Aug 1805, Wayland, Middlesex, Mass., m. 1 Apr 1829, in Framingham, Middlesex, Mass., **John Sanderson**.

77. **Margaret Howe** (35.Abigail[4], 11.Benjamin[3], 3.Joseph[2], 1.Francis[1]) (See marriage to number 68.)

78. **Nathan Dudley** (36.Ebenezer[4], 11.Benjamin[3], 3.Joseph[2], 1.Francis[1]) b. 20 Mar 1760, Sudbury, Middlesex, Mass., m. (1) 14 Mar 1787, in Wayland, Middlesex, Mass., **Jane Dudley**, (See marriage to number 72) m. (2) 12 Jun 1824, **Sylvia Washburn**. Nathan died 19 Feb 1838. After marriage, moved to Shepardstown, Maine. Info on Children from "Annals of Oxford." He was pensioned in 1819 for service in Mass. Continentals. "Annals of Oxford" has a marriage date of 14 Mar 1779, but I feel it is incorrect due to date of the first born. All the children below were found in the "Annals."
    Sylvia: She was the widow of Manassah Washburn.
    Children by Jane Dudley:

79. **David Dudley** (36.Ebenezer[4], 11.Benjamin[3], 3.Joseph[2], 1.Francis[1]) b. 1 Oct 1763, Sudbury, Middlesex, Mass., m. (1) 11 Sep 1791, **Rebecca Bucknam**, b. 1 Nov 1766, Worcester, Worcester, Mass., d. abt 1800, m. (2) 25 Nov 1802, **Charity Tuell**. David died Woodstock, Oxford, Maine. David first settled in Hebron, Maine, then moved to Paris, then to Woodstock. He lived on the hill farm, which, in 1882, was apparently still owned by the Dudley's (see "History of Woodstock."). No marriage records were found. He was in the Revolution, with the 1st Div. of Shepardsfield.
    Children by Rebecca Bucknam:

147.   i   **Daniel Dudley** b. abt 1792.

    ii **Rebecca Dudley** b. abt 1794, m. 1 Feb 1815, **E. Washburn**.
        E.: Was from Hebron.

    iii **David Dudley** b. 9 Sep 1796, d. 1820. He went to sea and never returned home.

    iv **Eliza Dudley** b. 13 Feb 1798, Paris, Oxford, Maine, m. 15 Nov 1844, in

Woodstock, Oxford, Maine, **Aaron Davis**. The IGI civil batch number M521471 states that a "Eliza Dudley" married Aaron Davis on 26 Oct 1843 in Woodstock. The "History of Woodstock." also reports this Dean Dudley lists her name as "Betsey."

   v **Clarissa Dudley** b. 13 Apr 1800, m. 7 Jun 1826, in Minot, Androscoggin, Maine, **Galen Soule**. IGI civil batch M520541 reports date of 17 May. I believe this was the intention date.
       Galen: Was from Oxford, Maine.
       Children by Charity Tuell:

148.   vi **Perrin Dudley** b. 3 Feb 1803.

   vii **Laodicea Dudley** b. 8 Nov 1805, Paris, Oxford, Maine, m. 10 Apr 1827, in Woodstock, Oxford, Maine, **Seth Perkins**.

   viii **Arvilla Dudley** b. 7 Dec 1807, m. 30 Dec 1830, in Woodstock, Oxford, Maine, **Eli Bryant**. Dean Dudley has a marriage date of 30 Nov. This could have been the intention date. My date comes from the IGI civil batch numbers...in this case M521471.

   ix **Ann Dudley** b. 19 Jun 1809, m. 25 Nov 1845, in Woodstock, Oxford, Maine, **John Day**. The IGI civil batch number M521471 has a marriage date of 25 May 1845 in Woodstock. As the IGI is famous for stating intention dates as marriage dates, I believe Dean Dudley is more accurate here.

   x **Alfred Dudley** b. 9 Jan 1811.

   xi **Charlotte Dudley** b. 1 Jun 1813, m. 27 Jun 1833, in Woodstock, Oxford, Maine, **Jonathan Day**. Charlotte died 12 Sep 1844. Dean Dudley has a marriage date of 15 May 1832. I sided with the IGI civil batch here.

   xii **Sidney Dudley** b. 9 Feb 1817, d. 11 Apr 1832.

149.   xiii **Gilbert Dudley** b. 19 Nov 1819.

150.   xiv **Ansel G. Dudley** b. 9 Feb 1821.

   xv **Josiah A. Dudley** b. 11 Mar 1823, d. 3 May 1832.

80. **Ebenezer Dudley** (36.Ebenezer[4], 11.Benjamin[3], 3.Joseph[2], 1.Francis[1]) b. 20 Apr 1771, Sudbury, Middlesex, Mass., m. 3 Jan 1799, in Roxbury, Norfolk, Mass., **Abigail Murdock**. Ebenezer died 2 Aug 1833, West Roxbury, Norfolk, Mass. Ebenezer died of "consumption."

       Children:

   i **Abigail Health Dudley** b. 21 Dec 1800, West Roxbury, Norfolk, Mass., m. 13 Oct 1835, in Roxbury, Norfolk, Mass., **John Brown**.
       John: Was from Billerica

   ii **Ebenezer Dudley** b. 25 Jan 1802, West Roxbury, Norfolk, Mass., m. 18 Jun 1826, in Roxbury, Norfolk, Mass., **Elizabeth F. Richards**, (daughter of **Lemuel R. Richards**).

   iii **Charity Murdock Dudley** b. 20 Jan 1804, West Roxbury, Norfolk, Mass., m.

(1) 24 Nov 1825, in Roxbury, Norfolk, Mass., **John A. Davis**, m. (2) **Samuel Briggs**.

Samuel: Was from Dorchester.

151.   iv   **William Davis Dudley** b. 1 Feb 1806.

152.   v   **Ephraim Murdock Dudley** b. 23 May 1808.

      vi   **Sarah Murdock Dudley** b. 3 Feb 1810, West Roxbury, Norfolk, Mass., m. 15 Jan 1835, in Roxbury, Norfolk, Mass., **Mottram V. Arnold**.

Mottram: Was from Brighton.

      vii **Ann Maria Dudley** b. 1 Mar 1812, West Roxbury, Norfolk, Mass.

      viii **Betsey S. Dudley** b. 25 May 1814, West Roxbury, Norfolk, Mass., d. 26 Jan 1837, West Roxbury, Norfolk, Mass.

      ix   **Charlotte Dudley** b. 26 Mar 1817, West Roxbury, Norfolk, Mass., m. **Alexander Mair**.

Alexander: Was from Boston.

      x   **Henry Dudley** b. 13 Jan 1821, West Roxbury, Norfolk, Mass.

81. **William Dudley** (37.William[4], 11.Benjamin[3], 3.Joseph[2], 1.Francis[1]) b. 25 Jul 1763, East Sudbury, Middlesex, Mass., occupation: Carpenter, m. (1) 7 July 1791, in Wayland, Middlesex, Mass., **Anna Moulton**, d. 5 Feb 1805, Wayland, Middlesex, Mass., m. (2) 26 Jun 1806, in Wayland, Middlesex, Mass., **Unity Rice**, b. 16 Dec 1771, (daughter of **Isaac Rice** and **Sarah Lamb**) d. 3 Mar 1835, Wayland, Middlesex, Mass. William died 29 Jun 1843, Wayland, Middlesex, Mass.

Anna: The Wayland Town Record says Ann died 8 Feb, The Church Record says 5 Feb. I believe she died 5 Feb as per church record as many towns record the BURIAL date.

Children by Anna Moulton:

      i   **John Moulton Dudley** b. 24 Oct 1791, Wayland, Middlesex, Mass., m. **Elizabeth Brown**. John died Sudbury, Middlesex, Mass. Dean Dudley is the only source for this marriage.

Elizabeth: Was from Scarborough, Maine.

153.   ii   **Samuel Dudley** b. 18 Apr 1793.

      iii **Clarissa Dudley** b. 9 Sep 1798, Wayland, Middlesex, Mass., m. 13 Feb 1825, in Dover, Rockingham, New Hampshire, **Thomas R. Hanson**, d. 28 Dec 1862, Weymouth, Norfolk, Mass., buried: Ashwood Cemetery, Weymouth, Mass. Clarissa died 17 Jun 1847, Weymouth, Norfolk, Mass. No death record found. **Thomas**: After Clarissa's death, he married Vira Chandler.

Children by Unity Rice:

154.   iv   **William Rice Dudley** b. 6 Mar 1807.

      v   **Sarah Ann Dudley** b. 25 May 1810, Wayland, Middlesex, Mass., d. 24 Mar 1844, Wayland, Middlesex, Mass. No children. She died of consumption.

155.   vi   **Benjamin Austin Dudley** b. 6 Sep 1811.

156.   vii **Nathaniel Curtis Dudley** b. 17 Jan 1813.

82. **Jason Dudley** (37.William[4], 11.Benjamin[3], 3.Joseph[2], 1.Francis[1]) b. abt 1772, East Sudbury, Middlesex, Mass., m. 14 Mar 1801, in East Sudbury, Middlesex, Mass., **Betsey Johnson**, (daughter of **Peter Johnson** and **Margaret Rice**) d. 18 Jun 1812, East Sudbury, Middlesex, Mass. Jason died 20 May 1812, East Sudbury, Middlesex, Mass. At Jason's death, the two oldest girls had Edmund Rice, their mothers grandfather, as their guardian. They also had a legacy from their grandfather Peter Johnson, in 1823. The Death record says Jason died "near age 40 y." Their marriage date is the intention date.

> *Children:*
> i   **Catherine C. Dudley**. Under 14 in 1813
> ii   **Mary E. Dudley**. Under 14 in 1813.
> iii   **Son**. Died young.
> iv   **Betsey Dudley** d. 13 Feb 1813, Wayland, Middlesex, Mass. Betsey died of "dropsey in the head", according to the VR.

83. **Abigail Dudley** (37.William[4], 11.Benjamin[3], 3.Joseph[2], 1.Francis[1]) m. 29 Nov 1799, in East Sudbury, Middlesex, Mass., **Paul Loker**, b. 2 Jul 1774, Sudbury, Middlesex, Mass., (son of **Isaac Loker** and **Dorothy Brintnal**) d. 12 Jun 1862, Wayland, Middlesex, Mass. Abigail died 19 Mar 1848, Wayland, Middlesex, Mass. The marriage date is the intention date.

> *Children:*
> i   **Otis Loker** b. 28 Mar 1803, Wayland, Middlesex, Mass., m. **Betsey Allen**. Otis died 22 Apr 1877, Wayland, Middlesex, Mass.
> ii   **Alpheus Dexter Loker** m. **Harriet Bowman**.
> iii   **Paul Loker** m. **Sarah B. Coggin**.

84. **Elizabeth Dudley** (39.John[4], 14.John[3], 4.John[2], 1.Francis[1]) b. 30 Nov 1763, Groton, Middlesex, Mass., m. 29 Oct 1789, in Westmoreland, Cheshire, New Hampshire, **Jonathan Knight**, (son of **Jonathan Knight** and **Mary Johnson**). Elizabeth died 29 Apr 1866. The "History of Westmoreland" states that she was "a remarkable woman. After the beginning of the Civil War, Elizabeth pieced a block for a quilt the ladies were making; in the center wrote: "Mrs Betsey Knight, age 100. She saw the Battle of Bunker Hill and hopes to see the end of this war" (the Civil War). Lived on Park Hill. Member of church in Westmoreland. Removed to Piermont, NH, c 1830."
Jonathan: Jonathan and Betsey had 12 children.

> *Children:*
> i   **Jonathan Knight** b. 25 Oct 1790, Westmoreland, Cheshire, New Hampshire, occupation: Physician, m. 14 Jan 1814, in Stoddard, Cheshire, N.H., **Dorothy "Dolly" Joslin**. Jonathan died 1 May 1879, Manchester, Hillsborough, N.H., buried: Piermont, Grafton, NH. He and Dorothy had 9 children.
> ii   **Josiah Knight** b. 8 Mar 1792, Westmoreland, Cheshire, New Hampshire, m.

20 Apr 1815, in Stoddard, Cheshire, N.H., **Betsey Joslin**. Josiah died 16 Mar 1882, St. Charles, Iowa. Had 5 children.

    iii **Curtis Knight** b. 15 Apr 1794, Westmoreland, Cheshire, New Hampshire, m. **Betsey Atwood**, d. North Bend, Indiana. Curtis died North Bend, Indiana. **Betsey**: Was of Cornish, NH.

    iv **Prentice Knight** b. 21 Jan 1797, Westmoreland, Cheshire, New Hampshire, m. **Melinda Gould**, d. Newbury, Vt. Prentice died Newbury, Vt. **Melinda**: Was from Hanover, NH.

85. **Nathan Dudley** (40.Peter⁴, 14.John³, 4.John², 1.Francis¹) b. 5 May 1766, Framingham, Middlesex, Mass., m. 30 Mar 1786, in Framingham, Middlesex, Mass., **Mercy Sheffield**. Nathan died Buffalo, N.Y.

Children:

157.   i **Aaron Dudley** b. 5 May 1786.

    ii **Sally Dudley** b. 5 May 1786, m. 28 Feb 1807, in Cambridge, Middlesex, Mass., **Paul Ellis**. They lived at Walpole. The marriage date is the intention date.

86. **Abraham Dudley** (40.Peter⁴, 14.John³, 4.John², 1.Francis¹) b. 14 Oct 1768, Framingham, Middlesex, Mass., d. 10 Sep 1846, Spencer, N.Y. He lived mostly in New York State.

Children:

    i **Polly Dudley** b. 5 Jul 1795, Boston, Suffolk, Mass., d. 23 Mar 1821.

    ii **Anson Dudley** b. 15 Mar 1798, Boston, Suffolk, Mass., d. 25 Aug 1822.

    iii **Abram Dudley** b. 22 Apr 1800, Boston, Suffolk, Mass.

    iv **Lemuel Dudley** b. 9 Apr 1802, Boston, Suffolk, Mass., m. **Margaret Miller**. Lived in Dix, N.Y. **Margaret**: Was from Dix, N.Y.

    v **Eunice Dudley** b. 24 Mar 1804, Boston, Suffolk, Mass., m. **John Pratt**. Lived in Burlington, N.Y.

    vi **Elizabeth Dudley** b. 5 Apr 1809, Boston, Suffolk, Mass., m. **Simon P. Chesley**. **Simon**: From Granville, Pa.

    vii **Joseph Dudley** b. 4 May 1816, Boston, Suffolk, Mass., m. **Frances Decker**. **Frances**: Was from Windham, N.Y.

87. **Daniel Dudley** (41.Daniel⁴, 14.John³, 4.John², 1.Francis¹) b. 27 Mar 1758, Concord, Middlesex, Mass., baptized: 2 Apr 1758, m. 23 Jun 1787, in Concord, Middlesex, Mass., **Lucy Vose**, b. ABT 1757, d. 26 Feb 1844, Wayland, Middlesex, Mass. Daniel died 22 July 1808, Woods Landing, Winslow?, Kennebec, Maine. Daniel owed a lot of money

when he died, but still left a considerable estate to his wife. He owed Dr. Moses Dudley $1,000, and William Dudley $8.52. Still, there was $1,142.29 left. Jacob Reeves was administrator of the estate, and sold 3 acres of woodland to Ephraim Dudley, 7 acres to Dr. Moses Dudley. A Sheep pasture went to Ephraim, and Dr. Moses owned most of the barn lot. Daniel and Lucy were married by Rev. Ezra Ripley. He died by drowning at Woods Landing, but it is uncertain where that is. Winslow VR shows the date.

Lucy: Death record states she was 87 at the time of her death.

> *Children:*
> i **Thomas Harling Dudley** b. 27 Mar 1788, Wayland, Middlesex, Mass., m. 25 Mar 1816, in Wayland, Middlesex, Mass., **Laura S. Barron**. Thomas died 8 May 1833, Wayland, Middlesex, Mass.
> Laura: Was "of Boston."
> ii **Joseph Dudley** b. 24 Sep 1789, Wayland, Middlesex, Mass.

158. iii **John Vose Dudley** b. ABT 1794.
159. iv **Lewis Dudley** b. 8 Jun 1799.
> v **Sally Dudley** m. 19 Oct 1823, in Wayland, Middlesex, Mass., **Artemas Greenwood**.
> Artemas: Was from Needham.

88. **James H. Dudley** (43.Francis[4], 14.John[3], 4.John[2], 1.Francis[1]) b. ABT 1775, Winslow, Kennebec, Maine, occupation: lumberman, m. 31 May 1806, in Machias, Washington, Maine, **Rosemund Finlason**, b. 4 Sep 1778, Machias, Washington, Maine, (daughter of **Wallace Finlason** and **Susanna Scott**) d. 28 Mar 1861, East Machias, Washington, Maine. James died AFT 1850, Maine. Signed 1812 petition with other settlers north of Bangor, ME, requesting protection from the Indians, who had burned a saw mill. James is found in Penobscot Co. deeds c1815, with brothers Daniel and Rowland, leasing Indian land from the Penobscot tribal agent, timbering it, and selling it back to the agent. He resided in unorganized townships, north of Bangor, Maine. He was a lumbeman in Miramichi, New Brunswick, Canada c 181-1820's. In 1850, age 75, he is in the household of son-in-law, Mark T. Scott, in Letter L Twp.

Rosemund: Surname also found as "Fenlason."

> *Children:*
160. i **Rowland Cushing Dudley** b. 25 Jul 1807.
161. ii **Mary H. Dudley** b. ABT 1809.
> iii **Rosamund F. Dudley** b. ABT 1811, Maine, m. 13 Jul 1834, in Lincoln, Penobscot, Maine, **Mark T. Scott**, b. ABT 1809, NB.
162. iv **James Madison Dudley** b. ABT Dec 1813.
163. v **Charles H. Dudley** b. 14 Apr 1818.

89. **Ann Williams Dudley** (43.Francis[4], 14.John[3], 4.John[2], 1.Francis[1]) b. ABT 1776, Winslow, Kennebec, Maine, m. INT 2 FEB 1799, in Winslow, Kennebec, Maine,

Zimri Heywood, b. 21 Jun 1774, Winslow, Kennebec, Maine, (son of **Zimri Heywood** and **Jane Foster**) d. 11 Mar 1814, Winslow, Kennebec, Maine. Ann died 12 Mar 1868, Canaan, Somerset, Maine.

> *Children:*
> i **Foster Moses Heywood** b. 26 Nov 1799, Winslow, Kennebec, Maine.
> ii **Charles Heywood** b. 7 Mar 1800, Winslow, Kennebec, Maine.
> iii **Eunice Heywood** b. 8 May 1802, Winslow, Kennebec, Maine.
> iv **Zimri Heywood** b. 19 Dec 1805, Winslow, Kennebec, Maine.
> v **Ann Heywood** b. 28 Feb 1808, Winslow, Kennebec, Maine.
> vi **Daniel Heywood** b. 11 Feb 1810, Winslow, Kennebec, Maine.
> vii **Lydia Heywood** b. 22 Apr 1812, Winslow, Kennebec, Maine.

90. **Rowland Dudley** (43.Francis[4], 14.John[3], 4.John[2], 1.Francis[1]) b. Winslow, Kennebec, Maine, occupation: lumberman, m. 22 Jun 1815, in Orono, Penobscot, Maine, **Ann Margaret McIntire**, b. ABT 1791, d. AFT 1860. Rowland died AFT 1836, Old Town, Penobscot, Maine. Their marriage intent was filed in Orono on Mar 3, 1815, and states that both are of "Board Eddy Plt." They were married in Old Town by "Jos" Butterfield, Justice of the Peace, and both are noted of "Piscataquis Settlement." Rowland is reported on the 1820 census of Passadumbeag, but not the 1830 Main U.S. Census. He fathered children up to 1836, based on the family residing with with widow Ann in the Old Town, Maine 1850 census.

> *Children:*
> i **Margaret Dudley** b. ABT 1819, Old Town, Penobscot, ME?.
> 164. ii **Rowland Dudley** b. 1820.
> iii **Caroline Pillsbury Dudley** b. 10 Feb 1826, Passadumkeag, Penobscot, Maine, m. 2 Dec 1852, in Passadumkeag, Penobscot, Maine, **George Washington Averill**.
> iv **Harriet Dudley** b. ABT 1828, Old Town, Penobscot, ME?.
> v **Eliza B. Dudley** b. ABT 1828, Old Town, Penobscot, ME?, d. 20 Aug 1840, Old Town, Penobscot, Maine, buried: Forest Hill Cemetery, Old Town, Maine.
> vi **Sarah Dudley** b. ABT 1830, Old Town, Penobscot, ME?.
> vii **Porter Dudley** b. ABT 1832, Old Town, Penobscot, ME?.
> viii **Cornelia Dudley** b. ABT 1836, Old Town, Penobscot, ME?.

91. **Joseph Dudley** (44.Samuel[4], 15.Samuel[3], 6.Samuel[2], 1.Francis[1]) b. 11 Jul 1765, Littleton, Middlesex, Mass., occupation: Mill owner, m. 16 Jun 1791, **Lucy Maynard**. Joseph died 1837, Waterford, Maine. Owned a mill and lived in the south part of Waterford. Settled there in 1798.

> *Children:*
> i **Hannah Dudley** b. 27 May 1792.
> ii **Rebecca Dudley** b. 29 Jun 1795.
> 165. iii **Joseph Dudley** b. 5 Feb 1798.

   iv **Israel Dudley** b. 1801.
166. v **James Dudley** b. 1803.
   vi **Samuel Dudley** b. 1805.
   vii **John Dudley** b. 1807.
   viii **Lucy Dudley** b. 1809, m. **Gee Harrison**.
     Gee: The History of Waterford records his name as Gee HARMON.
   ix **Mary Dudley** b. 1812.
   x **Hosea E. Dudley** b. 1822, m. **Fanny Barnes**.

92. **Josiah Dudley** (44.Samuel[4], 15.Samuel[3], 6.Samuel[2], 1.Francis[1]) b. 25 Dec
 1767, Littleton, Middlesex, Mass., occupation: Farmer, m. 6 Jul 1792, **Betsey Smith**, b. 1
 Apr 1772; (daughter of **Henry Smith** and **Lucretia**) d. 16 Sep 1851, Pamelia,
 Watertown P.O. Josiah died Mar 1858, Pamelia, N.Y.
   Children:
   i **Betsey Dudley** b. 11 Feb 1793, m. **Frederick Herrick**, occupation: Farmer,
    d. St. Lawrence Co., N.Y. Betsey and Frederick had a large family, but no record
    has been found of it.
   ii **Josiah Dudley** b. 28 Sep 1794, d. 1847, Ft. Wayne, Ia. Died unmarried.
167. iii **Polly Dudley** b. 4 Aug 1796.
168. iv **Henry Dudley** b. 20 May 1798.
169. v **Rebecca Dudley** b. 25 May 1800.
170. vi **Simeon H. Dudley** b. 12 May 1802.
   vii **Lucretia Dudley** b. 30 Jul 1804, m. **Randall Bingham**, occupation:
    Merchant. Lucretia died Aug 1877, Watertown, N. Y. Died s.p.
   viii **Fanny Dudley** b. 28 Oct 1806, m. **Hiram Converse**, occupation: Farmer.
    Fanny died 14 Dec 1883, near Watertown, N.Y.

93. **Stephen Dudley** (45.Stephen[4], 15.Samuel[3], 6.Samuel[2], 1.Francis[1]) b. 14 Nov
 1760, Littleton, Middlesex, Mass., m. 18 Jul 1781, **Rebecca Minard**, b. 1 Jan 1763,
 Grafton, Vt., (daughter of **Mr Minard** and **Deborah Leland**) d. 29 Sep 1828, Hannibal,
 N.Y. Stephen died Aug 1826, Cato, Cayuga Co., N.Y.
   Children:
   i **Sally Dudley** b. 1 Dec 1782, m. 1 Aug 1802, **Philip Marble**, occupation:
    Farmer of Cato, N.Y. Sally died 14 Apr 1821.
    Philip: Was from Shaftsbury, Vt.
171. ii **Lydia Dudley** b. 22 Dec 1784.
172. iii **Asa Dudley** b. 12 Nov 1786.
   iv **Rebecca Dudley** b. 5 Mar 1788, d. 1 Jul 1789.
   v **Clarissa Dudley** b. 15 Apr 1790, m. 18 Apr 1810, **Joel Northrop**,
    occupation: Farmer. Clarissa died Jun 1846.
173. vi **Sardis Dudley** b. 10 Jan 1792.

174.   vii **Lyman Dudley** b. 22 Nov 1793.

        viii **Mary Dudley** b. 26 Jul 1795, m. **Abel Prouty**, occupation: Farmer. Mary died 7 Sep 1829, Hannibal, N.Y. Was called Polly.

175.   ix **James Dudley** b. 12 Apr 1797.

176.   x **Ira Dudley** b. 22 Feb 1799.

177.   xi **Rebecca Dudley** b. 22 Apr 1801.

178.   xii **Stephen Merritt Dudley** b. 22 Mar 1803.

179.   xiii **Isaac Tichener Dudley** b. 16 Jan 1805.

180.   xiv **Electa Dudley** b. 6 Apr 1808.

94. **Joseph Dudley** (45.Stephen[4], 15.Samuel[3], 6.Samuel[2], 1.Francis[1]) b. 30 Sep 1766, Littleton, Middlesex, Mass. Moved first to Manchester, Vt, then in 1800 to Greenwich, Washington Co., N.Y. to Perry, Wyoming Co., abt 1830.

    Children:

        i **Jonathan A. Dudley** b. abt 1798. He went from Greenwich to Pennsylvania, and from there to Galesburg, Ill. He had sons when found in 1886, but no record of them or his wife exists.

181.   ii **Edward Dudley** b. 1800.

        iii **Harwood Dudley** b. abt 1802.

        iv **Martha Dudley** b. abt 1804, m. **Elijah True**.

        Elijah: Was "of Greenwich and Perry, N.Y., and Janesville, Wis."

95. **Peter Dudley** (45.Stephen[4], 15.Samuel[3], 6.Samuel[2], 1.Francis[1]) b. 29 Nov 1773, Littleton, Middlesex, Mass., occupation: General, m. 11 Mar 1800, **Lucy Barnard**, b. 7 Nov 1780, Westminster, Worcester, Mass., (daughter of **Benjamin Barnard** and **Mary Wood**) d. 24 Aug 1840. Peter died 13 Aug 1847, Peru, Bennington, Vt. Peter had 15 grandsons old enough to serve in the Civil War, and out of that 12 DID serve--7 were officers! Six were wounded, and 3 died.

    Children:

182.   i **Lucy Dudley** b. 6 Jun 1801.

183.   ii **Peter Dudley** b. 7 Jun 1803.

184.   iii **Stephen Dudley** b. 1 Jun 1805.

185.   iv **Elvira Dudley** b. 18 Jul 1807.

186.   v **Lydia Dudley** b. 12 Sep 1809.

        vi **Benjamin B. Dudley** b. 12 Aug 1811, d. 5 Sep 1813.

187.   vii **James M. Dudley** b. 19 Jul 1813.

188.   viii **Sophia Dudley** b. 13 Jun 1815.

189.   ix **Mary Dudley** b. 20 Sep 1817.

190.   x **Caroline Dudley** b. 3 Sep 1819.

        xi **Samuel Dudley** b. 8 Jun 1821, d. 26 Sep 1836.

191.   xii **Damietta Dudley** b. 5 Aug 1823.

192. xiii **Helen L. Dudley** b. 27 Jul 1826.

96. **Jonathan Dudley** (45.Stephen[4], 15.Samuel[3], 6.Samuel[2], 1.Francis[1]) b. 27 Sep 1778, Littleton, Middlesex, Mass. Dean Dudley says he was a "very intelligent, influential old gentleman." No record of his wife.

> *Children:*
> i **John H. Dudley**. Lived in Wisconsin.
> ii **Lydia Dudley**.
> iii **Patience Dudley**.
> iv **Lucy Dudley**. Lived in Indiana.
> v **Nancy Dudley**.
> vi **Stovell Bernard Dudley**.
> vii **Harriet Dudley**.
> viii **Hannah Dudley**.
> ix **Sophia Dudley**.
> x **Harwood Dudley**.

97. **Mary Dudley** (46.Francis[4], 16.Francis[3], 6.Samuel[2], 1.Francis[1]) b. 19 Dec 1771, Sutton, Worcester, Mass., m. **Jabez Stratton**. The marriage is not in the Sutton or Petersham V.R.'s.

> *Children:*
> i **Betsey Stratton** b. 25 Dec 1801, Athol, Worcestoer, Mass.
> ii **Mary (Polly) Stratton** b. 9 Dec 1803, Athol, Worcestoer, Mass.
> iii **Jabez Stratton** b. 7 Apr 1806, Athol, Worcestoer, Mass.
> iv **Charles Stratton** b. 14 Aug 1808, Athol, Worcestoer, Mass.
> v **Lyman Stratton** b. 8 Nov 1812, Athol, Worcestoer, Mass.

98. **Samuel Dudley** (46.Francis[4], 16.Francis[3], 6.Samuel[2], 1.Francis[1]) b. 1 Apr 1781, Sutton, Worcester, Mass., m. 20 Jun 1808, in West Boylston, Worcester, Mass., **Lydia Pierce**, b. 25 Apr 1784, d. 25 Aug 1866, Petersham, Worcester, Mass. Samuel died 10 Nov 1848, Petersham, Worcester, Mass. Samuel and Lydia were married by Robert B. Thomas, the Town Clerk.

> *Children:*
> i **Leonard Dudley** b. 23 Aug 1808, Petersham, Worcester, Mass., d. 11 Oct 1831.
> ii **Reuben Dudley** b. ABT 1809, occupation: Farmer, d. 28 Jun 1847, Douglas, Worcester, Mass. Reuben was 38 years old at his death, according to the VR.
193. iii **Marenia Dudley** b. 26 May 1811.
> iv **Samuel Dudley** b. 28 Jun 1813, Petersham, Worcester, Mass., d. 10 Nov 1815, Petersham, Worcester, Mass.
> v **Edwin Dudley** b. 18 Jan 1815, Petersham, Worcester, Mass., d. 14 Sep 1877.

    vi   **William Dudley** b. 22 Apr 1818, Petersham, Worcester, Mass., m. 27 Mar 1849, in Petersham, Worcester, Mass., **Lucy Witt**, (daughter of **Jairus Witt**). William died 28 Feb 1884.

194.   vii   **Marshall Dudley** b. 2 Sep 1820.

195.   viii **Harriet Dudley** b. 9 Nov 1823.

    ix   **Louisa Dudley** b. 27 Apr 1825, Petersham, Worcester, Mass., d. 1 Jan 1839, Petersham, Worcester, Mass.

196.   x   **Adeline Dudley** b. 9 Nov 1827.

99. **Joseph Dudley** (46.Francis⁴, 16.Francis³, 6.Samuel², 1.Francis¹) b. abt 1785, m. 28 Jun 1814, in Barre, Worcester, Mass., **Nancy Bigelow**, (daughter of **David Bigelow**). The marriage intention between Joseph and Nancy was filed at Petersham on 5 Jun 1814.

Children:

197.   i   **Amos Dudley** b. abt 1815.

198.   ii   **Emily Dudley** b. abt 1817.

    iii   **Otis Dudley** b. abt 1819, d. 12 Jul 1839, Petersham, Worcester, Mass. Drowned.

199.   iv   **William Dudley** b. abt 1820.

    v   **Russell Dudley** b. abt 1822, m. **Lucy J. Pease**. Died without children.

200.   vi   **Joseph Dudley** b. abt 1824.

201.   vii   **David Dudley** b. abt 1826.

    viii **Nancy Dudley** b. abt 1828, m. **Mr Conant**. Nancy had children, but there is no record of them.

    ix   **Simon Dudley** b. abt 1830, m. **Charlotte Bliss**. No children. **Charlotte**: "Of New Salem."

    x   **Sanford Dudley** d. 13 May 1835, Petersham, Worcester, Mass. Was discovered via a grave stone: "d. 13 May 1835, s. of Joseph and Nancy."

100. **Simon Dudley** (46.Francis⁴, 16.Francis³, 6.Samuel², 1.Francis¹) b. 23 Apr 1787, Sutton, Worcester, Mass., m. 5 Mar 1816, in Petersham, Worcester, Mass., **Clarissa Stowell**. Simon died ABT 1857.

Children:

202.   i   **Abel Stowell Dudley**.

    ii   **Joel F. Dudley**.

    iii   **Charles F. Dudley**.

    iv   **Eliza Ann Dudley**.

    v   **Mary Jane Dudley**.

101. **Lucy Dudley** (46.Francis⁴, 16.Francis³, 6.Samuel², 1.Francis¹) b. 16 Apr 1791, m. 21 Sep 1815, in Petersham, Worcester, Mass., **Walter Stratton**. Lucy wrote Dean

Dudley and told him she was the YOUNGEST of 9 children. She said two boys fell off a plank that was laid across the Blackstone river at night when they went for the cows and died--but she did NOT name the boys. The intention of marriage was filed 26 Aug 1815. As for her being the youngest of her siblings, the VR's do not support it.

Walter: Was of Athol, Mass.

> *Children:*
> i   **Joel Stratton**.
> ii **Austin Stratton**.
> iii **Emory Stratton**.
> iv **Lucy Ann Stratton**.
> v   **James Stratton**.
> vi **Hiram Stratton**.
> vii **Alvin Stratton**.
> viii **Clarissa Stratton**.
> ix **Charles Stratton**.

102. **Abel Dudley** (47.Abel[4], 17.David[3], 6.Samuel[2], 1.Francis[1]) b. 15 Sep 1780, Sutton, Worcester, Mass., m. 4 Feb 1802, in Grafton, Worcester, Mass., **Polly Drake**, b. Grafton, Worcester, Mass., d. 10 Feb 1817, Shrewsbury, Worcester, Mass. Abel died 10 Feb 1817, Shrewsbury, Worcester, Mass.

Polly: She was supposed to be a sister of Francis Drake. Able and Polly's marriage intention was filed in Sutton, VR 248, 18 Jun 1802.

> *Children:*
> i   **Clarinda Dudley** b. 29 Aug 1802, Sutton, Worcester, Mass., m. 16 Jan 1822, in Shrewsbury, Worcester, Mass., **Nahum Ball**. They lived in Woonsocket Falls, R.I.
>
> 203.   ii **Gerry Dudley** b. 20 Oct 1803.
> iii **David Dudley** b. 15 Jan 1805.
> iv **Eliza Dudley** b. 20 Aug 1806. Lived at Valley Falls, Rode Island.
> v   **Abigail Dudley** b. 2 Jan 1808. Called "Nabby." Lived in Valley Falls, Rhode Island.
> vi **Sumner Dudley** b. 4 Sep 1810, Sutton, Worcester, Mass., d. 12 Jul 1831. Was married, but no record.
> vii **Rufus H Dudley** b. 2 Oct 1813, Sutton, Worcester, Mass.
> viii **Mary Dudley** b. Shrewsbury, Worcester, Mass. Lived at Valley Falls, R.I.
> ix **Leonard Dudley** b. Shrewsbury, Worcester, Mass.
> x   **Caroline Dudley** b. Shrewsbury, Worcester, Mass. Married, and lived at Woonsocket Falls, R. I.
> xi **Sarah Dudley**. Married and lived at Valley Falls, R.I.
> xii **Harriet Dudley** b. Oxford, Worcester, Mass.
> xiii **Harrison Dudley** b. Shrewsbury, Worcester, Mass.

103. **Elijah Dudley** (48.Jonathan[4], 18.Jonathan[3], 6.Samuel[2], 1.Francis[1]) b. 26 Jul 1764, Sutton, Worcester, Mass., m. 30 Oct 1791, in Northbridge, Worcester, Mass., **Elizabeth Weld**. Elijah died 17 Sep 1805, Roxbury, Norfolk, Mass.
      Elizabeth: May also have been known as Isabel.
          Children:
- i   **Benjamin Dudley** b. 18 Dec 1792, Roxbury, Norfolk, Mass., d. 15 Mar 1814, Roxbury, Norfolk, Mass.
- ii   **Elizabeth C. Dudley** b. 24 Nov 1794, Roxbury, Norfolk, Mass., m. 27 Dec 1812, **Nathan Griggs**. Elizabeth died 31 Dec 1844, Cambridge, Middlesex, Mass.
- iii   **Lucinda E. Dudley** b. 24 Nov 1794, Roxbury, Norfolk, Mass., m. 16 Nov 1839, in Cambridge, Middlesex, Mass., **Jonathan W. Ford**. Was "of Boston" when married. The married date is the intention date.
- 204.   iv   **Sophia Dudley** b. 26 Nov 1799.
- v   **Caroline Dudley** b. 25 Jan 1802, Roxbury, Norfolk, Mass., d. 31 Oct 1802.

104. **Jonathan Dudley** (48.Jonathan[4], 18.Jonathan[3], 6.Samuel[2], 1.Francis[1]) b. 27 Feb 1766, Sutton, Worcester, Mass., occupation: Farmer, m. (1) 27 Nov 1788, in Sutton, Worcester, Mass., **Lydia Marble**, b. 18 Oct 1767, Sutton, Worcester, Mass., d. 7 Aug 1827, Sutton, Worcester, Mass., m. (2) 4 May 1829, in Shrewsbury, Worcester, Mass., **Lucy Eager**, b. ABT 1750, d. 26 Dec 1837, Sutton, Worcester, Mass. Jonathan died 30 Oct 1845, Sutton, Worcester, Mass. Jonathan owned a very lovely farm. Their marriage intention was filed 16 Apr 1829.
      Lucy: After Jonathan's death, lived with son Jason. She was from Shrewsbury according to the marriage intention.
          Children by Lydia Marble:
- 205.   i   **Simon Dudley** b. 14 Dec 1789.
- ii   **Polly Dudley** b. 10 Aug 1791, Sutton, Worcester, Mass., m. **Abram Chase**.
      Abram: Called "Esq." for Esquire, as he probably owned land. Was from Sutton.
- iii   **Lydia Dudley** b. 27 Apr 1793, Sutton, Worcester, Mass.
- 206.   iv   **Jonathan Dudley** b. 9 Jul 1798.
- v   **Hannah Dudley** b. 10 Nov 1801, Sutton, Worcester, Mass., m. 22 May 1827, in Northbridge, Worcester, Mass., **Josiah Adams**. The marriage date is the intention date.
- 207.   vi   **Elijah Dudley** b. 30 Jul 1803.
- vii   **Adaline Dudley** b. 4 May 1805, Sutton, Worcester, Mass., m. 10 Sep 1829, in Sutton, Worcester, Mass., **Nathaniel Dodge**.
- 208.   viii   **Jason Dudley** b. 6 Nov 1808.

ix **Almira Dudley** b. 26 Nov 1810, Sutton, Worcester, Mass., d. 4 Jan 1864, Sutton, Worcester, Mass.

x **Susan Dudley** b. 11 Dec 1812, Sutton, Worcester, Mass., m. 1 Jul 1840, in Sutton, Worcester, Mass., **Sumner Putnam**, b. 26 Jun 1807, Sutton, Worcester, Mass.

105. **Sally Dudley** (48.Jonathan[4], 18.Jonathan[3], 6.Samuel[2], 1.Francis[1]) b. 16 Aug 1790, Sutton, Worcester, Mass., m. 18 Apr 1813, **Reuben McKnight**. Sally died 25 May 1863, Providence, Rhode Island.

Children:

i **Diantha R. McKnight** b. 4 May 1814, Sutton, Worcester, Mass., m. 4 Oct 1838, **Alanson G. Hinds**.
Alanson: Was from Hubbardston, Mass.

ii **Lucy Dudley McKnight** b. 16 May 1818, Sutton, Worcester, Mass., m. 18 May 1845, **Henry E. Anthony**.
Henry: Was from Providence, R.I.

iii **Martha Prudence McKnight** b. 19 Jul 1820, Sutton, Worcester, Mass., m. 1 Jul 1841, **Nathaniel O. Chaffee**.
Nathaniel: Was from North Wilbraham, Mass.

106. **John Dudley** (49.John[4], 18.Jonathan[3], 6.Samuel[2], 1.Francis[1]) b. 19 Oct 1769, Sutton, Worcester, Mass., occupation: Captain, m. 20 Feb 1792, in Sutton, Worcester, Mass., **Deborah Marble**, b. 15 Mar 1771, Sutton, Worcester, Mass., (daughter of **Malachi Marble**) d. 1863. John died Feb 1858.

Children:

209. i **John Dudley** b. 3 Mar 1793.

ii **Sally Dudley** b. 21 Sep 1795, Sutton, Worcester, Mass., m. 30 Oct 1820, in Northbridge, Worcester, Mass., **Welcome Adams**. The marriage date is the intention date.

iii **Lomira Dudley** b. 29 Dec 1797, Sutton, Worcester, Mass., m. 1 Jun 1830, **Stephen Hunt**. Lomira died 8 Sep 1835, Sutton, Worcester, Mass. Death date from Wilkinsonville Cemetery, Sutton, Mass.

iv **Polly Dudley** b. 19 Feb 1800, Sutton, Worcester, Mass.

210. v **Leonard Dudley** b. 8 Mar 1802.

211. vi **James Dudley** b. 13 May 1805.

212. vii **Edward Morse Dudley** b. 12 Jan 1812.

107. **Joseph Dudley** (49.John[4], 18.Jonathan[3], 6.Samuel[2], 1.Francis[1]) b. 18 Sep 1773, Sutton, Worcester, Mass., m. 25 Mar 1794, in Sutton, Worcester, Mass., **Abigail Potter**, d. 7 Jan 1837, Sutton, Worcester, Mass.

Children:

        i   **Judith Dudley** b. 25 Sep 1794, Sutton, Worcester, Mass., m. 5 Nov 1812, in Sutton, Worcester, Mass., **John Blanchard**.

213.   ii **Silas Dudley** b. 1 Feb 1797.

214.   iii **Joseph Dudley** b. 3 May 1799.

108. **Pheobe Dudley** (50.Peter[4], 18.Jonathan[3], 6.Samuel[2], 1.Francis[1]) b. 21 Mar 1784, Sutton, Worcester, Mass., m. 22 Feb 1804, in Sutton, Worcester, Mass., **David Dudley**, b. 5 Jun 1781, Auburn, Worcester, Mass., (son of **David Dudley** and **Lois Whitney**) d. 3 Nov 1836, Sutton, Worcester, Mass. Pheobe died 7 Mar 1851, Sutton, Worcester, Mass. **David**: On his grave marker, called "Captain."

        Children:

        i   **Caleb Dudley** b. ABT 1805, Sutton, Worcester, Mass., d. 22 Oct 1830, Sutton, Worcester, Mass.

215.   ii **Peter Dudley** b. 1807.

      iii **Elbridge Gerry Dudley** b. 1810, Sutton, Worcester, Mass., d. 12 Apr 1834, Sutton, Worcester, Mass.

      iv **Betsey Emaline Dudley** b. 1812, Sutton, Worcester, Mass., d. 19 Apr 1834, Sutton, Worcester, Mass.

216.   v **David Tyler Dudley** b. 24 Sep 1817.

109. **John Dudley** (51.David[4], 21.Rogers[3], 6.Samuel[2], 1.Francis[1]) b. 27 Jan 1780, Auburn, Worcester, Mass., m. 20 Feb 1806, in Mendon, Worcester, Mass., **Huldah Gould**.

        Children:

        i   **Lois W. Dudley** m. 24 Dec 1834, in Grafton, Worcester, Mass., **Caleb Cutting**. Their marriage intentions, filled at Millbury, stated that Lois was from Grafton.

        ii **Susan Dudley** m. 24 Dec 1834, in Grafton, Worcester, Mass., **Francis P. Strong**.

110. **David Dudley** (51.David[4], 21.Rogers[3], 6.Samuel[2], 1.Francis[1]) (See marriage to number 108.)

111. **Luther Dudley** (51.David[4], 21.Rogers[3], 6.Samuel[2], 1.Francis[1]) b. 12 Jun 1783, Auburn, Worcester, Mass.

        Children:

        i   **Mary Ann Dudley**.

112. **Joseph Dudley** (51.David[4], 21.Rogers[3], 6.Samuel[2], 1.Francis[1]) b. 14 Mar 1790, Sutton, Worcester, Mass., occupation: Doctor, m. (1) **Eliza Eppes**, (daughter of **Deacon Richard Gregory**) m. (2) **Susanna Friend**, (daughter of **Thomas R. Ball**) m. (3) 1827, **Elizabeth Archer**, (daughter of **Col. Edward Archer**) d. 3 Jul 1879.

Joseph died 24 Sep 1831. Moved to Chesterfield Virginia in 1810/11, served in the War of 1812 under Captain Edward Archer. Was also a detective and friend to Andrew Jackson. Graduated University of Pennsylvania in Philadelphia in 1816, his graduating essay was on Typhus Fever. During the war, while in the south, he served and helped the Union, and was wounded 3 times, once badly in the face. He apparently had destruction on his home, but was unable to receive compensation for it. He helped Union soldiers return to the North in the War.

Eliza: She was apparently married before Joseph. No children.

Susanna: She was a widow when she married Joseph. No children.

> *Children by Elizabeth Archer:*
>
> i   **Joseph S. Dudley**. Graduated Virginia Medical College in Richmond, and died soon after. Was unmarried.
>
> ii   **Edward Chapman Dudley** b. 1828, d. 1832.

217.   iii **William Archer Dudley** b. 9 May 1829.

113. **Amasa Dudley** (51.David[4], 21.Rogers[3], 6.Samuel[2], 1.Francis[1]) b. 17 Oct 1792, Sutton, Worcester, Mass., m. 13 Oct 1814, in Northbridge, Worcester, Mass., **Ann Fletcher**, b. 22 Apr 1793, Northbridge, Worcester, Mass. Amasa died 20 Oct 1846, Uxbridge, Worcester, Mass. Amasa and Ann lived in Uxbridge, Mass, in a large brick house. The intention of marriage was filed in Millbury on 22 Sep 1814. Northbridge records the birth date in their VR.

> *Children:*

218.   i   **Joseph Amory Dudley** b. 15 Sep 1815.

219.   ii   **Paul Whitin Dudley** b. 3 Apr 1817.

> iii **William Neil Dudley** b. 20 Apr 1820, Northbridge, Worcester, Mass., d. 1 May 1822, Northbridge, Worcester, Mass.
>
> iv **William Henry Dudley** b. 23 Nov 1823, Northbridge, Worcester, Mass., occupation: Hardware dealer, m. 1 Jan 1850, **Susan Johnson**. William and Susan lived in Charlotte, Michigan. The intention of marriage was filed 15 Dec 1849 in Southborough, Middlesex, Mass, according to the VR.

114. **Samuel Dudley** (52.Benjamin[4], 23.William[3], 6.Samuel[2], 1.Francis[1]) b. 21 Dec 1781, Douglas, Worcester, Mass., m. 23 Feb 1805, in Douglas, Worcester, Mass., **Sarah Wallis**, b. 10 Jul 1785, Douglas, Worcester, Mass., (daughter of **Benjamin Wallis** and **Sarah Thayre**) d. 1824. Samuel died 16 Jul 1847, Douglas, Worcester, Mass., buried: Douglas Center Cemetery, Douglas, Mass. Executor of his fathers will. Marriage date is intention date.

Sarah: On some of her children's records, she appears as "Sally."

> *Children:*
>
> i   **Samuel Dudley** b. 24 Dec 1805, Douglas, Worcester, Mass., m. 1869, **Miss Alger**.

ii **Sarah Dudley** b. 15 Nov 1807, Douglas, Worcester, Mass.

iii **Azubah Dudley** b. 7 Aug 1810, Douglas, Worcester, Mass., m. 1 Jan 1835, in Douglas, Worcester, Mass., **Oliver W. Adams**.

iv **Benjamin Dudley** b. 7 Nov 1813, Douglas, Worcester, Mass., m. 19 May 1849, in Douglas, Worcester, Mass., **Nancy M Sibley**. Marriage date is intention date.

220.   v **Nelson Dudley** b. 16 Oct 1816.

115. **Benjamin Dudley** (52.Benjamin⁴, 23.William³, 6.Samuel², 1.Francis¹) b. 25 Feb 1784, Douglas, Worcester, Mass., m. (1) 2 Jan 1808, in Douglas, Worcester, Mass., **Polly Putnam**, d. 11 Sep 1815, Sutton, Worcester, Mass., m. (2) 1 Sep 1816, in Douglas, Worcester, Mass., **Olive Ellis**, b. 19 Jan 1795, d. 11 May 1880, Rochester, New York. Benjamin died 29 Sep 1828, Sutton, Worcester, Mass. Marriage date is intention date.

   Olive: After Benjamin's death, she married Abram Tabor of Providence, R.I. She was originally from Cape Cod, her ancestors arriving at Plymouth.

   Children by Olive Ellis:

221.   i **Mary Dudley** b. 22 Apr 1817.

ii **Olive Dudley** b. 25 Feb 1819, d. 15 Aug 1831. Died unmarried.

iii **Anna Dudley** b. 25 Aug 1821, d. 1843. Died unmarried.

iv **Phebe Dudley** b. 17 Dec 1824, Douglas, Worcester, Mass., m. 23 Jan 1844, in Woonsocket, RI, **Olney Arnold**. Phebe and Olney lived in Pawtucket, R.I. Phebe was so good at the business, she was recognized as a partner. She was active in various charities and church. Her husband always heeded her advice. He wrote a long poem to her that he read at a meeting in Providence in 1887.

v **Caroline E. Dudley** b. 7 May 1828, d. 14 Sep 1831. Died unmarried.

116. **David Dudley** (53.Paul⁴, 23.William³, 6.Samuel², 1.Francis¹) b. 11 Nov 1787, Douglas, Worcester, Mass., m. 26 Oct 1810, in Douglas, Worcester, Mass., **Hannah Walker**, b. 1788, d. 5 Jun 1872. David died 14 Sep 1829, Douglas, Worcester, Mass. I have another marriage date of 16 Dec. The VR shows the marriage date is intention date. There is no VR for his death in Douglas.

   Children:

222.   i **George Reed Dudley** b. 25 Jul 1811.

ii **Love Marie Dudley** b. 1814, m. **Edmund Carpenter**, b. Burrillville, RI. Love died 1835.

iii **Eliza J. Dudley** b. Feb 1817, Douglas, Worcester, Mass., d. Jun 1817, Douglas, Worcester, Mass.

iv **David W. Dudley** b. Oct 1818, Douglas, Worcester, Mass. Died young.

223.   v **Eliza J Dudley** b. 1823.

117. **John Dudley** (53.Paul⁴, 23.William³, 6.Samuel², 1.Francis¹) b. 8 Sep 1791,

Douglas, Worcester, Mass., m. 30 Sep 1810, in Douglas, Worcester, Mass., **Submit Hill**, b. 3 Mar 1790, Douglas, Worcester, Mass., (daughter of **Col. Moses Hill**). .

Children:

    i **Edwin Dudley** b. 9 Apr 1812, Douglas, Worcester, Mass., baptized: 9 Aug 1812, Douglas, Worcester, Mass., d. 26 Oct 1820, Douglas, Worcester, Mass. Birth date in VR with no year. Baptism date is recorded there. No VR for the death.

224.   ii **James Hill Dudley** b. 10 Dec 1814.

    iii **Emily Hill Dudley** m. 13 Oct 1842, in Douglas, Worcester, Mass., **Mowry Lapham**.
      Mowry: Was from Douglas.

118. **William Dudley** (53.Paul⁴, 23.William³, 6.Samuel², 1.Francis¹) b. 29 Oct 1793, Douglas, Worcester, Mass., occupation: Captain, m. (1) 18 Jan 1816, in Douglas, Worcester, Mass., **Harriot Craggin**, b. 29 Nov 1797, d. 12 Oct 1820, m. (2) 10 Jun 1822, **Mary Boyd Wilson**, b. 14 Feb 1801, d. 25 Nov 1826, m. (3) 9 Sep 1827, in Douglas, Worcester, Mass., **Sophronia Lincoln**, b. 13 May 1804, Leyden, d. 27 Jul 1865, Providence, Rhode Island. Dean Dudley lists most of William's children being born in Douglas, but no VR's were found there on any of them. He seems to have left after his first marriage, only to return for his third marriage. The intention was filed in Taunton on 1 May 1822.

Children by Harriot Craggin:

225.   i **William Dudley** b. 11 Nov 1816.

226.   ii **Charles Dudley** b. 19 Apr 1818.

227.   iii **Harriet Cragin Dudley** b. 9 Jan 1820.

Children by Mary Boyd Wilson:

    iv **Mary Dudley** b. 3 May 1823, d. 19 Jan 1829.

    v **Zilpha Ann Dudley** b. 23 Mar 1825, d. 1 Mar 1833.

    vi **Infant** b. 1826. Child's sex in unknown, it lived only 2 hours.

Children by Sophronia Lincoln:

    vii **Sophronia L. Dudley** b. 17 Jan 1829, d. 13 Oct 1846, Worcester, Worcester, Mass.

    viii **George Nelson Dudley** b. 12 Nov 1833, d. 5 Aug 1881. George married and had 2 sons, unrecorded.

    ix **Edwin R. Dudley** b. 28 Nov 1836, Leicester, d. 15 Feb 1881, Providence, Rhode Island. Married and had a daughter, no record.

228.   x **Mary Wilson Dudley** b. 21 Nov 1843.

    xi **Henry Holbrook Dudley** b. 9 Apr 1846, Worcester, Worcester, Mass., d. 11 Aug 1847, Worcester, Worcester, Mass.

119. **Willard Dudley** (53.Paul⁴, 23.William³, 6.Samuel², 1.Francis¹) b. 25 Nov 1796, Douglas, Worcester, Mass., m. 1 Dec 1819, in Douglas, Worcester, Mass., **Eunice**

Balcome, b. 23 Feb 1803, Douglas, Worcester, Mass., (daughter of **Ellis Balcome**). Please note that only ONE of their children is recorded in the Douglas VR's.

Children:

   i **Paul Dudley** b. abt 1821. Lived in Providence, R.I. There is no VR in Douglas on Paul.

   ii **Edwin Dudley** b. abt 1823. No VR in Douglas.

   iii **Dorothy Dudley** b. abt 1825, m. **Hawkins Mowry**. No VR in Douglas.

   iv **Francis Dean Dudley** baptized: 11 Oct 1829, Douglas, Worcester, Mass.

   v **Betsey Dudley** b. abt 1830. No VR in Douglas.

120. **Dorothy Dudley** (53.Paul[4], 23.William[3], 6.Samuel[2], 1.Francis[1]) b. 29 Mar 1802, Douglas, Worcester, Mass., m. 4 Dec 1822, in Douglas, Worcester, Mass., **Benjamin Hill**. The VR records her name as DORATHA, as it does her mothers name.

Children:

   i **Benjamin Hill**.

   ii **Emeline Hill**.

   iii **Eliza Ann Hill**.

   iv **Edwin Hill**.

121. **Harriot Dudley** (53.Paul[4], 23.William[3], 6.Samuel[2], 1.Francis[1]) b. 15 Dec 1804, Douglas, Worcester, Mass., m. 14 May 1823, in Douglas, Worcester, Mass., **Josiah Adams**, d. 19 Jan 1859. Harriot died 31 May 1861.

Children:

   i **Josiah Augustus Adams** b. 12 Mar 1824, Douglas, Worcester, Mass., m. **Fidelia**, d. 31 May 1861, Douglas, Worcester, Mass. Josiah died 19 Jan 1859, Douglas, Worcester, Mass.

122. **William Dudley** (54.Lemuel[4], 23.William[3], 6.Samuel[2], 1.Francis[1]) b. 27 Jun 1798, Douglas, Worcester, Mass., m. 30 Mar 1826, in Oxford, Worcester, Mass., **Lucy Putnam**, b. 3 Sep 1808, Sutton, Worcester, Mass., (daughter of **Cornelius Putnam**) d. 27 Apr 1888, Douglas, Worcester, Mass. William died 30 Aug 1879, Douglas, Worcester, Mass. There marriage intentions were published both in Douglas (VR 102) and Oxford. The marriage date is the intention date. Dean Dudley reports the death date in Douglas, but as the VR's only go to 1849, I could not confirm it.

Children:

229.   i **William Harrison Dudley** b. 19 Feb 1827.

230.   ii **Silas P Dudley** b. 3 Jul 1829.

       iii **Sarah Jane Dudley** b. 18 Oct 1848, Douglas, Worcester, Mass., m. 23 Nov 1870, in Thompson, Ct., **Jesse Thompson**. Sarah died 20 Mar 1920.

123. **Rueben Dudley** (54.Lemuel[4], 23.William[3], 6.Samuel[2], 1.Francis[1]) b. abt 1803,

Douglas, Worcester, Mass., m. 17 Mar 1828, in Douglas, Worcester, Mass., **Phebe Smith**, b. abt 1807. There is no VR confirmation on Reuben's birth.

Phebe: According to Dean Dudley, name may have been Viola.

        Children:

        i **Rueben Dudley** b. ABT. 1829, m. _____ **Hannah**, b. ABT. 1830.

124. **Nancy Wallis** (55.Hannah[4], 23.William[3], 6.Samuel[2], 1.Francis[1]) b. 17 Feb 1797, Douglas, Worcester, Mass., m. 20 May 1821, in Douglas, Worcester, Mass., **Alvah White**, b. 8 Jul 1798, Douglas, Worcester, Mass., d. 2 Sep 1846, Douglas, Worcester, Mass. Nancy died 22 Oct 1871.

        Children:

231.   i **Julie Ann White** b. 11 Sep 1836.

        ii **Danford White**.

        iii **Dandridge White**.

125. **Sarah Wallis** (57.Benjamin[4], 24.Lydia[3], 6.Samuel[2], 1.Francis[1]) (See marriage to number 114.)

126. **Persis Smith** (60.Robert[4], 25.Douglassa[3], 6.Samuel[2], 1.Francis[1]) b. 25 May 1802, Webster, Worcester, Mass., m. 23 Sep 1829, in Douglas, Worcester, Mass., **William Mellens**, b. ABT. 1800, Vermont.

        Children:

232.   i **Hannah Mellens** b. 1830.

127. **John Dudley** (63.Nathan[5], 26.Joseph[4], 10.Joseph[3], 3.Joseph[2], 1.Francis[1]) b. 18
Nov 1790, Lexington, Middlesex, Mass., baptized: 21 Nov 1790, Lexington, Middlesex,
Mass., occupation: Printer in Boston, m. **Esther Eliza Smith**.

> *Children:*
>   i **John W. Dudley** b. Lexington, Middlesex, Mass., d. Lexington, Middlesex,
>   Mass.
> ii **Eliza Dudley** b. Lexington, Middlesex, Mass., m. **George W. Fowle**.
> iii **Sarah Lewis Dudley** baptized: 31 Mar 1833, Bolton, Worcester, Mass., m.
>   **J.B. Holman**, occupation: Minister.
> iv **Martha Ann Dudley** baptized: 31 Mar 1833, Bolton, Worcester, Mass.

233.   v **Nathan Augustus Munroe Dudley** b. 20 Aug 1825.

> vi **Caroline Moore Dudley** baptized: 31 Mar 1833, Bolton, Worcester, Mass.
> vii **Andrew Jackson Dudley** b. 4 Mar 1829, Lancaster, Worcester, Mass.,
>   baptized: 31 Mar 1833, Bolton, Worcester, Mass., d. 30 Jul 1831, Lancaster,
>   Worcester, Mass.
> viii **Charles Henry Dudley** b. 15 Jul 1831, Lancaster, Worcester, Mass., baptized:
>   31 Mar 1833, Bolton, Worcester, Mass.
> ix **John Edwin Dudley** b. 28 Apr 1834, Lancaster, Worcester, Mass., baptized: 23
>   Apr 1837, Bolton, Worcester, Mass.

128. **Samuel R. Dudley** (64.Samuel[5], 31.James[4], 10.Joseph[3], 3.Joseph[2],
1.Francis[1]) b. 16 Jun 1793, Bethel, Vt., m. **Ms. Gilbert**, (daughter of **Zalmon
Gilbert**). They had 10 children, but were all dead except those listed below in 1892

> *Children:*
>   i **Lorenzo G. Dudley** b. abt 1815.
> ii **Esther Ann Dudley**.
> iii **Mary Dudley**.

129. **James Dudley** (65.Paul[5], 31.James[4], 10.Joseph[3], 3.Joseph[2], 1.Francis[1]) b. 23
Sept 1797, Acton, Middlesex, Mass., m. 18 Nov 1824, in Littleton, Middlesex, Mass., **Mary
Ann Proctor**.

> *Children:*
>   i **Mary A. Dudley** b. 1825, d. 13 Sep 1839, Concord, Middlesex, Mass.
> ii **James H. Dudley** b. 1827. Lived in Boston.
> iii **Leonard Dudley** b. 1829, buried: 1831, at sea.
> iv **Maria E. Dudley** b. 28 Apr 1832, Lexington, Middlesex, Mass. Lived in
>   Boston.
>   v **Paul A. Dudley** b. 8 Feb 1842.

130. **Paul Dudley** (65.Paul[5], 31.James[4], 10.Joseph[3], 3.Joseph[2], 1.Francis[1]) b. 19 Sep 1799, Acton, Middlesex, Mass., m. 26 Apr 1827, in Concord, Middlesex, Mass., **Rebecca Adams**, b. 27 Dec 1801, (daughter of **Paul Adams**) d. 26 May 1871, Concord, Middlesex, Mass. Paul died 6 Mar 1882, Acton, Middlesex, Mass. There are three childrens deaths in the V.R.'s: Paul, Apr 6, 1836....Paul, Apr 8, 1836...Paul, Oct 12, 1839. The first two are probable twins, and all are listed with the fathers' name Paul. It is highly likely they all belong to this family, but without birth confirmation, I could not list them. Repeating a name was quite common at this time.

Children:
  i **Paul Adams Dudley** b. 26 Feb 1843, Acton, Middlesex, Mass., occupation: Soldier, d. 20 Mar 1865, City Point, Va. Enlisted in the Union Army in 1862. Was in the 1st Mass. Heavy Artillery.

131. **John L. Dudley** (65.Paul[5], 31.James[4], 10.Joseph[3], 3.Joseph[2], 1.Francis[1]) b. 27 Oct 1805, Acton, Middlesex, Mass., m. **Rebecca Brown**. John died Nov 1841. **Rebecca**: Was from Andover.

Children:
  i **Marcus L. Dudley** b. Dighton.
  ii **Eliza Dudley** b. Baltimore, Maryland, d. Baltimore, Maryland.
  iii **Maria Dudley** b. Baltimore, Maryland. Also lived at Baltimore.
  iv **Rebecca B. Dudley** b. Baltimore, Maryland.
  v **Jane C. Dudley** b. Baltimore, Maryland.
  vi **John L. Dudley** b. 1839, Baltimore, Maryland, d. 28 Nov 1840, Baltimore, Maryland.
  vii **Theexina Dudley** b. Baltimore, Maryland.
  viii **Melissa Dudley** d. 16 Mar 1844, Baltimore, Maryland. Found in the Baltimore Sun.

132. **Josiah P. Dudley** (65.Paul[5], 31.James[4], 10.Joseph[3], 3.Joseph[2], 1.Francis[1]) b. 22 May 1808, Acton, Middlesex, Mass., occupation: Carpenter, m. (1) 9 Sep 1839, in Concord, Middlesex, Mass., **Deborah Bosworth**, m. (2) **Aroline Fry**. The marriage date for Josiah and Deborah is the intention date.

Children by Deborah Bosworth:
  i **Deborah B. Dudley** b. 1842.
Children by Aroline Fry:
  ii **Sophia Elizabeth Dudley** b. 9 Nov 1845, Lowell, Middlesex, Mass.
  iii **Daughter Dudley** b. 16 Dec 1847, Lowell, Middlesex, Mass.
  iv **Georgiana Dudley** b. Dec 1848, Lowell, Middlesex, Mass.

133. **Asa P. Dudley** (65.Paul[5], 31.James[4], 10.Joseph[3], 3.Joseph[2], 1.Francis[1]) b. 13 Nov 1811, m. 3 Nov 1839, in Acton, Middlesex, Mass., **Almira Bright**.

Children:

234. i **Charles G. B. Dudley** b. 23 May 1843.

134. **James Heywood Dudley** (67.Samuel[5], 32.Benjamin[4], 10.Joseph[3], 3.Joseph[2],
1.Francis[1]) b. 30 Mar 1810, Lincoln, Middlesex, Mass., occupation: Cordwainer, m.
Susan Moulton. James and Susan had about $400. each from father Samuel's estate.
Their aunt Abigail also left them a legacy in 1820.
Susan: Susan was probably the sister of Dexter Moulton, who married James' sister
Caroline.

Children:
  i **Caroline Augusta Dudley** b. 15 Jan 1842, Lincoln, Middlesex, Mass.
  ii **Mary Abby Dudley** b. 27 Apr 1844, Lincoln, Middlesex, Mass.
  iii **George Alfred Dudley** b. 16 Apr 1846, Lincoln, Middlesex, Mass.

135. **Joseph Dudley** (68.Nahum[5], 33.Joseph[4], 11.Benjamin[3], 3.Joseph[2], 1.Francis[1])
b. ABT 1780, m. **Mary Page**. Joseph died 31 Dec 1830, Westmoreland, Cheshire, New
Hampshire, buried: 2 Jan 1831, North Cemetery, Westmoreland, N.H. He died of
consumption.
Mary: She was of Concord, Mass.

Children:
  i **Mary Dudley** b. 9 Sep 1810, Westmoreland, Cheshire, New Hampshire, m.
  Rolston G. Tyler.
235. ii **Herbert Dudley** b. 27 Jul 1812.
  iii **Margaret Dudley** b. 28 Aug 1814, Westmoreland, Cheshire, New Hampshire,
  m. **James Barney**.
  iv **Caroline Dudley** b. 15 Jul 1816, Westmoreland, Cheshire, New Hampshire, m.
  Ansel Davis.
  v **Fanny Dudley** b. 31 Jan 1819, Westmoreland, Cheshire, New Hampshire, m.
  George Barber.
  vi **Selina Dudley** b. 16 Mar 1821, Westmoreland, Cheshire, New Hampshire.
  vii **Semira Dudley** b. 16 Mar 1821, Westmoreland, Cheshire, New Hampshire.
  viii **Warren Dudley** b. 4 Apr 1823, Westmoreland, Cheshire, New Hampshire.
  Settled in Orange, New Hampshire.
  ix **George Dudley** b. 4 Feb 1827, Westmoreland, Cheshire, New Hampshire.

136. **Moses Dudley** (68.Nahum[5], 33.Joseph[4], 11.Benjamin[3], 3.Joseph[2], 1.Francis[1])
b. 18 Oct 1794, Westmoreland, Cheshire, New Hampshire, occupation: Selectman, m. 9 Nov
1819, in Westmoreland, Cheshire, New Hampshire, **Persis Pratt**, (daughter of **Rev.
Pratt** and **Persis Little**). Moses died 16 Apr 1874, Westmoreland, Cheshire, New
Hampshire. Moses was a Selectman in Westmoreland for the years 1832, 1833, 1835, and
1849. He was a delegate to the Constitutional Convention in 1850.

Children:

236.   i   **Allen Pratt Dudley** b. 16 Dec 1819.
      ii   **Hannah Dudley** b. 27 May 1821, Westmoreland, Cheshire, New Hampshire, m. Aug 1838, **Charles B. Holbrook**, occupation: Physician.
237.   iii   **Charles P. Dudley** b. 25 Dec 1822.
238.   iv   **William L. Dudley** b. 20 Dec 1824.
      v   **Persis M. Dudley** b. 20 Nov 1830, Westmoreland, Cheshire, New Hampshire, m. 3 Oct 1850, in Westmoreland, Cheshire, New Hampshire, **Romanzo W. Thompson**.

137. **Josiah Wellington Dudley** (70.Luther⁵, 33.Joseph⁴, 11.Benjamin³, 3.Joseph², 1.Francis¹) b. 23 Jan 1792, Wayland, Middlesex, Mass., m. 11 Nov 1815, in Woodstock, Oxford, Maine, **Polly Fuller**, (daughter of **Aaron Fuller**). According to Dean Dudley, he "removed to Paris, and died there at an advanced age." "History of Woodstock" says he was an "enterprising and energetic business man." He was "entrusted with responsible town offices...was filled to the acceptance of his townsmen." Note that his middle name is spelled "Willington" in the Wayland VR, but "Wellington" in most other sources.
Polly: Was from Paris.

     Children:

239.   i   **Wellington Dudley** b. 8 Jun 1817.
      ii   **Maria Dudley** b. 11 Mar 1819, m. **Eben S. Chapin**.
        Eben: Was from Stafford, Ct.
     iii   **Emily Dudley** b. 5 Oct 1820, d. 1838.
     iv   **Julia A. Dudley** b. 20 Mar 1822, m. **Edward P. Chase**.
        Edward: Was from Portland.
     v   **Mary Dudley** b. 27 Aug 1825, m. **Josiah B. Snow**.
        Josiah: Was from Orleans, Mass.
240.   vi   **Smith Dudley** b. 8 Jun 1827.

138. **Moses Dudley** (70.Luther⁵, 33.Joseph⁴, 11.Benjamin³, 3.Joseph², 1.Francis¹) b. 11 Oct 1794, Wayland, Middlesex, Mass., m. in Woodstock, Oxford, Maine, **Welthea Benson**. Moses died Paris, Oxford, Maine. Was only a few years in Woodstock, then moved to Paris where he died.
Welthea: Married William O. Pearson after Moses' death.

     Children:

      i   **Charles Dudley**.
      ii   **Mary A. Dudley**.
     iii   **James B. Dudley** m. **Nellie Bryant**, (daughter of **Christopher Bryant**).
     iv   **Moses Dudley**.
     v   **Ruth Dudley**.

139. **Nathan Dudley** (72.Jane[5], 34.Benjamin[4], 11.Benjamin[3], 3.Joseph[2], 1.Francis[1])
b. 21 May 1795, m. 27 Jan 1816, **Sarah Churchill**.
Children:
  i   **Benjamin C. Dudley** b. 17 Dec 1816.
  ii **Caleb Dudley** b. 24 Nov 1819.
  iii **Nathan Dudley** b. 12 Mar 1823, m. 12 Jan 1853, **Sarah Soule**.
  iv **Samuel Dudley** b. 28 Feb 1826.
  v   **Simon G. Dudley**.
  vi **William Dudley**.

140. **Ebenezer Dudley** (72.Jane[5], 34.Benjamin[4], 11.Benjamin[3], 3.Joseph[2],
1.Francis[1]) b. 19 Jan 1798, m. 8 May 1824, **Ruth Churchill**.
Children:
  i   **Seth Benson Dudley** b. 13 Jul 1825, m. 24 Dec 1854, **Hannah E.
      Churchill**.
  ii **Sarah G.B.B. Dudley** b. 2 Jul 1829.
  iii **Jane Dudley** b. 1831.
  iv **Daniel Dudley** b. 1833.
  v   **Harrison Dudley** b. 1842.
  vi **Rawson Dudley** b. 1844.

141. **Abijah Dudley** (73.Benjamin[5], 34.Benjamin[4], 11.Benjamin[3], 3.Joseph[2],
1.Francis[1]) baptized: 25 Aug 1799, Sudbury, Middlesex, Mass., occupation: Captain, m.
Susan Trull, b. ABT 1799, d. 13 Jun 1877, buried: Sudbury, Middlesex, Mass. Abijah
died 24 Apr 1840, Sudbury, Middlesex, Mass.
Children:
  i   **Sarah Dudley** d. 14 Apr 1840, Sudbury, Middlesex, Mass.
  ii **Emily Langdon Dudley** b. 8 Nov 1818, Sudbury, Middlesex, Mass., m. 18 Oct
      1838, in Sudbury, Middlesex, Mass., **Jonas D. Morse**.
  iii **Amos Augustus Dudley** b. 17 Jun 1821, Sudbury, Middlesex, Mass., d. 11 Apr
      1822, Sudbury, Middlesex, Mass.
  iv **Amos Augustus Dudley** b. 23 Mar 1823, Sudbury, Middlesex, Mass.
241. v   **Lyman Gardner Dudley** b. 3 Apr 1825.
  vi **Samuel Edwin Dudley** b. 8 Jul 1827, Sudbury, Middlesex, Mass., m. 12 Apr
      1849, in Marlborough, Middlesex, Mass., **Jane M. Morse**.
  vii **George Gerry Dudley** b. 7 May 1830, Sudbury, Middlesex, Mass., d. 1 Oct
      1832, Sudbury, Middlesex, Mass.

142. **Benjamin Dudley** (73.Benjamin[5], 34.Benjamin[4], 11.Benjamin[3], 3.Joseph[2],
1.Francis[1]) b. 25 Oct 1799, baptized: 3 Nov 1799, Sudbury, Middlesex, Mass., m. (1) 14
Oct 1824, in Chelmsford, Middlesex, Mass., **Betsey Proctor Byam**, b. 20 Dec 1803,

(daughter of **Solomon Byam**) d. 28 Nov 1837, Chelmsford, Middlesex, Mass., m. (2) 28 Jun 1838, in Chelmsford, Middlesex, Mass., **Martha Hale (Barrett) Parkhurst**, b. 5 Mar 1801, Billerica, Middlesex, Mass., (daughter of **Stephen Barrrett** and **Lucy**).

    Martha: This is Martha's 2nd marriage. Her first was to a Mr. Parkhurst, possibly Micajah. Dean Dudley has her name was Nancy....but no Nancy was found.

        Children by Betsey Proctor Byam:

      i **Elizabeth Ann Dudley** b. 23 Jul 1825, m. 1846, in Chelmsford, Middlesex, Mass., **Rufus D. Spaulding**. Dean Dudley had a death date of 27 July 1837 for Elizabeth. However, to have been born, married, and died before 12 years of age would have been a major accomplishment, even in those days of early marriage. In addition, a marriage intent date of 18 Oct 1846--9 years after her death---was found.

242.   ii **Otis Byam Dudley** b. 8 Mar 1827.

      iii **Sarah Jane Dudley** b. 3 Feb 1830, m. 2 Feb 1853, **Rev. William J. Parkhurst**.

243.   iv **George Henry Dudley** b. 18 Mar 1836.

143. **Caleb Dudley** (74.John[5], 34.Benjamin[4], 11.Benjamin[3], 3.Joseph[2], 1.Francis[1])
b. 11 Feb 1797, Framingham, Middlesex, Mass. Note that Dean Dudley lists a child Nathan to this family. However, that Nathan (whom married a "Miss Hatsat") was married 4 Jul 1819 in Petersham (VR 89), making it impossible for Nathan to be Caleb's son. I have, therefore, removed him.

        Children:

      i **Caleb Dudley**. Lived in Petersham.

      ii **John Dudley**. Lived in Petersham.

      iii **Mary Ann Dudley** m. **Mr. Burnett**. Lived in South Orange, Mass.

144. **John P. Dudley** (75.Jonathan[5], 34.Benjamin[4], 11.Benjamin[3], 3.Joseph[2], 1.Francis[1]) b. 13 Aug 1797, Beverly, Essex, Mass., m. 17 May 1818, in Danvers, Essex, Mass., **Huldah Herrick**. John died 18 Nov 1827, Wenham, Essex, Mass.
Huldah: According to the Danvers V.R., she filed intentions to marry Charles Kent of Rowley, 14 Mar 1829--after John's death.

        Children:

244.   i **John Dudley** b. 14 Dec 1818.

      ii **Ruth Dudley** b. 11 Feb 1821, Danvers, Essex, Mass., m. 31 Dec 1837, in Wenham, Essex, Mass., **William Cook**.

      iii **Hannah E. Dudley** b. 27 Nov 1824, Danvers, Essex, Mass., m. **Francis Dodge**.
         Francis: Was from Hamilton.

      iv **Josiah Dudley** b. 27 Feb 1827, Danvers, Essex, Mass.

145. **Josiah Dudley** (75.Jonathan[5], 34.Benjamin[4], 11.Benjamin[3], 3.Joseph[2], 1.Francis[1]) b. 7 Dec 1799, Beverly, Essex, Mass., occupation: Cordwainer, m. 15 Apr 1821, in Danvers, Essex, Mass., **Sally Wells**.

> *Children:*
> i   **Elvira Judson Whipple. Dudley** b. 5 Apr 1822, Danvers, Essex, Mass., m. 15 Jun 1842, in Beverly, Essex, Mass., **Benjamin C. Putman**.
> ii   **Samuel Ober Dudley** b. 21 Jan 1824, Danvers, Essex, Mass., d. 9 Feb 1844, Beverly, Essex, Mass.
> iii   **Lucretia P. Wells Dudley** b. 23 Dec 1826, Beverly, Essex, Mass.
> iv   **Mary Porter Dudley** b. 22 Jan 1828, Danvers, Essex, Mass., m. 12 Jun 1848, in Salem, Essex, Mass., **James Radcliff**, b. ABT 1824, (son of **George Radcliff** and **Mary**) occupation: Cordwainer.
>   **James**: Was from Standish, Maine. Was 25 y/o when he married.
> v   **Sarah Elizabeth Dudley** b. 27 Feb 1830, Danvers, Essex, Mass., m. abt 1850, **Edward Allen**.
> vi   **Josiah Francis Dudley** b. 27 Oct 1831, Beverly, Essex, Mass., d. 1843, Beverly, Essex, Mass. A strange entry. The Beverly Vital Records says he died of "vorioloid" at age 12. The Danvers VR says he was BORN at Danvers 2 Oct 1831
> vii   **Hannah Carter. Dudley** b. 6 Aug 1833, Danvers, Essex, Mass.
> viii **Sophronia Warren Dudley** b. 16 Feb 1836, Danvers, Essex, Mass., d. 10 Mar 1843, Beverly, Essex, Mass. According to the Beverly Vital Records, she died of "scarlet fever, age 7."
> ix   **Allen Webb Dudley** b. 30 May 1838, Beverly, Essex, Mass.
> x   **Harriet Maria Dudley** b. 30 Aug 1840, Beverly, Essex, Mass., d. 28 Mar 1843, Beverly, Essex, Mass. The Beverly and Danvers V.R.'s disagree with each other on her birth date. Beverly has 1840, Danvers 1841. Her death record says she died of "scarlet fever, age 2y, 6m." That would, then, confirm Beverly's VR.
> xi   **Harriet Sophronia Dudley** b. 13 Jul 1843, Beverly, Essex, Mass., d. 30 Mar 1849, Danvers, Essex, Mass. Died of scarlet fever
> xii   **Melicent Eldora Dudley** b. 28 Apr 1845, Danvers, Essex, Mass.

146. **Joseph Dudley** (76.Josiah[5], 34.Benjamin[4], 11.Benjamin[3], 3.Joseph[2], 1.Francis[1]) baptized: 20 Dec 1807, Wayland, Middlesex, Mass., m. (1) **Lovina Lackey**, m. (2) 5 Dec 1842, in Hopkinton, Middlesex, Mass., **Eliza Ann Bixby**.

> *Children by Eliza Ann Bixby:*
> i   **Ann E. Dudley** b. 11 Oct 1843, Westborough, Middlesex, Mass.
> ii   **Charles Bixby Dudley** b. 4 Feb 1845, Westborough, Middlesex, Mass.
> iii **Adiel Harvey Dudley** b. 6 Aug 1847, Westborough, Middlesex, Mass.
> iv **Henrietta Maria Dudley** b. 26 May 1848, Westborough, Middlesex, Mass.

147. **Daniel Dudley** (79.David[5], 36.Ebenezer[4], 11.Benjamin[3], 3.Joseph[2],

1.Francis[1]) b. abt 1792, m. (1) 28 Nov 1816, **Lovisa Hathaway**, b. 1794, d. 1835, m. (2) 9 Jun 1835, **Jane Churchill**. According to the "History of Woodstock", the marriages are reversed, and Polly should be the first wife. The "Annals of Oxford" list the children, but only those below by name, and says "and others", and states that the marriages, as listed here, are correct.

Children by Lovisa Hathaway:
- i **Laura M. Dudley**.
- ii **Samuel H. Dudley**.
- iii **Daniel I. Dudley**.
- iv **Oliver P. Dudley**.

148. **Perrin Dudley** (79.David[5], 36.Ebenezer[4], 11.Benjamin[3], 3.Joseph[2], 1.Francis[1]) b. 3 Feb 1803, Paris, Oxford, Maine, m. 30 May 1828, in Woodstock, Oxford, Maine, **Pauline Felt**, b. 7 Aug 1811, Woodstock, Oxford, Maine, (daughter of **Joshua Felt**) d. 30 Nov 1890, Woodstock, Oxford, Maine. Perrin died 1897. Inherited the homestead of his father at Woodstock, Me., and occupied it from 1820 onward. He was one of the most prominent and esteemed citizens. Went through the grades in the military, rising to Colonel. In the Civil War, he drilled the troops at Bryant's Pond, and nearly every one of his soldiers enlisted (he was in the militia at the time). According to Dean Dudley, "he gave his children a good start in life." Marriage date is from Dean Dudley, place from IGI civil batch.

Children:
- i **Otis S. Dudley** b. 25 Jan 1829, Woodstock, Oxford, Maine, d. 2 May 1830.
- ii **Jairus Dudley** b. 7 Oct 1831, Woodstock, Oxford, Maine, m. 3 Jul 1860, **Amanda M. Clark**, (daughter of **Norman Clark**). Jairus died 1881, Bethel, Oxford, Maine.
- iii **Angelina Dudley** b. 20 Jul 1833, Woodstock, Oxford, Maine, m. 4 Jul 1853, **Albion P. Bowker**.
- iv **Clementine Dudley** b. 8 May 1835, Woodstock, Oxford, Maine, d. 15 Aug 1838.
- v **Margaret Dudley** b. 2 Jun 1837, Woodstock, Oxford, Maine, d. 15 Jul 1839.
- vi **Otis S. Dudley** b. 11 Apr 1839, Woodstock, Oxford, Maine, m. 21 Jun 1862, **Mahala Curtis**.
- vii **Adelia Dudley** b. 29 Mar 1841, Woodstock, Oxford, Maine, m. 26 Dec 1861, **Jeremiah Curtis**. Adelia died 4 Aug 1876.
- 245. viii **Ansel Dudley** b. 11 Apr 1844.
- ix **Amanda M. Dudley** b. 31 Mar 1846, Woodstock, Oxford, Maine, m. 1 Jan 1868, **James Sheran**.
- x **Evelyn O. Dudley** b. 20 Dec 1849, Woodstock, Oxford, Maine, m. 7 Nov 1869, **Freeland Young**.
- xi **Perrin A. Dudley** b. 14 Dec 1853, Woodstock, Oxford, Maine, d. 16 Sep 1855.

149. **Gilbert Dudley** (79.David⁵, 36.Ebenezer⁴, 11.Benjamin³, 3.Joseph²,
1.Francis¹) b. 19 Nov 1819, m. 5 Mar 1844, in Woodstock, Oxford, Maine, **Mahala Curtis**. Perrin is the only known child. There were probably others. The IGI batch number M521471 lists a marriage date of 14 Jan 1844. As it is notorious for stating the intention date as the marriage date, I believe Dean Dudley's date is more accurate here.
> *Children:*
> i **Perrin Dudley.**

150. **Ansel G. Dudley** (79.David⁵, 36.Ebenezer⁴, 11.Benjamin³, 3.Joseph²,
1.Francis¹) b. 9 Feb 1821, occupation: Farmer, m. **Augusta Curtis**, (daughter of **Noah Curtis**).
> *Children:*
> i **Edwin A. Dudley** b. 2 May 1857.
> ii **Nellie A. Dudley** b. 2 May 1857. Twin to Edwin.
> iii **Dora E. Dudley** b. 7 Nov 1861.

151. **William Davis Dudley** (80.Ebenezer⁵, 36.Ebenezer⁴, 11.Benjamin³, 3.Joseph²,
1.Francis¹) b. 1 Feb 1806, West Roxbury, Norfolk, Mass., m. **Elizabeth Lufkin**, b. 13 Jul 1818, d. 29 Oct 1867. William died 31 Apr 1849, Roxbury, Norfolk, Mass. The death record says he died of "lung fever at the alms house." Yes, the death date IS 31 April, according to the VR.
Elizabeth: Poor Elizabeth lost her husband and 2 children within one month.
> *Children:*
> 246.   i **George Henry Dudley** b. 8 Apr 1841.
> ii **Charles Eaton Dudley** b. 21 Jun 1843, d. 25 May 1849, Roxbury, Norfolk, Mass.
> iii **William Davis Eaton Dudley** b. 3 Oct 1845, Roxbury, Norfolk, Mass., d. Jun 1849, Roxbury, Norfolk, Mass.

152. **Ephraim Murdock Dudley** (80.Ebenezer⁵, 36.Ebenezer⁴, 11.Benjamin³,
3.Joseph², 1.Francis¹) b. 23 May 1808, West Roxbury, Norfolk, Mass., occupation: Yeoman, m. 7 May 1835, in Roxbury, Norfolk, Mass., **Elmira Swallow**, (daughter of **John S. Swallow**).
> *Children:*
> i **Wayne B. Dudley** b. 3 Jun 1848, Roxbury, Norfolk, Mass.

153. **Samuel Dudley** (81.William⁵, 37.William⁴, 11.Benjamin³, 3.Joseph²,
1.Francis¹) b. 18 Apr 1793, Wayland, Middlesex, Mass., occupation: Colonel, m. 25 Feb 1819, in Framingham, Middlesex, Mass., **Nancy Brown**, b. ABT 1775, d. 28 Aug 1825, Portland, Cumberland, Maine. Samuel died New York. Was murdered in New York. When

married, he was "of Dover, N.H." No records found other than marriage in Framingham--did they reside in Dover?

Children:

247.　　i　**Anne Elizabeth Dudley**.

154. William Rice Dudley (81.William[5], 37.William[4], 11.Benjamin[3], 3.Joseph[2], 1.Francis[1]) b. 6 Mar 1807, Wayland, Middlesex, Mass., m. 5 May 1833, in Lincoln, Middlesex, Mass., **Mary P. Sherman**. Marriage intentions were filed in Wayland on 17 Mar 1833. He was of "E. Sudbury" at the time.
Mary: From Lincoln.

Children:

i　**Lucy Ann Dudley** b. 12 Jan 1834, Wayland, Middlesex, Mass.

ii　**Mary Elizabeth Dudley** b. May 1836, Wayland, Middlesex, Mass., d. 29 Feb 1844, Wayland, Middlesex, Mass. Dean Dudley records name as Elizabeth, but she appears in Wayland death record, and grave record, as Mary Elizabeth. Her death record says she died of "dropsy in the head" at "7y, 9m."

155. Benjamin Austin Dudley (81.William[5], 37.William[4], 11.Benjamin[3], 3.Joseph[2], 1.Francis[1]) b. 6 Sep 1811, Wayland, Middlesex, Mass., occupation: Mason, m. 8 May 1839, in Wayland, Middlesex, Mass., **Rosalie A. Heard**.

Children:

i　**Rosalia Austin Dudley** b. 8 Jan 1846, Wayland, Middlesex, Mass.

ii　**Edward M. Dudley** b. Wayland, Middlesex, Mass. Edward does not appear in the Wayland V.R.'s. Source is Dean Dudley only.

156. Nathaniel Curtis Dudley (81.William[5], 37.William[4], 11.Benjamin[3], 3.Joseph[2], 1.Francis[1]) b. 17 Jan 1813, Wayland, Middlesex, Mass., occupation: farmer, m. (1) 14 Mar 1837, in Wayland, Middlesex, Mass., **Philindia Damon**, b. abt 1816, d. 19 May 1838, Wayland, Middlesex, Mass., m. (2) 27 Jun 1844, in Framingham, Middlesex, Mass., **Anna S. Maynard**, b. abt 1825.
Philindia: Dean Dudley records a death of 16 April. It appears she may have died as a result of childbirth.
Anna: From Framingham. Her and Nathaniel's intention was filed June 1 in Wayland (VR 68).

Children by Philindia Damon:

i　**Evelin Augusta Dudley** b. Wayland, Middlesex, Mass., d. 1838, Wayland, Middlesex, Mass. There are a number of death dates possible for this child, or there may have been more than one child at the birth. The gravestone says 8 June 1838, the town record says 7 May, and the church record records April. It appears that the mother, Philindia, may have died as a result. The Wayland VR says she was "9 m" (months) old and died Apr.

Children by Anna S. Maynard:
   ii **Anna M. Dudley** b. 26 Apr 1845, Wayland, Middlesex, Mass.
  iii **Caroline Elizabeth Dudley** b. 18 Sep 1847, Wayland, Middlesex, Mass.

157. **Aaron Dudley** (85.Nathan[5], 40.Peter[4], 14.John[3], 4.John[2], 1.Francis[1]) b. 5 May 1786, m. 19 Nov 1807, in Hopkinton, Middlesex, Mass., **Sophia Frail**, b. 30 Mar 1786, Hopkinton, Middlesex, Mass. Moved to North Leverett, Mass.
       Children:
        i **Martha G. Dudley** b. 15 Oct 1808, North Leverett, Hampshire, Mass., d. 4 Oct 1863.
248.   ii **Aaron Dudley** b. 20 Nov 1810.
249.   iii **Samuel F. Dudley** b. 31 Oct 1812.
250.   iv **Isaac Dudley** b. 28 Feb 1815.
251.   v **Luther Dudley** b. 6 Sep 1817.
       vi **Hannah S. Dudley** b. 17 Sep 1819, North Leverett, Hampshire, Mass.
     vii **S. Maria Dudley** b. 25 Jul 1821, North Leverett, Hampshire, Mass.
252. viii **William E. Dudley** b. 26 Apr 1823.
      ix **James Ransom Dudley** b. 25 Aug 1825, North Leverett, Hampshire, Mass., d. 27 Jan 1859.
       x **Nathan Dudley** b. 15 Mar 1828, North Leverett, Hampshire, Mass., d. 30 May 1837. Was killed by having been thrown from a horse he was riding to plow. His skull was broken.

158. **John Vose Dudley** (87.Daniel[5], 41.Daniel[4], 14.John[3], 4.John[2], 1.Francis[1]) b. ABT 1794, m. 18 Jul 1819, in Wayland, Middlesex, Mass., **Eliza Harrington**. John died 17 Oct 1837, Wayland, Middlesex, Mass. His gravestone states he was 43 at his death.
       Children:
        i **Moses Dudley** b. 3 Jan 1820, Wayland, Middlesex, Mass.
       ii **James Winthrop Dudley** b. 27 Mar 1824, Wayland, Middlesex, Mass., m. 6 Sep 1848, in Framingham, Middlesex, Mass., **Margaret Collins**, b. ABT 1824. James' and Margaret's marriage intention was filed 19 Aug 1848 in Wayland. **Margaret**: Birth date from marriage record, states she was 25.
      iii **Ellen Dudley** b. ABT 1834, Wayland, Middlesex, Mass., d. 23 Apr 1842, Wayland, Middlesex, Mass. Death record states she was 8 years old at death.

159. **Lewis Dudley** (87.Daniel[5], 41.Daniel[4], 14.John[3], 4.John[2], 1.Francis[1]) b. 8 Jun 1799, Wayland, Middlesex, Mass., m. 7 Jan 1819, in Wayland, Middlesex, Mass., **Margaret Winch**, d. 11 May 1878, Wayland, Middlesex, Mass. Lewis died 16 Jan 1838, Wayland, Middlesex, Mass. Was drowned in Johnson Pond, often called now "Dudley Pond." He left $2,626 in real Estate, and $387.37 in personal estate. The children were noted in the will. There are no VR records for them.

Children:

   i **Mary B. Dudley** b. ABT 1826, m. 1 Nov 1848, in Wayland, Middlesex, Mass., **William V. Chaloner**, b. ABT 1817, (son of **Thomas Chaloner** and **Lucy Chaloner**) occupation: carpenter. Her marriage record stated she was 22 when married.
       William: Marriage record states he was 31 when married.
   ii **Elizabeth M. Dudley** m. 1 Apr 1841, in Wayland, Middlesex, Mass., **David Spofford**.
   iii **Martha J. Dudley** m. **Samuel Adams**.
   iv **Maria Dudley** m. 1835, **George W. Stone**. Marriage intentions were filed 3 May 1835 in Wayland (68). No marriage record found.
       George: Was "of Sudbury".

253.   v **Caroline W. Dudley** b. Mar 1829.
   vi **Julia Ann Dudley**.
   vii **Lewis Dudley**.
   viii **Edwin A. Dudley**.

160. **Rowland Cushing Dudley** (88.James[5], 43.Francis[4], 14.John[3], 4.John[2], 1.Francis[1]) b. 25 Jul 1807, Winslow, Kennebec, Maine, occupation: farmer/lumberman, m. 9 Oct 1831, in Alexander, Washington, Maine, **Sarah "Sally" Fenlason**, b. 14 Apr 1812, Machias, Washington, Maine, (daughter of **Mark Fenlason** and **Sally M. Elsemore**) d. BEF 1870, Maine. Rowland died AFT 1880. He resided in Alexander, Maine c1830; then at Woodville Plt c1834-1849; in Wesley about 1850, then back to Woodville by 1860. He was in Princeton by 1870 and then no further mention in the census'. He was living in the household of his son-in-law Randall Day in the US 1870 census in Princeton, Maine, but no wife is mentioned. One son, Roland (age 15 at the time) is noted as present.
       Children:

   i **Daniel Harden Dudley** b. 29 Aug 1832, Alexander, Washington, Maine, d. 28 Jan 1833, Alexander, Washington, Maine.
   ii **Bethiah Dudley** b. 23 Dec 1833, Alexander, Washington, Maine, d. BEF 1847. Died young.
   iii **Ann Mariah Dudley** b. ABT 1836, Maine, m. **Samuel Barrows**. She is found as "Ann M." in the 1850 census, as "Mariah" in the 1860 census.
   iv **John S. Dudley** b. ABT 1838, Maine. Middle name "Scott?"
   v **Catharia Dudley** b. ABT 1840, Alexander, Washington, Maine. She is found in the 1850 census as "Casiah." Not present in the 1860 census.

254.   vi **Nancy Emma Dudley** b. 1 Jan 1842.
255.   vii **Mark Fenlason Dudley** b. 17 Dec 1844.
   viii **Rosemund Dudley** b. ABT 1846, Maine, m. 13 Jul 1864, in Mattawamkeag, Penobscot, ME, **Orris Moore Wellman**, b. 1 Nov 1836, Searsmont, Washington, ME, d. 29 Feb 1912, Calais, Washington, Maine. Rosemund died

BEF 1867. The Wellman Genealogy says she died shortly after marriage. No known issue.

Orris: He married (3) Joan Fisher b 17 Apr 1862, Perry, ME. Yes, he married Dudley sisters.

256.   ix   **Bethiah Dudley** b. ABT 1847.

        x   **Rowland Cushing Dudley** b. ABT 1854, Maine.

161. **Mary H. Dudley** (88.James[5], 43.Francis[4], 14.John[3], 4.John[2], 1.Francis[1]) b. ABT 1809, Maine, m. 10 Dec 1829, in Passadumkeag, Penobscot, Maine, **Charles H. Scott**, b. ABT 1807, Maine, d. BET 1860-1870, Maine. Mary died 1886, Maine, buried: Elsemore Cemetery, Twp#18, Maine. She is found in the 1870 census in East Machias, ME, a widow.

    Charles: Resided in Woodville, Penobscot, ME c1837-1860, based on census records.

       Children:

     i   **James M. Scott** b. ABT 1832, W. Indian Twp [Woodville], Penobscot, ME.

    ii   **Mary H. Scott** b. ABT 1835, W. Indian Twp [Woodville], Penobscot, ME.

   iii   **Charles H. Scott** b. ABT 1838, W. Indian Twp [Woodville], Penobscot, ME, m. 11 Nov 1866, in Maine, **Lydia Andrews**. Charles died 10 Jun 1915, Plantation 18, Washington, ME, buried: Elsemore Cemetery, Twp#18, Maine.

   iv   **Rosamund Fenlason Scott** b. 2 Mar 1841, W. Indian Twp [Woodville], Penobscot, ME, m. 27 Jul 1862, in Maine, **Ira Lowell Cook**. Rosamund died 24 Dec 1911.

    v   **Stephen D. Scott** b. 3 Jun 1843, W. Indian Twp [Woodville], Penobscot, ME, m. (1) 25 Jan 1868, in Maine, **Julia Elsemore**, m. (2) 13 Apr 1881, in Maine, **Louisa Lowery**. Stephen died Jul, 1936, Princeton, Washington, Maine, buried: Baring Cemetery, Baring, Maine. Not in this family in 1850 census, but present in 1860 census.

   vi   **Mark T. Scott** b. 10 Feb 1846, W. Indian Twp [Woodville], Penobscot, ME, m. 20 DEC 1869, in East Machias, Washington, Maine, **Judith R. "Julia" Elsemore**, b. 22 Jun 1850, East Machias, Washington, Maine, (daughter of **Cyrus F. Elsemore and Lucy C. _____**) d. 14 Dec 1873, Plantation 18, Washington, ME. Mark died 30 Jan 1928, Plantation 18, Washington, ME, buried: Scott Lot, Jacksonville, ME.

   vii   **Theodore Scott** b. ABT 1849, Maine, m. 28 Nov 1877, in Maine, **Julia Etta Lund**. Theodore died in the West.

  viii   **Elmira Scott** b. ABT 1850, W. Indian Twp [Woodville], Penobscot, ME, m. **James Bagley**.

   ix   **Lorenzo Dudley "Cub" Scott** b. 16 Aug 1854, W. Indian Twp [Woodville], Penobscot, ME, m. **Abbie Myria Elsemore**, b. Oct 1862, East Machias, Washington, Maine, (daughter of **Charles Elsemore** and **Sarah Elizabeth**) d. 1 May 1886, East Machias, Washington, Maine. Lorenzo died 7 Nov 1939,

Jacksonville, East Machias, Wash., ME.

162. **James Madison Dudley** (88.James[5], 43.Francis[4], 14.John[3], 4.John[2],
1.Francis[1]) b. ABT Dec 1813, Maine, occupation: lumberman, m. 18 Jun 1840, in
Howland, Penobscot, Maine, **Julia A. Kimball**, b. 20 Mar 1820, Sebec, Piscataquis, ME,
(daughter of **Robert Kimball** and **Lydia Adams**) d. 22 Jun 1906, Buxton, York, ME.
James died 23 May 1896, Scarborough, Cumberland, ME, buried: Scarborough, Cumberland,
ME. He is listed called "James 2nd" in the "History of Penobscot County, Maine" which
notes that about 1840, he built a sawmill on Eagle Stream close to the Penobscot River in
Woodville Plt (E. Indian Twp). He later operated a farm in in West Enfield, Maine. James
resided with his children in Cumberland County, Maine, in his old age. His cause of death is
listed as suicide. Note that diptheria ravaged this family in 1860, taking 3 of its last 4
children.
Julia: A letter dated 19 Nov 1896 to Julia from brother, John T. Kimball of Lincoln,
Maine, implies her husband, James, is dead and sends regards to her sons, John and Charles
(apparently she is residing with one of them). It also mentions her daughter, Sophronia,
apparently still living, but no clues as to her residence.

Children:

  i   **Lydia Ellen Dudley** b. 10 May 1841, Howland?, Penobscot, ME.
  ii **Sophronia Pierce Dudley** b. 1 Jun 1842, of Howland, Penobscot, ME, d. 14
      Oct 1843, Maine.
  iii **Sophronia Pierce Dudley** b. 13 Sep 1843, Lincoln, Penobscot, Maine, d. AFT
      1896.
257. iv **John T. Dudley** b. 26 Jun 1845.
  v   **Charles Francis Dudley** b. 23 Mar 1847, Lincoln, Penobscot, Maine, d. 29 Jan
      1927, Portland, Cumberland, Maine. Charles was living with his parents, age 32,
      in the West Enfield, Maine 1880 Census. He settled in Portland, Maine about
      1917.
  vi **James Madison Dudley** b. 12 Nov 1849, Lincoln, Penobscot, Maine, d. 21
      Aug 1850, Maine. James is not in the 1850 census.
  vii **Julia Ann Dudley** b. 15 May 1850, Lincoln, Penobscot, Maine.
  viii **James Madison Dudley** b. 21 Jun 1852, Lincoln, Penobscot, Maine, d. 30 May
      1860, Mattawamkeag, Penobscot, ME. James died of diptheria.
  ix **Mary A. Dudley** b. 27 Mar 1854, Lincoln, Penobscot, Maine, d. 28 May 1860,
      Mattawamkeag, Penobscot, ME. Died of diphtheria.
  x   **Melvin V. Dudley** b. 14 Oct 1856, Lincoln, Penobscot, Maine. Melvin
      removed to Cumberland County, Maine after 1880.
  xi **Milton T. Dudley** b. 13 Aug 1858, Lincoln, Penobscot, Maine, d. 7 May 1860,
      Mattawamkeag, Penobscot, ME. Died of diphtheria. Death record,
      Mattawamkeag: died age 1 yr 6 mo.

163. **Charles H. Dudley** (88.James[5], 43.Francis[4], 14.John[3], 4.John[2], 1.Francis[1]) b. 14 Apr 1818, Miramichi, New Brunswick, Canada, occupation: lumberman, m. (1) 3 Oct 1840, in Passadumkeag, Penobscot, Maine, **Abigail H. Sibley**, b. 1 Apr 1823, Passadumkeag, Penobscot, Maine, (daughter of **Peter Sibley** and **Elizabeth Whitton**) d. 11 May 1888, Stacyville, Penobscot, Maine, buried: Stacyville, Penobscot, Maine, m. (2) 9 Jul 1894, in Stacyville, Penobscot, Maine, **Elizabeth A. Sibley**, b. 14 Apr 1820, Maine, (daughter of **Peter Sibley** and **Elizabeth Whitton**) d. 12 May 1900, Passadumkeag, Penobscot, Maine, buried: Village Cemetery, Passadumkeag, ME. Charles died 14 Apr 1897, Passadumkeag, Penobscot, Maine, buried: Stacyville, Penobscot, Maine. Charles was a Civil War veteran, serving in the 30th Maine Regiment, 4th Battery (1865-1866). Yes, he did marry two sisters.

Abigail: She is found wife of Charles H. Dudley, age 28 1850 USC; age 38 1860 USC Stacyville 1870 USC age 46. Gravestone: d age 66 yrs, 8 days.

Elizabeth: On gravestone: ROUNDY, Elizabeth A. wife of J.P Roundy April 14 1820 - May 12 1900. She was the widow of Rev. Joshua P. Roundy and sister of Charles H. Dudley's first wife, Abigail.

Children by Abigail H. Sibley:

258.　　i　**Silence H. Dudley** b. ABT 1841.
259.　　ii　**Mary E. Dudley** b. ABT 1842.
　　　　iii　**Jane Dudley** b. ABT 1843, Maine. She appears in this family's household only in the 1860 census.
260.　　iv　**Ira B. Dudley** b. 10 Oct 1845.
261.　　v　**James Hunter Dudley** b. 29 Jan 1849.
262.　　vi　**Hannah H. Dudley** b. ABT 1850.
263.　　vii　**Charles H. Dudley** b. 11 May 1852.
　　　　viii　**Matilda Ann Dudley** b. 24 Feb 1858, Winn?, Penobscot, ME, m. 23 Aug 1873, in Stacyville, Penobscot, Maine, **Francis "Frank" E. Ellis**, b. 4 Mar 1851, Maine, (son of **Monoah Ellis**). Matilda and Frank moved to Seattle, Washington.
264.　　ix　**Abigail (Eliza?) Dudley** b. 20 Jul 1859.

164. **Rowland Dudley** (90.Rowland[5], 43.Francis[4], 14.John[3], 4.John[2], 1.Francis[1]) b. 1820, Maine, m. 16 Oct 1854, in Old Town, Penobscot, Maine, **Sarah P. Hunt**, b. 1836, Maine, d. 1909, Old Town, Penobscot, Maine, buried: Forest Hill Cemetery, Old Town, Maine. Rowland died 1894, Old Town, Penobscot, Maine, buried: Forest Hill Cemetery, Old Town, Maine. Resided in household of widowed mother, Ann Dudley, in 1850 Old Town census, age 28. He may have had other children, as yet unidentified. Marriage date is the date of the Certificate--usually issued within one week of marriage.

Children:

　　　　i　**Ellis C. Dudley** b. 1855, Old Town, Penobscot, Maine, d. 1856, Old Town, Penobscot, Maine, buried: Forest Hill Cemetery, Old Town, Maine.

ii　**Lewis C. Dudley** b. 1857, Old Town, Penobscot, Maine, d. 1857, Old Town, Penobscot, Maine, buried: Forest Hill Cemetery, Old Town, Maine.

iii　**Frank R. Dudley** b. 1860, Old Town, Penobscot, Maine, d. 1890, Old Town, Penobscot, Maine, buried: Forest Hill Cemetery, Old Town, Maine.

iv　**Nellie E. Dudley** b. 1864, Old Town, Penobscot, Maine, d. 1883, Old Town, Penobscot, Maine, buried: Forest Hill Cemetery, Old Town, Maine.

v　**Howard H. Dudley** b. 1872, Old Town, Penobscot, Maine, d. 1872, Old Town, Penobscot, Maine, buried: Forest Hill Cemetery, Old Town, Maine.

165. **Joseph Dudley** (91.Joseph[5], 44.Samuel[4], 15.Samuel[3], 6.Samuel[2], 1.Francis[1])
b. 5 Feb 1798, m. **Abigail Morse**. Lived near the mill in the south part of Waterford.
Children:
i　**Joseph W. Dudley** m. **Elizabeth Earles**.
ii　**Albert Dudley**.
iii　**Samuel Dudley**.
iv　**Israel Dudley** m. **Thirza Kilgore**.
v　**Matilda Dudley**.

166. **James Dudley** (91.Joseph[5], 44.Samuel[4], 15.Samuel[3], 6.Samuel[2], 1.Francis[1])
b. 1803, occupation: Farmer and Miller, m. **Lucinda Dillingham**. James lived near the mill at Harrison.
Children:
i　**Lucinda D. Dudley** m. **C. Jefferds**.
ii　**James E. Dudley** m. **Eliza Burns**.
iii　**Nancy J. Dudley** m. **Stephen Pattee**.
iv　**Charlotte Dudley**. There is a discrepancy between Dean Dudley and the "History of Waterford." The Waterford book records a "Charles M." here.
v　**Samuel Dudley**.
vi　**John Dudley** m. **Susan Backman**.
　　Susan: Her name comes from the "History of Waterford."
vii　**Lewis F. Dudley** m. 14 Jul 1875, in Harrison, Cumberland, Maine, **Amy Fernald**.
viii　**Frederick E. Dudley**.

167. **Polly Dudley** (92.Josiah[5], 44.Samuel[4], 15.Samuel[3], 6.Samuel[2], 1.Francis[1])
b. 4 Aug 1796, m. 20 Feb 1820, **William Mather**, occupation: Farmer, d. abt 1862, Adams, Jefferson Co., N.Y. Polly died abt 1862. William and Polly settled at Adams, N.Y.
Children:
i　**Milo S. Mather** b. 8 Jan 1821, occupation: farmer, m. 14 Mar 1849, **Adelia S. Hunting**.
ii　**Simeon Mather** b. 10 Jun 1822, occupation: Farmer, m. 1847, **Mary E.**

Green.
- iii **George Mather** b. 4 Oct 1824, occupation: Farmer, m. 11 Dec 1867, **Jame Murray**. Lived on the homestead of his father in Adams, Jefferson County, N.Y. **Jame**: The first name spelling is odd on this one, it is probably JAMIE.
- iv **Betsey Mather** b. 21 Jun 1827, m. 15 Feb 1849, **Mero B. Hunting**. Betsey died 23 May 1850.
- v **Eliza Mather** b. 9 Mar 1830, m. 22 Aug 1852, **J.E. Green**. Eliza died 15 Sep 1853. Probably died in childbirth.
- vi **Malvina Mather** b. 9 Jun 1832, d. 12 Dec 1875. Unmarried.
- vii **William Mather** b. 20 Aug 1834, occupation: Farmer, m. 21 Sep 1876, **Eunice G. Bull**.

168. **Henry Dudley** (92.Josiah^5, 44.Samuel^4, 15.Samuel^3, 6.Samuel^2, 1.Francis^1)
b. 20 May 1798, buried: Jan 1876. We do not know the name of Henry's wife. His 3 sons were all living in Grand Junction, Green Co., Iowa.
> *Children:*
> - i **Enos Dudley**.
> - ii **Smith Dudley**.
> - iii **Andrew Dudley**.

169. **Rebecca Dudley** (92.Josiah^5, 44.Samuel^4, 15.Samuel^3, 6.Samuel^2, 1.Francis^1)
b. 25 May 1800, m. **Asa Otis**, occupation: Farmer, d. 26 Mar 1871, Pamelia, N.Y. After Asa's death, went to live with her daughter in South Champion, N.Y.
> *Children:*
> - i **Daughter** m. **Theodore Waldo**. Her name is unknown. She had 2 sons and 2 daughters.

170. **Simeon H. Dudley** (92.Josiah^5, 44.Samuel^4, 15.Samuel^3, 6.Samuel^2, 1.Francis^1) b. 12 May 1802, m. **Chloe Felt**. Simeon died abt 1886. He lived in Fort Wayne, Indiana, and the children were probably born there.
> *Children:*
> - i **Charles Dudley**.
> - ii **Adelia Dudley**.

171. **Lydia Dudley** (93.Stephen^5, 45.Stephen^4, 15.Samuel^3, 6.Samuel^2, 1.Francis^1)
b. 22 Dec 1784, m. 18 Dec 1809, in Cato, Cayuga Co., N.Y., **Isaac Kinney**, occupation: Farmer of Chicago, Ill. Lydia died 18 Dec 1876. All children born at Chicago.
> *Children:*
> - i **Lydia Kinney** m. **Mr Vint**.
> - ii **Elijah Kinney** m. **Olive**.
> - iii **Lois Kinney** m. **Asa Watson**.

      iv **Clara Kinney** m. **Waters Northrop**.

      v **Marietta Kinney** m. **Peter Northrop**.

      vi **Isaac Kinney** m. **Eveline**.

172. **Asa Dudley** (93.Stephen[5], 45.Stephen[4], 15.Samuel[3], 6.Samuel[2], 1.Francis[1])
    b. 12 Nov 1786, occupation: Farmer and sheriff, m. 17 Sep 1807, in Cato, Cayuga Co., N.Y.,
    Lovina Alcot. Asa died 22 Sep 1868. Was the Sheriff of Bloomingdale, Ill.
        Children:

        i **Myron Dudley** m. abt 1847, in Napierville, Ill., **Lucinda Willey**. Myron
          and Lucinda had four children, but no records.

        ii **Harriet Dudley** m. **Orange Kent**. Harriet and Orange had four children.

265.   iii **Lavina Dudley**.

        iv **Maria Dudley** m. **Stephen Penyer**. No children.
          Stephen: Was from Chicago.

266.   v **Caroline Dudley**.

        vi **Susan Dudley** m. **Noah Barnes**. Susan and Noah had 4 or 5 children at
          Bloomingdale, Ill.

        vii **Emily Dudley** m. **Berlin Godfrey**. Emily and Berlin had 3 or 4 children in
          Bloomingdale.
          Berlin: Of Bloomindale, Ill.

        viii **Catherine Dudley**. Died unmarried at 18.

173. **Sardis Dudley** (93.Stephen[5], 45.Stephen[4], 15.Samuel[3], 6.Samuel[2],
    1.Francis[1]) b. 10 Jan 1792, occupation: Farmer, m. (1) 13 Feb 1816, in Cato, Cayuga Co.,
    N.Y., **Anstis Ferris**, d. 1825, m. (2) **Mary Ferris**, d. 8 Feb 1863, Meridian, N.Y., m.
    (3) **Harmony Smith**. Sardis died 26 Jan 1876.
    Harmony: No children.
        Children by Anstis Ferris:

267.   i **Elmina Dudley** b. 23 Nov 1817.

268.   ii **Isaac Vaughn Dudley** b. Dec 1819.

269.   iii **Edwin Dudley** b. Aug 1822.

        iv **Angeline Dudley** b. Aug 1822. Died young.

        v **Zipporah A. Dudley** b. 19 Nov 1824.
        Children by Mary Ferris:

270.   vi **Anstis A. Dudley** b. 1827.

        vii **Emily Dudley** b. 25 Feb 1830, d. 1847.

271.   viii **Betsey A. Dudley** b. 10 Jun 1832.

        ix **Julia Letitia Dudley** b. May 1834, d. 17 May 1837, Cato, Cayuga Co., N.Y.

        x **Ira L. Dudley** b. 16 Jun 1836, m. (1) **Mary Northrop**, d. 25 Oct 1862, m.
          (2) **Addie Drew**, d. 20 Nov 1879, Illinois. Ira had a third wife, no record.

        xi **Edgar M. Dudley** b. 17 Sep 1838, m. 2 Sep 1875, **Cassie Vose**. Lived at

Chicago. No children.

xii   **Celestia Emogene Dudley** b. Aug 1840, d. 1842.

xiii   **Angeline Dudley** b. 2 Dec 1842, m. **Lorin Colten**. Had 2 children, lived in Meridian.

xiv   **Frank Dudley** b. 9 Dec 1845, m. **Lottie Whitney**. Lived at Jordan, N.Y. No children.

xv   **Theron Dudley** b. 9 Dec 1845, m. **Ella Seymour**. Had 4 sons at Meridian.

xvi   **Jay W. Dudley** b. 12 Jun 1851, m. 1874, **Lilian Morley**. No children. Lived in Meridian.

174. **Lyman Dudley** (93.Stephen[5], 45.Stephen[4], 15.Samuel[3], 6.Samuel[2], 1.Francis[1])
b. 22 Nov 1793, occupation: Farmer, m. 31 Dec 1815, in Hannibal, N.Y., **Susann Burnham**. Lyman died 1875. Death date could be 1876. Lived in Mansfield, Ohio.
Children:

272.   i   **Lorenzo Dudley** b. abt 1817.

         ii   **Orison Dudley** b. abt 1819, m. **Kate**. Orison died Dayton, Ohio. Kate and Orison had two children at Dayton, Ohio.

        iii   **Hannah Dudley** m. **Mr. Willard**.
           Mr.: Was from Cleveland

        iv   **Eliza A. Dudley** m. (1) **Mr. Johns**, m. (2) **Mr. Stocking**. Eliza had one child with Mr. Johns, and 5 with Mr. Stocking.

175. **James Dudley** (93.Stephen[5], 45.Stephen[4], 15.Samuel[3], 6.Samuel[2], 1.Francis[1])
b. 12 Apr 1797, occupation: Farmer, m. **Lucy Chappel**. James died 1882.
Children:

         i   **Addison Dudley**. Was married and had two children, no record.

        ii   **Charles Dudley**.

        iii   **Ann Dudley**. Was married twice and lived in Chicago. No records.

176. **Ira Dudley** (93.Stephen[5], 45.Stephen[4], 15.Samuel[3], 6.Samuel[2], 1.Francis[1]) b.
22 Feb 1799, occupation: Minister, m. (1) 18 Dec 1821, in Cato, Cayuga Co., N.Y.,
Margaret Ferris, d. 4 Sep 1865, buried: Hannibal, N.Y., m. (2) 26 Apr 1870, in Rockford,
Ill, **Mrs. R. M. Hervey**. Ira died 6 Oct 1883, Meridian, N.Y., buried: Hannibal, N.Y.
Lived and preached at Baldwinsville, N.Y. and St. Charles, Ill. His wife, by the way, WAS
the sister of Ira's brother Sardis' 1st two wives.
Children by Margaret Ferris:

273.   i   **Mary Ann Dudley** b. 3 Jun 1823.

274.   ii   **Angeline A. Dudley** b. 25 Feb 1825.

        iii   **Herbert Stephen Dudley** b. 14 Oct 1827, d. 30 Aug 1849, Albany, N.Y. Died unmarried of Cholera at Albany Normal School. Had studied law in the office of M.B. Church.

275.   iv   **Emily Z. Dudley** b. 23 Mar 1830.
276.   v   **Judson H. Dudley** b. 8 Apr 1832.
277.   vi   **George P. Dudley** b. 16 Apr 1838.

177. **Rebecca Dudley** (93.Stephen⁵, 45.Stephen⁴, 15.Samuel³, 6.Samuel²,
    1.Francis¹) b. 22 Apr 1801, m. 1 Apr 1824, in Hannibal, N.Y., **Abner Loomis**.
        Children:
        i   **Abner Loomis**. He married and had four children.

178. **Stephen Merritt Dudley** (93.Stephen⁵, 45.Stephen⁴, 15.Samuel³, 6.Samuel²,
    1.Francis¹) b. 22 Mar 1803, occupation: Farmer, m. 11 Oct 1827, in Hannibal, N.Y.,
    Lucy Dudley. Stephen died Mar 1841, Orland, Ind.
        Children:
278.   i   **Myra A. Dudley** b. Oct 1828.
279.   ii   **Jonathan Merritt Dudley** b. 7 Sep 1830.
        iii **Sophia Dudley**. Died in infancy.
        iv   **George Stephen Dudley** b. 10 Mar 1834, Hannibal, N.Y., m. 1869, in Suisun,
            Solano, California, **Emma Leopold**. George and Emma moved to Seattle,
            Washington, and had two children--no record.
        v   **Lucinda E. Dudley** b. 25 Aug 1835, Hannibal, N.Y., m. **Aaron Bodley**.
            Lucinda died Aug 1876, Dixon, California. No children.
        vi   **Grove Hall Dudley** b. 11 Sep 1838, Orland, Ind. Served the Union Army for
            three years during the Civil War, with Sherman from Vicksburg to surrender of
            Johnston in North Carolina. He belonged to Company B, 100th Indiana Regiment.
            Was married with six children, and lived in Orland, Indiana on his fathers
            homestead. No record of wife and children.

179. **Isaac Tichener Dudley** (93.Stephen⁵, 45.Stephen⁴, 15.Samuel³, 6.Samuel²,
    1.Francis¹) b. 16 Jan 1805, occupation: Farmer, m. May 1828, in Hannibal, N.Y., **Irena
    Lockwood**. Isaac died 17 Nov 1835, Branch, Mich.
        Children:
        i   **Caroline Dudley**.
        ii **Angeline Dudley**.

180. **Electa Dudley** (93.Stephen⁵, 45.Stephen⁴, 15.Samuel³, 6.Samuel²,
    1.Francis¹) b. 6 Apr 1808, Oswego, N.Y., m. **Isaiah Andrus**, occupation: Farmer.
    Electa died 9 Aug 1839, Oswego, N.Y.
        Children:
        i   **Lois Andrus**.
        ii   **Jane Andrus**.
        iii **John Andrus**.

181. **Edward Dudley** (94.Joseph[5], 45.Stephen[4], 15.Samuel[3], 6.Samuel[2], 1.Francis[1])
b. 1800, m. 1824, **Martha Force**, b. 1 Feb 1803, Washington Co., N.Y., d. 23 Mar 1889,
Warsaw, N.Y. Edward died 31 Jul 1837, Perry, N.Y.
Martha: Martha married James. B. Farmer of Perry after Edward's death.
> *Children:*
> i **Harwood A. Dudley** b. 5 Mar 1825, occupation: Magazine Owner. Editor and
> proprietor of the Western New Yorker Magazine. Was Called "Major", probably
> due to status in the Civil War.

182. **Lucy Dudley** (95.Peter[5], 45.Stephen[4], 15.Samuel[3], 6.Samuel[2], 1.Francis[1]) b. 6
Jun 1801, occupation: Teacher, m. 16 Nov 1826, **John True**, d. 4 Nov 1875. Lucy died
10 Aug 1874. Was educated, and became a school teacher, 1st in Vermont, and then in
Perry, Genesee Co., N.Y. where she was very successful. After her marriage, they moved to
Chautauqua County, where she was a pioneer school teacher, the County being mostly new
settlements. She became influential and highly respected.
> *Children:*
> i **Lucy Ellen True** b. 22 Feb 1841, m. 22 Feb 1869, **John Wesley Pease**, b.
> 15 Mar 1834.
> ii **Lydia Caroline True** b. 3 Oct 1843, m. 1 Jul 1863, **Anthony Kane**. Lydia
> died 3 May 1881.

183. **Peter Dudley** (95.Peter[5], 45.Stephen[4], 15.Samuel[3], 6.Samuel[2], 1.Francis[1]) b. 7
Jun 1803, occupation: Farmer, m. (1) 25 Nov 1830, **Delia Davis**, d. Oct 1836,
Manchester, Vt., m. (2) 29 Apr 1838, **Phebe Norton**, m. (3) 10 Jul 1856, **Sophia L.
Vance**. Peter died 10 Jan 1883, Bennington, Vt. Peter owned a farm until his 1st wife's
death, then moved to Londonderry, Vt, and ran a hotel. Sold that, and moved to Rutland and
became Station Master, Post master AND hotel keeper. He lost his Post office when he
became a Republican and voted for Fremont in 1856 (says Dean Dudley). Sold his Rutland
property and moved to Manchester, Vt in 1861, and bought a farm. In his old years, he sold
the farm, bought a home, and retired "with competency." He was proud of his children's role
in the Civil War.
Delia: As Delia died the same month as the birth of the twins, we may suppose that she
probably died as a result of child birth.
Sophia: No children. She continued to live on the homestead after Peter's death.
> *Children by Delia Davis:*
> i **Edwin D. Dudley** b. 16 Jul 1831, d. 21 Nov 1888.
> ii **Charles P. Dudley** b. 22 May 1833, occupation: Lt Col, m. abt 1863, **Helen
> M. Frost**, d. 1876. Charles died 7 Apr 1854, Fredericksburg, Va. First enlisted
> in the 1st Vermont Regiment for 3 months, and later raised a company in answer
> to the call from President Lincoln. Was chosen Captain of "Equinox Company",

composed of 100 men. Rose to the rank of Major, and then died from a wound received at the battle of Spottsylvania Court House. He was recommended for the rank of Lt. Colonel posthumously by the Governor of Vermont. He died in the arms of his wife.

Helen: No children.

iii **Charles P. Dudley** b. 24 Jan 1835, d. 21 May 1864.

iv **James S. Dudley** b. 3 Oct 1836. Was in the Civil War, and was a Lieutenant in the Regular Army.

v **Delia C. Dudley** b. 3 Oct 1836, d. 9 May 1863.

Children by Phebe Norton:

vi **Norton T. Dudley** b. 10 Sep 1839, occupation: Soldier, d. 30 Oct 1864. He died at the Confederate prison at Salisbury, N.C., after being taken prisoner.

184. **Stephen Dudley** (95.Peter[5], 45.Stephen[4], 15.Samuel[3], 6.Samuel[2], 1.Francis[1])
b. 1 Jun 1805, m. 16 Jun 1834, **Lydia Davis**, b. 3 Mar 1811, d. 13 May 1873. Stephen died 21 Oct 1876.

Children:

i **Benjamin Barnard Dudley** b. 1 Apr 1835, Peru, Bennington, Vt., d. 16 Apr 1836, Peru, Bennington, Vt.

ii **Daughter** b. 1 Apr 1835, Peru, Bennington, Vt., d. 13 Apr 1835, Peru, Bennington, Vt.

280. iii **Myron Samuel Dudley** b. 20 Feb 1837.

iv **George Byron Dudley** b. 21 Feb 1839, Peru, Bennington, Vt., d. 29 Jul 1863.

v **Lucy Barnard Dudley** b. 26 Apr 1841, Peru, Bennington, Vt., d. 29 Apr 1865.

vi **Harlan Elmer Dudley** b. 23 May 1843, Peru, Bennington, Vt. Was in the 16th Vermont Volunteers in the Civil War, and was severely wounded at the Battle of Gettysburg. He had 3 amputations, and was never again in good health. He was a pensioner.

vii **Helen Estelle Dudley** b. 23 May 1843, Peru, Bennington, Vt.

viii **Homer A. Dudley** b. 20 Sep 1845, Peru, Bennington, Vt. Was in Company E of the 5th Vermont Veteran Volunteers and served throughout the Civil War.

ix **Lydia Caroline Dudley** b. 31 Dec 1849, Peru, Bennington, Vt.

x **Stephen Guilford Dudley** b. 24 Apr 1854, Peru, Bennington, Vt., d. 15 Aug 1866.

185. **Elvira Dudley** (95.Peter[5], 45.Stephen[4], 15.Samuel[3], 6.Samuel[2], 1.Francis[1]) b. 18 Jul 1807, occupation: Teacher, m. 1831, **Johnson Montgomery**, occupation: Farmer. Elvira died 12 May 1863. Elvira loved history and politics, and was well informed on may subjects. Along with her husband, she hid and helped many escaped slaves. All their children of age fought in the Civil War, the youngest being 15.

Johnson: Helped to form the Republican party in 1854. Was an ardent abolitionist.

Children:

 i **Peter Dudley Montgomery** b. Oct 1833, Attica, N.Y. Was promoted to Major by the end of the Civil War, was wounded twice.

 ii **Amanda Montgomery** b. 1835.

 iii **Ezra A. Montgomery** b. 1837, occupation: 1st Lieu., d. 1863. Was a member of the 42nd Illinois Volunteers, died at Chickamauga.

 iv **Celestia Montgomery** b. 1839.

 v **Helen D. Montgomery** b. 1841.

 vi **Charles Montgomery** b. 1841.

 vii **Candia Montgomery** b. 1845.

 viii **Jok Montgomery** b. 1847.

 ix **Robert Morris Montgomery** b. 12 May 1849, Eaton Rapids, occupation: Teacher/Attorney.

186. **Lydia Dudley** (95.Peter[5], 45.Stephen[4], 15.Samuel[3], 6.Samuel[2], 1.Francis[1]) b. 12 Sep 1809, m. 15 May 1834, **David Arnold**, b. 17 Mar 1811, occupation: Farmer/Lawyer, d. 15 Jan 1881. Lydia died 2 Apr 1886.

  Children:

 i **George J. Arnold** b. 23 May 1835, occupation: Doctor, m. 6 Nov 1861, **Anna E. Bullard**. George died 1882. George served as a Dr in the Civil War and privately.

 ii **Charles E. Arnold** b. 8 Jan 1837, occupation: Lawyer, d. 8 Mar 1880. Unmarried.

 iii **Lydia Ann Frances Arnold** b. 26 Apr 1839, m. 5 Sep 1866, **Charles A. Starbuck**.

 iv **Samuel Dudley Arnold** b. 26 Mar 1841, occupation: Soldier, m. 29 May 1867, **Elenora Tenney**. Samuel was in the battle of Gettysburg.

 v **David Pratt Arnold** b. 9 Apr 1843.

 vi **Lucy Caroline Arnold** b. 29 Jan 1845, m. 26 Nov 1863, **Jonathan W. Melendy**.

 vii **Helen Wheeler Arnold** b. 12 Sep 1847, d. 14 Mar 1850.

 viii **Mary Elizabeth Arnold** b. 19 Oct 1849, m. 29 May 1870, **George E. Robinson**.

187. **James M. Dudley** (95.Peter[5], 45.Stephen[4], 15.Samuel[3], 6.Samuel[2], 1.Francis[1]) b. 19 Jul 1813, occupation: lawyer, m. 14 Jun 1843, **Maria Swartwout**, b. 9 Jan 1820, d. 4 Mar 1882. James first attended Burr and Burton Seminary in Manchester Vt, then began to study law. He was admitted to practice law in N.Y. in 1845. In 1854 he moved to Johnstown, and formed a partnership. He was an Episcopalian, and vestryman. He was well respected by peers and townspeople.

  Children:

281.   i **Edgar Swartwout Dudley** b. 14 Jun 1845.

    ii **Ella Caroline Dudley** b. 24 Aug 1847, Oppenheim, N.Y., m. 10 Sep 1870, **James Alfred Dennison**, b. 10 Sep 1846, occupation: Lawyer.

    iii **James Guilford Dudley** b. 5 Feb 1850, Oppenheim, N.Y., occupation: Civil Engineer, d. 8 Jan 1889, Lincoln, Nebraska.

    iv **Harwood Dudley** b. 11 Sep 1852, Oppenheim, N.Y., occupation: Lawyer. Graduated Union College, N.Y. and Albany Law School.

    v **John Harold Dudley** b. 11 Sep 1852, Oppenheim, N.Y.

    vi **Mary Eliza Dudley** b. 19 Dec 1859, Johnstown, m. 2 Jun 1881, **Charles Carroll Edmunds**, b. 18 Jun 1853, Green Bay, Wisconsin, occupation: Episcopal Priest.
    Charles: Graduated Seminary in New York in 1880, was Rector of Christ Church, Herkimer, N.Y. since 1885.

188. **Sophia Dudley** (95.Peter[5], 45.Stephen[4], 15.Samuel[3], 6.Samuel[2], 1.Francis[1]) b. 13 Jun 1815, m. 21 May 1835, **Nelson Curtis**, b. 14 Feb 1801, Sandgate, Vt., occupation: Tailor, d. 18 Dec 1884, Hoosic, Vt. Sophia died 1891.
Children:

    i **Frances Josephine Curtis** b. 1 Apr 1836, Hoosic, Vt., m. 18 Dec 1859, **John H. Bennett**.

    ii **James Dudley Curtis** b. 21 Mar 1840, Hoosic, Vt., m. 22 Dec 1864, **Elenora D. Simpson**. Was a private in the Civil War.

    iii **George Dexter Curtis** b. 6 Mar 1844, Hoosic, Vt., m. 5 Dec 1867, **Eve Esther Barton**.

    iv **Charles Lee Curtis** b. 8 Sep 1846, Hoosic, Vt., m. 13 Nov 1880, **Emily V. Jones**.

    v **Edwin M. Curtis** b. 5 Jul 1849, Hoosic, Vt., m. 9 Jul 1872, **Amret F. Barnes**.

189. **Mary Dudley** (95.Peter[5], 45.Stephen[4], 15.Samuel[3], 6.Samuel[2], 1.Francis[1]) b. 20 Sep 1817, m. 30 Sep 1841, **Jessie Rider**, b. 23 Sep 1812, occupation: Farmer, d. 11 Apr 1886. Mary died 11 Apr 1881.
Children:

    i **Mary Helen Rider** b. 7 Oct 1842, m. 14 May 1865, **Henry Stiles**.

    ii **Jesse Leroy Rider** b. 8 Jul 1844, d. 5 Jan 1847.

    iii **Carrie Lucy Rider** b. 21 Sep 1846, m. 24 Jan 1872, **Egbert S. Garfield**.

    iv **James Leroy Rider** b. 22 Jan 1849, m. 30 Nov 1875, **Lucy E. Kenny**. James died 31 Jul 1879.

    v **Charles Edward Rider** b. 8 Apr 1851, d. 3 Aug 1854.

    vi **Guilford Dudley Rider** b. 20 Jun 1853.

    vii **Julia Frances Rider** b. 4 Jul 1855, m. 22 Mar 1876, **Leroy H. Haseltine**.

190. **Caroline Dudley** (95.Peter[5], 45.Stephen[4], 15.Samuel[3], 6.Samuel[2], 1.Francis[1]) b. 3 Sep 1819, m. Nov 1842, **Charles Lee**, occupation: Lawyer. Caroline died 18 Apr 1851.

> *Children:*
> i **Aurora Lee** b. 19 Aug 1845, m. **W.W. Quinn**.
> ii **Hobart Lee** b. Jul 1847.

191. **Damietta Dudley** (95.Peter[5], 45.Stephen[4], 15.Samuel[3], 6.Samuel[2], 1.Francis[1]) b. 5 Aug 1823, m. 20 Dec 1843, **Isaiah Bates**, b. 3 Aug 1817. Damietta died 15 Jan 1876.

> *Children:*
> i **Elizabeth Bates** b. 18 Dec 1844, m. 5 Sep 1870, **Luther Feere**.
> ii **Emma Caroline Bates** b. 19 Feb 1848.
> iii **Mary Helen Bates** b. 21 May 1850, d. 17 Aug 1867.
> iv **Myron Dudley Bates** b. 12 Mar 1854, m. **Mary Barber**, b. Mar 1846.

192. **Helen L. Dudley** (95.Peter[5], 45.Stephen[4], 15.Samuel[3], 6.Samuel[2], 1.Francis[1]) b. 27 Jul 1826, m. (1) 27 Sep 1847, **Leonard C. Holton**, b. 8 Jan 1812, d. 1 Oct 1870, m. (2) 22 Jul 1873, **Martin Brachall**, b. 26 Jul 1808.

> *Children by Leonard C. Holton:*
> i **Abbie Holton** b. 22 Jul 1848, m. 24 Dec 1872, **Henry Donne**, b. 16 Aug 1840, Bristol, England. Abbie died 17 Jun 1875.
> ii **Frank Dudley Holton** b. 28 Jul 1850, m. 10 May 1884, **Jane Shedd**.
> iii **Henry C. Holton** b. 23 Oct 1853, m. 11 Oct 1883, **Urania Ames**.
> iv **James William Holton** b. 7 Nov 1859, occupation: Telegraph/Train Dispatch., m. 24 May 1882, **Elizabeth Sanders**.

193. **Marenia Dudley** (98.Samuel[5], 46.Francis[4], 16.Francis[3], 6.Samuel[2], 1.Francis[1]) b. 26 May 1811, Petersham, Worcester, Mass., m. 18 May 1836, in Petersham, Worcester, Mass., **Alfred Atwood**, (son of **Barney Atwood**). Marenia died 15 Apr 1889.
Alfred: Was "of Barre".

> *Children:*
> i **Charles Atwood**.
> ii **Frederick Atwood**.
> iii **Carrie Atwood**.
> iv **Lucas Atwood**.
> v **Frank Atwood**.
> vi **Cora Atwood**.

194. **Marshall Dudley** (98.Samuel[5], 46.Francis[4], 16.Francis[3], 6.Samuel[2], 1.Francis[1]) b. 2 Sep 1820, Petersham, Worcester, Mass., m. 16 Jun 1880, **Elsie M. Howe**, (daughter of **George W. Howe**). Marshall died 23 Sep 1890.

> *Children:*
> i **George M. Dudley**.

195. **Harriet Dudley** (98.Samuel[5], 46.Francis[4], 16.Francis[3], 6.Samuel[2], 1.Francis[1]) b. 9 Nov 1823, Petersham, Worcester, Mass., m. 9 Nov 1847, in Petersham, Worcester, Mass., **Albert Carruth**, (son of **Jonas Carruth**).

> *Children:*
> i **Louisa Carruth**.
> ii **George Albert Carruth**. Died young.

196. **Adeline Dudley** (98.Samuel[5], 46.Francis[4], 16.Francis[3], 6.Samuel[2], 1.Francis[1]) b. 9 Nov 1827, Petersham, Worcester, Mass., m. 26 Jun 1852, **Ethan Cheney**, (son of **Artemas Cheney**).

> *Children:*
> i **Charles Cheney**.
> ii **Jennie Cheney**.
> iii **Lulu Cheney**.

197. **Amos Dudley** (99.Joseph[5], 46.Francis[4], 16.Francis[3], 6.Samuel[2], 1.Francis[1]) b. abt 1815, m. 28 Dec 1841, in Petersham, Worcester, Mass., **Susan Braman**. Was "of Gardner."

> *Children:*
> i **Lewis Dudley**.
> ii **Ellen Dudley**.
> iii **Fred Dudley**. Died young.
> iv **Charles Albert Dudley** b. 7 Apr 1845, Petersham, Worcester, Mass., d. 3 Sep 1845, Petersham, Worcester, Mass. Here is another odd entry. One record had "Albert," another "Charles A." Albert's record has a 7 May birth date, and Charles as 7 April. (VR 21) I believe they are the same child, with one being a birth, and perhaps the other the baptism. There is enough similarity of name to warrant it. Charles' record indicates he died in September at 4 m., 27 days, (VR 174) which works out to 7 April.

198. **Emily Dudley** (99.Joseph[5], 46.Francis[4], 16.Francis[3], 6.Samuel[2], 1.Francis[1]) b. abt 1817, m. 6 Apr 1837, in Petersham, Worcester, Mass., **Chandler Moore**. Chandler: "Of Erving." Dean Dudley records the name as "Charles."

> *Children:*
> i **Louisa Moore**.

  ii **Fred Moore**.
  iii **Josephine Moore**.
  iv **Nancy Moore**.
  v **Ellen Moore**.

199. **William Dudley** (99.Joseph[5], 46.Francis[4], 16.Francis[3], 6.Samuel[2], 1.Francis[1])
  b. abt 1820, m. **Juliette Green**.
  Juliette: "Of Shrewsbury."
    Children:
    i **Frederick Dudley**. Died without children.

200. **Joseph Dudley** (99.Joseph[5], 46.Francis[4], 16.Francis[3], 6.Samuel[2], 1.Francis[1])
  b. abt 1824, m. **Orinna Forbes**.
  Orinna: "Of Hardwick."
    Children:
    i **George Dudley**.
    ii **Carrie Dudley**.
    iii **Mary Dudley**.
    iv **Nellie Dudley**.
    v **Juliette Dudley**.

201. **David Dudley** (99.Joseph[5], 46.Francis[4], 16.Francis[3], 6.Samuel[2], 1.Francis[1]) b.
  abt 1826, m. **Fannie Bliss**.
  Fannie: "Of Ware."
    Children:
    i **Frank Dudley**.

202. **Abel Stowell Dudley** (100.Simon[5], 46.Francis[4], 16.Francis[3], 6.Samuel[2],
  1.Francis[1]) m. 8 Dec 1840, in Shirley, Middlesex, Mass., **Hannah Fales**. The marriage
  also appears on the Templeton, Worcester, Mass VR.
    Children:
    i **George Henry Dudley** b. 15 Dec 1842, Shirley, Middlesex, Mass. His birth
     also shows on the Templeton, Worcester, Mass VR.

203. **Gerry Dudley** (102.Abel[5], 47.Abel[4], 17.David[3], 6.Samuel[2], 1.Francis[1]) b. 20
  Oct 1803, Shrewsbury, Worcester, Mass., m. 18 Nov 1827, in Shrewsbury, Worcester,
  Mass., **Betsey K. Bellows**. Gerry died 25 Jan 1835, Shrewsbury, Worcester, Mass. The
  Wayland VR's spell his name GARY.
    Children:
    i **Harriet Lovisa Dudley** b. 15 Apr 1828, Shrewsbury, Worcester, Mass.
    ii **Abigail Frances Dudley** b. 2 Jun 1829, Shrewsbury, Worcester, Mass., m. 29

Apr 1847, in Wayland, Middlesex, Mass., **William M. Richards**, (son of
Eliakim Richards and **Fanny**) occupation: Shoemaker.

   iii **Mary Ann Dudley** b. 16 Aug 1831, Shrewsbury, Worcester, Mass.

204. **Sophia Dudley** (103.Elijah[5], 48.Jonathan[4], 18.Jonathan[3], 6.Samuel[2],
    1.Francis[1]) b. 26 Nov 1799, Roxbury, Norfolk, Mass., m. 7 Jan 1827, in Boston, Suffolk,
Mass., **Thomas N. Kingsbury**, occupation: Grain Dealer.
        Children:
     i **Thomas Kingsbury** b. 16 Feb 1828, Boston, Suffolk, Mass.
    ii **Franklin Kingsbury** b. 10 Oct 1829, Boston, Suffolk, Mass.
   iii **Lucinda Kingsbury** b. 12 Feb 1832, Boston, Suffolk, Mass.
   iv **Isabel Kingsbury** b. 13 Sep 1833, Boston, Suffolk, Mass., d. 4 Sep 1835,
        Boston, Suffolk, Mass.
    v **George W. Kingsbury** b. 27 Jun 1837, Boston, Suffolk, Mass.
   vi **Isabel W. Kingsbury** b. 25 May 1842, Boston, Suffolk, Mass.

205. **Simon Dudley** (104.Jonathan[5], 48.Jonathan[4], 18.Jonathan[3], 6.Samuel[2],
    1.Francis[1]) b. 14 Dec 1789, Sutton, Worcester, Mass., m. 28 Dec 1817, in Northbridge,
Worcester, Mass., **Betsey Adams**, b. 3 Jun 1792, Northbridge, Worcester, Mass.,
(daughter of **Jacob Adams**). Simon and Betsey's marriage intentions were filed 4 Dec
1817 in Sutton (VR 248).
        Children:
     i **Sarah Elizabeth Dudley** b. 3 Jan 1818, Sutton, Worcester, Mass., m. 6 Dec
        1843, in Millbury, Worcester, Mass., **Benjamin L Harden**.
    ii **Louisa Mariah Dudley** b. 23 Mar 1820.
   iii **Martha Ann Dudley** b. 6 Sep 1823, Sutton, Worcester, Mass.
   iv **Simon Dudley** b. 16 Dec 1828, Sutton, Worcester, Mass., d. 16 Aug 1832,
        Sutton, Worcester, Mass.

206. **Jonathan Dudley** (104.Jonathan[5], 48.Jonathan[4], 18.Jonathan[3], 6.Samuel[2],
    1.Francis[1]) b. 9 Jul 1798, Sutton, Worcester, Mass., m. 6 Jun 1825, in Oxford, Worcester,
Mass., **Sarah R. Torrey**, b. Oxford, Worcester, Mass., (daughter of **John Torrey**).
Jonathan died 8 Dec 1847, Sutton, Worcester, Mass.
        Children:
282.   i **Edwin Augustus Dudley** b. 22 Jun 1827.
    ii **Ann Elizabeth Dudley** b. 2 Jan 1831, Sutton, Worcester, Mass., m. 25 May
        1853, **R C Hall**.

207. **Elijah Dudley** (104.Jonathan[5], 48.Jonathan[4], 18.Jonathan[3], 6.Samuel[2],
    1.Francis[1]) b. 30 Jul 1803, Sutton, Worcester, Mass., m. (1) **Elizabeth W. Fisk**, b. ABT.
1815, Ludlow, Hampden, Mass., d. 25 Nov 1840, Millbury, Worcester, Mass., m. (2) 6 Oct

1841, in Southbridge, Worcester, Mass., **Eleanor M. Haynes**, b. 10 Nov 1814, Southbridge, Worcester, Mass., (daughter of **Henry Haynes**) d. 21 Jan 1848, Millbury, Worcester, Mass.

Elizabeth: Elizabeth and Elijah's marriage intentions were filed 18 Sep 1841, in Millbury, according to Millbury VR 76.

Eleanor: Name may be spelled Hains. Eleanor and Elizah's marriage intentions were filed 18 Sep 1841 according to Millbury VR 76. Her birth date is based on the death V.R. (136) which states she was "33y 2m 11d."

Children by Elizabeth W. Fisk:

    i **Thomas H Dudley** b. 10 Oct 1838, Millbury, Worcester, Mass.

Children by Eleanor M. Haynes:

    ii **Charles Haynes Dudley** b. 18 Aug 1842, Millbury, Worcester, Mass.

    iii **Susan E Dudley** b. 1 Jan 1848, Millbury, Worcester, Mass., d. 2 Jan 1848, Millbury, Worcester, Mass.

208. **Jason Dudley** (104.Jonathan[5], 48.Jonathan[4], 18.Jonathan[3], 6.Samuel[2], 1.Francis[1]) b. 6 Nov 1808, Sutton, Worcester, Mass., m. 14 Jun 1843, in Leicester, Worcester, Mass, **Mary A. Daniels**, (daughter of **Cyrus Daniels**).

Children:

283.   i **George Jason Dudley** b. 17 Feb 1849.

    ii **Mary E Dudley** m. 9 Oct 1867, **Frank J Dadmun**.

209. **John Dudley** (106.John[5], 49.John[4], 18.Jonathan[3], 6.Samuel[2], 1.Francis[1]) b. 3 Mar 1793, Sutton, Worcester, Mass., m. 1 Jan 1840, **Mary Woodbury**, b. 8 Jul 1796, Sutton, Worcester, Mass.

Children:

    i **John W Dudley** b. 30 Nov 1840, Sutton, Worcester, Mass.

    ii **Mary W. Dudley** b. 26 Jul 1844, Sutton, Worcester, Mass., m. 20 Mar 1878, **Charles J. Dudley**, occupation: Captain.

Charles: He was a Captain in the civil war.

210. **Leonard Dudley** (106.John[5], 49.John[4], 18.Jonathan[3], 6.Samuel[2], 1.Francis[1]) b. 8 Mar 1802, Sutton, Worcester, Mass., m. 1832, in Sutton, Worcester, Mass., **Elizabeth Fisher**, b. Warwick, RI, (daughter of **Harmon C. Fisher**). Leonard died 12 May 1842. Leonard and Elizabeth's marriage intentions was filed 17 Nov 1832 in Sutton (VR 249).

Children:

    i **Leonard F Dudley** b. 13 Jan 1837, Sutton, Worcester, Mass.

    ii **Abby G Dudley** b. 1 Mar 1841, Sutton, Worcester, Mass.

211. **James Dudley** (106.John[5], 49.John[4], 18.Jonathan[3], 6.Samuel[2], 1.Francis[1]) b. 13 May 1805, Sutton, Worcester, Mass., m. 21 Sep 1834, in Charlton, Worcester, Mass,

Dolly Towne, b. Charlton, Worcester, Mass. James died 19 Dec 1844, Sutton, Worcester, Mass. The marriage date is the intention date.

> *Children:*
> i **Jane Lomira Dudley** b. 25 Dec 1835, Sutton, Worcester, Mass.
284. ii **John Leonard Dudley** b. 20 Aug 1837.
> iii **Sarah Louisa Dudley** b. 14 Feb 1839, Sutton, Worcester, Mass., d. 26 Sep 1840, Sutton, Worcester, Mass.
> iv **James Marius Dudley** b. 6 Mar 1841, Sutton, Worcester, Mass.
> v **Ann Elicia Towne Dudley** b. 10 Mar 1843, Sutton, Worcester, Mass.

212. **Edward Morse Dudley** (106.John[5], 49.John[4], 18.Jonathan[3], 6.Samuel[2], 1.Francis[1]) b. 12 Jan 1812, Sutton, Worcester, Mass., m. 27 Mar 1839, in Sutton, Worcester, Mass., **Betsey S Bartlett**, b. Shrewsbury, Worcester, Mass.

> *Children:*
> i **Mary Elizabeth Dudley** b. 16 Nov 1839, Sutton, Worcester, Mass.
> ii **Edward Bartlett Dudley** b. 17 Oct 1842, Sutton, Worcester, Mass.

213. **Silas Dudley** (107.Joseph[5], 49.John[4], 18.Jonathan[3], 6.Samuel[2], 1.Francis[1]) b. 1 Feb 1797, Sutton, Worcester, Mass., m. 28 Feb 1829, **Charlotte K. Armsbury**, b. 2 Jun 1805, Mendon, Worcester, Mass., d. 7 Dec 1877. Silas died 15 Nov 1882. Birth confirmed by gravestone.

> *Children:*
285. i **Edward Dudley** b. 15 Dec 1829.
> ii **Silas Dudley** b. 1839, d. 1899, buried: Swandale Cemetery, Mendon, Mass.
> iii **Charlotte Eliza Dudley** b. 12 Jun 1841, d. 29 Jan 1844, Mendon, Worcester, Mass.
> iv **Mary Elizabeth Dudley** b. 24 Jan 1845, m. 1 Dec 1874, **James L Greenleaf**.

214. **Joseph Dudley** (107.Joseph[5], 49.John[4], 18.Jonathan[3], 6.Samuel[2], 1.Francis[1]) b. 3 May 1799, Sutton, Worcester, Mass., m. 30 Apr 1829, in Boylston, Worcester, Mass., **Lois Longley**, b. 26 May 1805, East Boylston, Worcester, Mass., d. 6 Oct 1886, Sutton, Worcester, Mass. Joseph died 25 Feb 1866, Sutton, Worcester, Mass. Joseph and Mary's marriage intention was filed 2 March, 1829 in Sutton (VR 249). Death date from monument at Wilkinsonville Cemetery, Sutton.
Lois: Birth and death dates from Wilkinsonville Cemetery, Sutton.

> *Children:*
> i **James E. Dudley** b. ABT 1833, d. 10 May 1866, Sutton, Worcester, Mass. Death date from Wilkinsonville Cemetery, Sutton. States "son of Joseph."
> ii **Eliza Ann Dudley** b. abt 1835, Sutton, Worcester, Mass., d. 5 Jan 1836, Sutton, Worcester, Mass.

iii **Mary Eliza Dudley** b. ABT 1835, Sutton, Worcester, Mass., d. 5 Jan 1836.

iv **Jane Augusta Dudley** b. ABT. 1840, Sutton, Worcester, Mass., d. 11 May 1845, Northbridge, Worcester, Mass. Jane died of consumption.

v **Edwin Augustine Dudley** b. ABT Aug 1843, Northbridge, Worcester, Mass., d. 5 Feb 1845, Northbridge, Worcester, Mass., buried: Wilkinsonville Cemetery, Sutton, Mass. Name based upon Cemetery Inscription. His name in the VR is Edwin AUGUSTUS. Birth date based on death record: "2y, 7m, 27 days."

vi **Emma Ruth Dudley** b. 25 Jun 1844, Northbridge, Worcester, Mass., d. 12 Nov 1853, Sutton, Worcester, Mass. Death date from Wilkinsonville Cemetery, Sutton.

vii **Edwin Dudley** b. 29 May 1846, Northbridge, Worcester, Mass.

viii **Seth Francis Dudley** b. 17 Dec 1848, Northbridge, Worcester, Mass.

215. **Peter Dudley** (108.Pheobe[5], 50.Peter[4], 18.Jonathan[3], 6.Samuel[2], 1.Francis[1]) b. 1807, Sutton, Worcester, Mass., m. 2 Dec 1829, in Sutton, Worcester, Mass., **Juliette Robinson**. Peter died 31 Jul 1840, Sutton, Worcester, Mass.
Children:

i **Caleb Fisher Dudley** b. 27 Nov 1830, Sutton, Worcester, Mass.

ii **Charles Henry Dudley** b. 10 Mar 1833, Sutton, Worcester, Mass.

iii **Sarah Prince Dudley** b. 30 Nov 1834, Sutton, Worcester, Mass.

iv **Mary Carlisle Dudley** b. 13 Apr 1837, Sutton, Worcester, Mass., m. **H L Ainsworth**.

v **Marcus Morton Dudley** b. Sutton, Worcester, Mass., baptized: 28 Jun 1840, Sutton, Worcester, Mass.

216. **David Tyler Dudley** (108.Pheobe[5], 50.Peter[4], 18.Jonathan[3], 6.Samuel[2], 1.Francis[1]) b. 24 Sep 1817, Sutton, Worcester, Mass., m. (1) 29 Nov 1838, in Sutton, Worcester, Mass., **Lucy Larkin Wilder**, b. 19 May 1819, d. 5 Feb 1857, Sutton, Worcester, Mass., m. (2) 1 Jun 1869, **Anne E. Leland**, b. 16 Feb 1836, d. 1 Mar 1883, Sutton, Worcester, Mass. David died 5 Sep 1896, Sutton, Worcester, Mass. Birth and Death dates are from his monument at Wilkinsonville Cemetery, Sutton.
Lucy: Birth and death dates from Wilkinsonville Cemetery.
Anne: Birth and death dates from Wilkinsonville Cemetery.
Children by Lucy Larkin Wilder:

286.   i **Henry Tyler Dudley** b. 27 Apr 1841.

ii **Augusta L Dudley** b. 21 Aug 1847, Sutton, Worcester, Mass., m. **W.S. Hale**. Augusta died 30 Jan 1886, Sutton, Worcester, Mass. Birth, death, and marriage from Wilkinsonville Cemetery.

iii **Frederick C Dudley** b. 24 Aug 1851, m. 22 Oct 1872, **Angie Anderson**.

iv **Sumner A Dudley** b. 15 Mar 1854.

v **Charles F Dudley** b. 3 Apr 1856, d. 27 Mar 1857, Sutton, Worcester, Mass.

217. **William Archer Dudley** (112.Joseph⁵, 51.David⁴, 21.Rogers³, 6.Samuel²,
   1.Francis¹) b. 9 May 1829, Petersburg, Va., m. (1) 18 Aug 1852, **Lydia Ann Gorham**, d.
   17 Feb 1853, Petersburg, Va., m. (2) 22 Oct 1856, divorced 1861, **Mary Virginia Todd**,
   m. (3) 1 Jun 1869, **Elizabeth Wilson Boothe**. Graduated Medical University of
   Pennsylvania in Philadelphia 1851, his essay was on cholera infantum.
   Mary: Mary had one daughter, and it died young. She got a divorce from William
   because he was a "Unionist".
   Children by Elizabeth Wilson Boothe:
      i **Joseph Hugh Norwell Dudley** b. 18 Apr 1870, d. 10 Nov 1874.
     ii **David Ed. Wm. Sam. Rogers Fran. Dudley** b. 25 Feb 1878. Without a doubt,
         the LONGEST Dudley name in history: David Edward William Samuel Rogers
         Francis Dudley.
     iii **Child** b. 1881, d. 1882.
     iv **Chester Arthur Dudley** d. 1882. Died young.
      v **Elizabeth Lois Whitney Dudley** b. 1884. Died young.

218. **Joseph Amory Dudley** (113.Amasa⁵, 51.David⁴, 21.Rogers³, 6.Samuel²,
   1.Francis¹) b. 15 Sep 1815, Albany, N.Y., occupation: Wholesale Druggist, m. (1) 10 May
   1839, in Rome, NY, **Frances M. Blair**, b. ABT 1817, (daughter of **Dr. Arab Blair**) d. 2
   Sep 1844, Rome, NY, buried: 4 Sep 1844, m. (2) 1 Oct 1846, in Rome, NY, **Ann Frances
   Draper**, (daughter of **Virgil Draper**) d. 15 Apr 1871, New York, N.Y. Joseph died 22
   Apr 1884, New York, N.Y. Joseph's middle name may have been Amasa. In his will, he
   leaves sizable sums to two churches (a Presbyterian and a Puritan), and various women's
   groups.
   Frances: She died at the home of her father. Funeral date was in the VR.
   Children by Frances M. Blair:
   287.   i **Anna Lauretta Dudley** b. 5 Jan 1844.
           Children by Ann Frances Draper:
          ii **James Whitin Dudley** b. 1847, Rome, NY, d. 9 Sep 1848, Rome, NY.
         iii **Eliza Holmes Dudley** b. 7 Jun 1850, m. 13 Oct 1874, in New York, N.Y.,
             William S. Lyon, d. 10 Nov 1879, New York, N.Y. Eliza died 10 Nov 1879.
   288.   iv **Charles Virgil Dudley** b. 2 Sep 1852.
   289.   v **William Blair Dudley** b. 25 Nov 1857.

219. **Paul Whitin Dudley** (113.Amasa⁵, 51.David⁴, 21.Rogers³, 6.Samuel²,
   1.Francis¹) b. 3 Apr 1817, Amsterdam, N.Y., occupation: Merchant, m. 19 Oct 1842, in
   Uxbridge, Worcester, Mass., **Sarah Ann Tobey**, b. 23 Dec 1819. Paul died 1 Jul 1872,
   Whitinsville, Worcester, Mass.
   Sarah: Her birth date was found in the Northbridge VR, but no birth place.
   Children:

290.   i **Henry Merchant Dudley** b. 12 Aug 1846.
       ii **Frederic Amasa Dudley** b. 13 Jun 1850, d. 25 Aug 1853.
      iii **Arthur Whitin Dudley** b. 21 Nov 1853, d. 12 Mar 1854.
      iv **Herbert Hale Dudley** b. 9 Mar 1855, occupation: Merchant. Lived in Whitinsville.
       v **Sarah Jane Dudley** b. 17 May 1859.
      vi **Walter Whitin Dudley** b. 12 Oct 1864.

220. **Nelson Dudley** (114.Samuel[5], 52.Benjamin[4], 23.William[3], 6.Samuel[2], 1.Francis[1]) b. 16 Oct 1816, Douglas, Worcester, Mass., m. 31 May 1843, in Douglas, Worcester, Mass., **Betsey P. Elliot**.
      Children:
       i **Nelson G. Dudley** b. 21 Jan 1845, Douglas, Worcester, Mass.
      ii **Son** b. 13 Jan 1847, Douglas, Worcester, Mass. This child is recorded, but for some reason not named, in the VR.

221. **Mary Dudley** (115.Benjamin[5], 52.Benjamin[4], 23.William[3], 6.Samuel[2], 1.Francis[1]) b. 22 Apr 1817, m. **Samuel M. Millard**. Mary died 20 Jun 1855.
      Children:
       i **Mary Elizabeth Millard**.
      ii **Cornelius F. Millard**.
      iii **Anna D. Millard** b. 1844.

222. **George Reed Dudley** (116.David[5], 53.Paul[4], 23.William[3], 6.Samuel[2], 1.Francis[1]) b. 25 Jul 1811, Douglas, Worcester, Mass., m. (1) 27 Dec 1832, in Douglas, Worcester, Mass., **Susan Robbins**, d. 1844, m. (2) 13 Sep 1845, in Louisville, Kentucky, **Emma Lofland**.
      Children by Susan Robbins:
       i **Eugene Dudley** b. 1832.
      Children by Emma Lofland:
291.   ii **Emma Dudley** b. 2 Jul 1846.
      iii **Anna Dudley** b. 27 Dec 1847, d. 6 Dec 1854, Covington, Ky.
292.   iv **George Hiram Dudley** b. 29 Dec 1849.
293.   v **Kate Dudley** b. 12 Nov 1851.
      vi **William Lofland Dudley** b. 16 Apr 1859, Covington, Ky., occupation: Chemical Scientist.

223. **Eliza J Dudley** (116.David[5], 53.Paul[4], 23.William[3], 6.Samuel[2], 1.Francis[1]) b. 1823, Douglas, Worcester, Mass., m. 1848, **Dutee Smith**, b. Burrillville, RI. Eliza died 7 Dec 1867.
      Children:

     i **Luella M Smith** b. 1850, Douglas, Worcester, Mass., m. 15 Apr 1876,
       Moses H Balcome, b. Douglas, Worcester, Mass.

    ii **George H. Smith** b. 1854.

   iii **Clara H. Smith** b. 1858.

224. **James Hill Dudley** (117.John[5], 53.Paul[4], 23.William[3], 6.Samuel[2],
    1.Francis[1]) b. 10 Dec 1814, Douglas, Worcester, Mass., baptized: 26 Mar 1815, Douglas,
    Worcester, Mass., m. 28 Sep 1836, in Hampton, CT, **Eliza Avery Prentiss**, b. 3 Mar 1819,
    Hampton, CT.
         Children:
  294.   i **Arthur James Dudley** b. 7 May 1839.

        ii **Louesa Maria Dudley** baptized: 17 Jul 1842, Douglas, Worcester, Mass.

225. **William Dudley** (118.William[5], 53.Paul[4], 23.William[3], 6.Samuel[2],
    1.Francis[1]) b. 11 Nov 1816, occupation: Alderman, Librarian, m. 22 Jul 1851, **Elizabeth
    Morse**, b. Providence, Rhode Island. William died 2 Jul 1879, Madison Wis. Was
    Secretary of the Wisconsin Historical Society. Was State Librarian under Gov. Farwell in
    Wisconsin.
         Children:
        i **Charles L. Dudley** b. 10 Jul 1857, Madison Wis., occupation: Superintendent,
          m. 7 Oct 1880, **Mary V. Patten**. Charles died 2 Nov 1883, Chicago, Illinois.
          Graduated from the state University in Madison 1877, and from the Law
          Department in 1880. Bought an interest in a "manufactory" in Cragin, a suburb of
          Chicago. He had no children.

226. **Charles Dudley** (118.William[5], 53.Paul[4], 23.William[3], 6.Samuel[2],
    1.Francis[1]) b. 19 Apr 1818, occupation: Dry Goods Retail, m. 28 Oct 1846, **Clara
    Danforth Wilmarth**, b. 10 Jun 1819. Charles died 2 Oct 1889, Providence, Rhode Island.
    Lived in Providence, R.I.
         Children:
  295.   i **William Aldrich Dudley** b. 7 Dec 1847.
  296.   ii **Annie W. Dudley** b. 25 Sep 1849.

       iii **Harriet C. Dudley** b. 4 Feb 1859, m. 25 Apr 1889, **Edward F. Sibley**.

227. **Harriet Cragin Dudley** (118.William[5], 53.Paul[4], 23.William[3], 6.Samuel[2],
    1.Francis[1]) b. 9 Jan 1820, m. 21 Oct 1847, **George R Barker**, b. abt 1825, d. 19 Jun
    1865, Cornville, Somerset, Maine.
         Children:
        i **Harriet C D Barker** b. 23 Mar 1852, Cornville, Somerset, Maine, d. 15 Sep
          1876, Douglas, Worcester, Mass.
       ii **John Freemont Barker** b. 9 Apr 1856, Cornville, Somerset, Maine, m. 17 Oct

1883, in Roseburg, Oregon, **Annie Jones**.
    iii **Charles Dudley Barker** b. 2 Oct 1857, Cornville, Somerset, Maine, m. 20 Nov 1889, in Providence, Rhode Island, **Maud M. Tucker**.

228. **Mary Wilson Dudley** (118.William[5], 53.Paul[4], 23.William[3], 6.Samuel[2], 1.Francis[1]) b. 21 Nov 1843, Worcester, Worcester, Mass., m. 23 Oct 1863, **David A. Yeaw**. Mary died 15 Jan 1882, Providence, Rhode Island.
    Children:
    i **Clara Dudley Yeaw** b. 21 Oct 1866, m. **Harry M. Gyles**.

229. **William Harrison Dudley** (122.William[5], 54.Lemuel[4], 23.William[3], 6.Samuel[2], 1.Francis[1]) b. 19 Feb 1827, Douglas, Worcester, Mass., m. 22 Aug 1855, in Sutton, Worcester, Mass., **Harriet Amelia Frink**, b. 27 May 1838, Stafford, CT, d. 28 May 1878, Ellington, CT. William died 27 Jun 1887.
    Children:
297.   i **Gustavus Harrison Dudley** b. 29 Oct 1855.
    ii **Ella Marie Dudley** b. 3 Jun 1858, Willington, CT, m. 12 Dec 1878, **George W Sweet**, b. 12 Dec 1845, Hinkley, OH, d. 11 Jun 1910. Ella died 3 Mar 1929, Carlyle, MT.
    iii **Lucy Ann Dudley** b. 17 Feb 1861, Willington, CT, d. 16 Sep 1861, Willington, CT.
    iv **Marie Louise Dudley** b. 1 May 1863, m. 5 Aug 1877, **George Taft Smith**, b. Burrillville, RI. Marie died 28 Jul 1920.

230. **Silas P Dudley** (122.William[5], 54.Lemuel[4], 23.William[3], 6.Samuel[2], 1.Francis[1]) b. 3 Jul 1829, Douglas, Worcester, Mass., m. 8 Nov 1855, in Douglas, Worcester, Mass., **Julie Ann White**, b. 11 Sep 1836, Webster, Worcester, Mass., (daughter of **Alvah White** and **Nancy Wallis**) d. 30 Nov 1896, Woonsocket, RI. Silas died 23 Jan 1891, Douglas, Worcester, Mass.
    Children:
    i **Dandredge W Dudley** b. 30 May 1856, Douglas, Worcester, Mass., m. **Rachel Thompson**.
298.   ii **Charles Dudley** b. 19 Jun 1858.
299.   iii **Ida May Dudley** b. 15 Aug 1864.
300.   iv **Lucy Jane Dudley** b. 22 Oct 1866.
    v **Alva Putnam Dudley** b. 17 Feb 1867, Douglas, Worcester, Mass., m. **Carrie Buttrick**. Alva died 8 Mar 1926.
    vi **Marie Abigail Dudley** b. 24 Jul 1878, Douglas, Worcester, Mass., m. **Oscar Rawson**.

231. **Julie Ann White** (124.Nancy[5], 55.Hannah[4], 23.William[3], 6.Samuel[2],

1.Francis[1]) (See marriage to number 230.)

232. **Hannah Mellens** (126.Persis[5], 60.Robert[4], 25.Douglassa[3], 6.Samuel[2],
1.Francis[1]) b. 1830, Webster, Worcester, Mass., m. 6 Mar 1853, in Webster, Worcester,
Mass., **Reuben Dudley**, b. 1829, Webster, Worcester, Mass. Hannah died abt 1899.
Children:
301.   i **Sarah Anne Dudley** b. 7 Jun 1853.

233. **Nathan Augustus Munroe Dudley** (127.John⁶, 63.Nathan⁵, 26.Joseph⁴,
10.Joseph³, 3.Joseph², 1.Francis¹) b. 20 Aug 1825, baptized: 31 Mar 1833, Bolton,
Worcester, Mass., occupation: General, m. 12 Nov 1845, in Roxbury, Norfolk, Mass.,
Elizabeth Gray Jewett. Nathan died AFT 1889. Nathan was baptized at the Hillside
church in Bolton, and it fell under Lancaster's jurisdiction, and appears there also. He was a
General in the Army (a career man) and retired 20 Aug 1889.
> *Children:*
> i   **Granville Winthrop Dudley** b. 24 Jul 1848, Roxbury, Norfolk, Mass.

234. **Charles G. B. Dudley** (133.Asa⁶, 65.Paul⁵, 31.James⁴, 10.Joseph³,
3.Joseph², 1.Francis¹) b. 23 May 1843, Acton, Middlesex, Mass., m. 12 Jan 1859, in
Baltimore, Maryland, **Clara J. Peters**.
> *Children:*
> i   **Charles G.B. Dudley** b. Nov 1869, d. 20 Aug 1870, Baltimore, Maryland.

235. **Herbert Dudley** (135.Joseph⁶, 68.Nahum⁵, 33.Joseph⁴, 11.Benjamin³,
3.Joseph², 1.Francis¹) b. 27 Jul 1812, Westmoreland, Cheshire, New Hampshire,
occupation: farmer, m. (1) Jun 1878, in Westmoreland, Cheshire, New Hampshire, **Eliza J.
Dodge**, m. (2) 1836, **Mary B. Scott**.
Eliza: Was from Dummerston, Vt.
> *Children by Mary B. Scott:*
> i   **Mary C. Dudley** b. 28 Mar 1839, Westmoreland, Cheshire, New Hampshire,
>   m. 19 May 1878, in Westmoreland, Cheshire, New Hampshire, **William C.
>   Smith**.

236. **Allen Pratt Dudley** (136.Moses⁶, 68.Nahum⁵, 33.Joseph⁴, 11.Benjamin³,
3.Joseph², 1.Francis¹) b. 16 Dec 1819, Westmoreland, Cheshire, New Hampshire,
occupation: Lawyer, m. 16 Nov 1841, in Westmoreland, Cheshire, New Hampshire, **Mary
S. Wheelock**. Went to California about 1855.
> *Children:*
> i   **Mary G. Dudley** b. 9 Sep 1842, Westmoreland, Cheshire, New Hampshire, d.
>   10 Jul 1844, Westmoreland, Cheshire, New Hampshire.
> ii   **Henry L. Dudley** b. 21 Jun 1844, Westmoreland, Cheshire, New Hampshire, d.
>   11 Aug 1847, Westmoreland, Cheshire, New Hampshire.
> iii **Charles Allen Dudley** b. 20 Mar 1846, Westmoreland, Cheshire, New
>   Hampshire, d. 11 Dec 1873, Westmoreland, Cheshire, New Hampshire.
> iv   **Edward Thomas Dudley** b. 2 Feb 1848, Chesterfield, Cheshire, New
>   Hampshire, m. 17 Oct 1878, in California, **Sarah N. Triplett**. Moved to
>   California about 1877.

Sarah: Was from Solano Co., California.

    v   **Arthur William Dudley** b. 5 Jun 1850, Chesterfield, Cheshire, New Hampshire, d. 11 Feb 1853, Chesterfield, Cheshire, New Hampshire.

    vi   **Alice Josephine Dudley** b. 1 Mar 1852, Chesterfield, Cheshire, New Hampshire.

    vii   **Anna Charlotte Dudley** b. 3 Apr 1854, Chesterfield, Cheshire, New Hampshire.

    viii   **John Wheelock Dudley** b. 10 Nov 1860, California, d. 27 Jun 1877, California.

237. **Charles P. Dudley** (136.Moses[6], 68.Nahum[5], 33.Joseph[4], 11.Benjamin[3], 3.Joseph[2], 1.Francis[1]) b. 25 Dec 1822, Westmoreland, Cheshire, New Hampshire, m. 14 May 1846, **Lydia J. Davis**. Lived in San Francisco, California.

    Children:

    i   **Ellen Maria Dudley** b. 14 Mar 1847, Lowell, Middlesex, Mass., m. 30 Mar 1865, in San Francisco, California, **Levi N. Turner**.

    ii   **Anna Gertrude Dudley** b. 5 Apr 1852, California, m. 14 Sep 1871, in San Francisco, California, **W. Baxter Hall**.
       W.: His name is listed differently in various sources. This came from the "History of Westmoreland."

    iii   **Charles Davis Dudley** b. 14 Nov 1855, Mokelumne Hill, Calif., d. 19 Jan 1856, California.

    iv   **William Moses Dudley** b. 5 Apr 1858, California.

    v   **Emma Eunice Dudley** b. 2 Nov 1860, California, d. 6 Jun 1867, California.

    vi   **Hannah A. Dudley** b. 11 Feb 1863, California, d. 25 Nov 1865, California.

238. **William L. Dudley** (136.Moses[6], 68.Nahum[5], 33.Joseph[4], 11.Benjamin[3], 3.Joseph[2], 1.Francis[1]) b. 20 Dec 1824, Westmoreland, Cheshire, New Hampshire, occupation: Lawyer, m. 11 Nov 1858, in California, **Mary Caroline Doak**, (daughter of **Thomas Doak** and **Betsey Mead**). Went to Stockton, California in 1849.

    Children:

    i   **Elizabeth Mead Dudley** b. 16 Aug 1860, California.

    ii   **William Little Dudley** b. 13 Jun 1869, California.

    iii   **Mary Frances Dudley** b. 26 Nov 1872, California.

239. **Wellington Dudley** (137.Josiah[6], 70.Luther[5], 33.Joseph[4], 11.Benjamin[3], 3.Joseph[2], 1.Francis[1]) b. 8 Jun 1817, m. **Ann Chandler Bent**, (daughter of **Otis Bent**). Wellington died 1 Apr 1883, Litchfield, Minn.

    Children:

    i   **Mary Aldrich Dudley** b. 10 Nov 1841, m. in Litchfield, Minn., **Joseph Fryburger**. The "History of Paris" records her middle name as

"Adalaide."

    ii **Josiah W. Dudley** b. 28 Oct 1843, m. **Jennie Gorton**. Settled in Genesee, Minn.

   iii **Clara Maria Dudley** b. 8 Jan 1848, m. **F.Q. Elliott**. Settled in Norway, Maine.

   iv **John Hancock Dudley** b. 10 Jun 1857, m. in Meadville, Minn, **Olie Wakefield**. Settled in Meadville, Minn.

240. **Smith Dudley** (137.Josiah⁶, 70.Luther⁵, 33.Joseph⁴, 11.Benjamin³, 3.Joseph², 1.Francis¹) b. 8 Jun 1827, m. **Lydia H. Stearns**, (daughter of **William Stearns**). Smith died 23 Feb 1883.
       Children:
    i **Charles Smith Dudley** b. 10 Dec 1858, m. **Carrie Clapp**.
    ii **James Stearns Dudley** b. Feb 1862.
   iii **Ella Louisa Dudley** b. 12 Apr 1865.
   iv **Emily Gertrude Dudley** b. Aug 1869.

241. **Lyman Gardner Dudley** (141.Abijah⁶, 73.Benjamin⁵, 34.Benjamin⁴, 11.Benjamin³, 3.Joseph², 1.Francis¹) b. 3 Apr 1825, Sudbury, Middlesex, Mass., occupation: Yeoman, m. 23 Sep 1847, in Natick, Norfolk, Mass., **Mary Jane McIntire**, b. ABT 1828, (daughter of **Henry McIntire** and **Mary McIntire**).
Mary: Birth date based upon marriage record stating 19 yrs old.
       Children:
    i **Lyman H. Dudley** b. 21 Jan 1849, Weston, Middlesex, Mass.

242. **Otis Byam Dudley** (142.Benjamin⁶, 73.Benjamin⁵, 34.Benjamin⁴, 11.Benjamin³, 3.Joseph², 1.Francis¹) b. 8 Mar 1827, Cambridge, Middlesex, Mass., occupation: Blacksmith, m. 13 Aug 1846, in Chelmsford, Middlesex, Mass., **Martha Ann Byam**, b. 28 Jun 1830, Cambridge, Middlesex, Mass., (daughter of **Ezekiel Byam** and **Charlotte Byam**).
Martha: Her birth date is based on the marriage record which states she is 16 years old at her marriage.
       Children:
    i **Martha Ann Dudley** b. 12 Oct 1846, Baptist Village, Chelmsford, Mass., d. 12 May 1848, Chelmsford, Middlesex, Mass. Died of "Lung Fever." The Cambridge VR also records the birth.
    ii **Clifton O. Dudley** b. 30 Jun 1849.
   iii **Clifford George Dudley** b. 30 Jun 1849.
   iv **Ellen Louise Dudley** b. 5 Nov 1851.
    v **Charles Bateman Dudley** b. 31 Jan 1860, d. 8 Dec 1863.

243. **George Henry Dudley** (142.Benjamin[6], 73.Benjamin[5], 34.Benjamin[4], 11.Benjamin[3], 3.Joseph[2], 1.Francis[1]) b. 18 Mar 1836, m. 26 Oct 1856, **Hittie D. Lapham**.

Children:
- i **Gilford Henry Dudley** b. 17 Sep 1857, d. 27 Sep 1857.
- ii **Gilbert Herbert Dudley** b. 17 Sep 1857. It is not known whether he died the same day.
- iii **Lora Lillian Dudley** b. 2 Nov 1860.
- iv **Ada Lizzie Dudley** b. 22 Feb 1865.
- v **Grace Betsy Dudley** b. 27 Aug 1867.
- vi **Mattie Louise Dudley** b. 6 Feb 1870.

244. **John Dudley** (144.John[6], 75.Jonathan[5], 34.Benjamin[4], 11.Benjamin[3], 3.Joseph[2], 1.Francis[1]) b. 14 Dec 1818, Danvers, Essex, Mass., m. 29 Nov 1838, in Wenham, Essex, Mass., **Rebecca P. Shattuck**.
Rebecca: Was from Wenham.

Children:
- i **Emily Ann Dudley** b. 16 Feb 1844, Wenham, Essex, Mass.
- ii **Mary Anna Dudley** b. 12 Aug 1848, Wenham, Essex, Mass.

245. **Ansel Dudley** (148.Perrin[6], 79.David[5], 36.Ebenezer[4], 11.Benjamin[3], 3.Joseph[2], 1.Francis[1]) b. 11 Apr 1844, Woodstock, Oxford, Maine, m. 4 Mar 1868, in Woodstock, Oxford, Maine, **Josephine E. Childs**, b. 1850, Paris, Oxford, Maine.

Children:
- i **Olivia D. Dudley** b. 1875.
- ii **Carl Childs Dudley** b. 1877.

246. **George Henry Dudley** (151.William[6], 80.Ebenezer[5], 36.Ebenezer[4], 11.Benjamin[3], 3.Joseph[2], 1.Francis[1]) b. 8 Apr 1841, South Boston, Suffolk, Mass., m. 18 Jan 1862, **Elizabeth Andrews**, b. 1 Apr 1840, South Boston, Suffolk, Mass., d. 15 Sep 1887, South Boston, Suffolk, Mass. George died 8 Mar 1902, Dorchester, Norfolk, Mass.

Children:
- 302.   i **Charles Eaton Dudley** b. 11 Jul 1863.
- ii **Lillian Isabelle Dudley** b. 29 Mar 1866, South Boston, Suffolk, Mass.
- iii **Charlotte Elizabeth Dudley** b. 10 Nov 1868, South Boston, Suffolk, Mass., d. 3 Apr 1896, South Boston, Suffolk, Mass.
- iv **George Henry Dudley** b. 9 July 1872, South Boston, Suffolk, Mass., d. 26 Oct 1872, South Boston, Suffolk, Mass.
- v **William Henry Franklin Dudley** b. 4 Nov 1876, South Boston, Suffolk, Mass., d. 14 Apr 1877, South Boston, Suffolk, Mass.

247. Anne Elizabeth Dudley (153.Samuel[6], 81.William[5], 37.William[4], 11.Benjamin[3], 3.Joseph[2], 1.Francis[1]) m. 23 Dec 1841, in Weymouth, Norfolk, Mass., **Isaiah Warren Thayer**, b. 2 Jan 1818, Weymouth, Norfolk, Mass., (son of **Isaiah Thayer**). Anne and Warren lived in Beloit, Wisconsin. No birth record, or any record, of Anne or J. Warren exist in Mass. All data from Dean Dudley.

Isaiah: Dean Dudley lists him as "J. WARREN THAYER."

> *Children:*
> i **Celestia N. Thayer** b. 15 Sep 1838, Weymouth, Norfolk, Mass.
> ii **Henry Adams Thayer** b. 18 Jul 1843, Weymouth, Norfolk, Mass.

248. Aaron Dudley (157.Aaron[6], 85.Nathan[5], 40.Peter[4], 14.John[3], 4.John[2], 1.Francis[1]) b. 20 Nov 1810, North Leverett, Hampshire, Mass., m. 22 Oct 1835, **Emeline Maynard**.

> *Children:*
> i **Nathan A. Dudley** b. 27 Aug 1837, m. 24 May 1868, **Melissa A. Felton**, b. 19 Apr 1843.
> ii **Asher H. Dudley** b. 4 Aug 1841, m. 14 Jun 1870, **Addie E. Spear**, b. 26 Jan 1851, d. 20 Oct 1883.
> 303. iii **Elbridge H. Dudley** b. 26 Apr 1844.

249. Samuel F. Dudley (157.Aaron[6], 85.Nathan[5], 40.Peter[4], 14.John[3], 4.John[2], 1.Francis[1]) b. 31 Oct 1812, North Leverett, Hampshire, Mass., occupation: Colonel, m. (1) 8 Mar 1838, **Jemina Prouty**, b. 16 Mar 1819, d. 7 Apr 1880, m. (2) **R. Blackmar**.

R.: She was a widow at her marriage.

> *Children by Jemina Prouty:*
> 304. i **George S. Dudley** b. 20 Jan 1839.
> ii **Richard A. Dudley** b. 23 Mar 1841, Shutesbury, Franklin, Mass., m. **Melinda B. Armstrong**, b. 8 Jan 1843.
> iii **Sophia J. Dudley** b. 8 Jun 1843, Shutesbury, Franklin, Mass.
> iv **Meriel O. Dudley** b. 10 Jun 1843, Shutesbury, Franklin, Mass., d. 9 Jul 1849.
> v **Angeline M. Dudley** b. 26 Aug 1845, Shutesbury, Franklin, Mass., m. **Christopher Clapp**.
> vi **Rosella V. Dudley** b. 8 Jul 1850, Shutesbury, Franklin, Mass., m. **George A. Paul**, b. 10 Jun 1847.
> vii **Alfred P. Dudley** b. 18 Jul 1853, Shutesbury, Franklin, Mass., m. 16 Jan 1877, **Alma A. Fairbanks**, b. 6 Aug 1853.
> viii **Arthur B. Dudley** b. 18 Dec 1855, Shutesbury, Franklin, Mass., m. 29 May 1879, **Eva S. Bartlett**, b. 10 Jan 1861.

250. Isaac Dudley (157.Aaron[6], 85.Nathan[5], 40.Peter[4], 14.John[3], 4.John[2], 1.Francis[1]) b. 28 Feb 1815, North Leverett, Hampshire, Mass., m. 29 Jun 1841, **Harriet L.**

Montague, b. 11 Mar 1818. Isaac died 17 Oct 1875.

    Children:
- i   **Henry I. Dudley** b. 27 Mar 1843, Wendell, Franklin, Mass., m. 8 Apr 1880, **Anne B. Hunt**, b. 1 Aug 1839, occupation: Widow.
- ii   **Alice M. Dudley** b. 17 Jun 1849, North Leverett, Hampshire, Mass., m. 25 Dec 1873, **Charles E. Thompson**, b. 30 May 1849.
- iii   **Vesta L. Dudley** b. 15 Mar 1856, North Leverett, Hampshire, Mass., m. 30 Jun 1878, **Clarence S. Goodnow**, b. 5 Feb 1855.

251. **Luther Dudley** (157.Aaron^6, 85.Nathan^5, 40.Peter^4, 14.John^3, 4.John^2, 1.Francis^1) b. 6 Sep 1817, North Leverett, Hampshire, Mass., occupation: Captain, m. 6 Jun 1843, **Asamena Clark**, b. 25 Jun 1822.

    Children:
- i   **Tremain Dudley** b. 26 Jul 1844, North Leverett, Hampshire, Mass., m. 3 Mar 1869, **Ellen M. Spear**.
- ii   **Clifford Dudley** b. 10 Mar 1846, North Leverett, Hampshire, Mass., m. Nov 1880, **Jessie Heston**.
- iii   **Myra Dudley** b. 1 Feb 1849, North Leverett, Hampshire, Mass.
- iv   **Herbert Dudley** b. 18 Nov 1850, North Leverett, Hampshire, Mass., d. 6 Oct 1868.
- v   **Mary Dudley** b. 28 Mar 1854, North Leverett, Hampshire, Mass., m. 17 Aug 1878, **John C. Holston**, b. 7 Oct 1850.
- vi   **Emmons L. Dudley** b. 8 Jun 1858, North Leverett, Hampshire, Mass.

252. **William E. Dudley** (157.Aaron^6, 85.Nathan^5, 40.Peter^4, 14.John^3, 4.John^2, 1.Francis^1) b. 26 Apr 1823, North Leverett, Hampshire, Mass., m. 21 Feb 1849, **Mary Ann Perry**.

    Children:
- i   **Lester W. Dudley** b. Aug 1850, North Leverett, Hampshire, Mass.
- ii   **Miner C. Dudley**.
- iii   **Jennie Dudley** b. North Leverett, Hampshire, Mass., m. **James Richardson**.
- iv   **Hattie Dudley**. Died young.
- v   **Hattie Dudley**.
- vi   **Ellis Dudley** b. Montague, Franklin, Mass.
- vii   **Child** b. Montague, Franklin, Mass.

253. **Caroline W. Dudley** (159.Lewis^6, 87.Daniel^5, 41.Daniel^4, 14.John^3, 4.John^2, 1.Francis^1) b. Mar 1829, Wayland, Middlesex, Mass., m. 16 Aug 1849, in Wayland, Middlesex, Mass., **Isaac Myrick Thompson**, b. 1828, Unity, Waldo, Maine, (son of **William Thompson** and **Mary**) occupation: teamster, d. abt 1871. Caroline died 30 Nov 1871, Hopkinton, Middlesex, Mass.

Children:

    i **Edwin F. Thompson** b. 1850, Wayland, Middlesex, Mass., d. 1850, Wayland, Middlesex, Mass.

   ii **Emma Thompson** b. 1853, Hopkinton, Middlesex, Mass.

  iii **Frederick Louis Thompson** b. 2 Sep 1855, Hopkinton, Middlesex, Mass., m. **Mary Isabel Cairn**, b. 26 Oct 1863, Sand Springs, Delaware, Iowa, d. 2 Dec 1952, San Francisco, California. Frederick died 22 Apr 1892, Neligh, Antelope, Nebraska.

  iv **Carrie Thompson** b. abt 1860, Hopkinton, Middlesex, Mass.

254. **Nancy Emma Dudley** (160.Rowland⁶, 88.James⁵, 43.Francis⁴, 14.John³, 4.John², 1.Francis¹) b. 1 Jan 1842, Woodville Plt, Penobscot, ME, m. 4 Jul 1861, in Wesley, Washington, Maine, **Randall Hall Day**, b. 29 Mar 1837, Wesley, Washington, Maine, (son of **Joel Day** and **Elizabeth Eleanor Jones**) occupation: farmer, guide, d. 22 May 1906, Princeton, Washington, Maine, buried: West St. Cemetery, Princeton, ME. Nancy died 28 Apr 1917, Waterville, Kennebec, Maine, buried: West St. Cemetery, Princeton, ME.

        Children:

    i **Edgar Foreston Day** b. 22 Jan 1862, Wesley, Washington, Maine. Unmarried.

   ii **Ella Day** b. 16 Sep 1863, Wesley, Washington, Maine, d. 24 Sep 1865, Milltown, Calais, Washington, ME.

  iii **Rosie Day** b. 8 Sep 1865, Wesley, Washington, Maine, d. 31 Jan 1867, St. Stephen, Charlotte, NB.

  iv **Orris Melvin Day** b. 12 Mar 1868, St. Stephen, Charlotte, NB, d. 24 Aug 1869, Princeton, Washington, Maine.

   v **Orrin Elroy Day** b. 15 Jan 1870, Princeton, Washington, Maine, d. 16 Dec 1877, Princeton, Washington, Maine.

  vi **Beatrice May Day** b. 28 Apr 1872, Princeton, Washington, Maine, m. 28 Sep 1889, in Princeton, Washington, Maine, **William Edward Choate**.

 vii **infant son Day** b. 31 May 1874, Princeton, Washington, Maine, d. 15 Jun 1874, Princeton, Washington, Maine.

viii **infant son Day** b. 1 Jan 1876, Princeton, Washington, Maine, d. 21 Jan 1876, Princeton, Washington, Maine.

  ix **Silas Alonzo Day** b. 6 May 1878, Princeton, Washington, Maine, occupation: hydroelectric engineer, m. 4 Sep 1907, in Blue Hill, Maine, **Angie N. Hinckley**, b. 26 Jun 1882, California. Silas died Feb 1964, New Jersey.

   x **Cleveland Randall Day** b. 15 May 1881, Princeton, Washington, Maine, occupation: hydro engineer, m. 15 Sep 1909, in Princeton, Washington, Maine, **Alice Edna Pike**, b. 16 Jun 1882, Princeton, Washington, Maine, (daughter of **William Franklin "Frank" Pike** and **Olivia Maria Porter**) occupation: elem. teacher, d. 16 Feb 1957, Oakland, Kennebec, Maine. Cleveland died 10 Oct

1967, Waterville, Kennebec, Maine.

255. **Mark Fenlason Dudley** (160.Rowland[6], 88.James[5], 43.Francis[4], 14.John[3], 4.John[2], 1.Francis[1]) b. 17 Dec 1844, Woodville, Penobscot, Maine, m. 4 Mar 1866, in Milltown, Calais, Washington, ME, **Elizabeth Eleanor Day**, b. 21 Sep 1842, Wesley, Washington, Maine, (daughter of **Joel Day** and **Elizabeth Eleanor Jones**) d. 6 Dec 1923, Stacyville, Penobscot, Maine. Mark died 17 Dec 1925, Stacyville, Penobscot, Maine. A Private in Co. F, 1st Maine Volunteers, enlisted April 1864, discharged July 12, 1865 at Portland, ME, participated in battles at Cedar Creek, Fisher Hill, Snicker's Gap, and Petersburg. Wounded at Petersburg. Resided Princeton, Wesley and Stacyville, ME.
> *Children:*
> i **Mary Elizabeth Dudley** b. 4 Dec 1866, Princeton, Washington, Maine, m. 7 Jan 1883, in Sherman, Penobscot, ME, **Wallace Percy Gerald**, b. 21 Oct 1855, Canaan, Somerset, Maine, (son of **David Gerald** and **Ellen Clark**). Mary died 21 Nov 1901, Lee, Penobscot, Maine. Mary resided Lee, ME., and had 5 children born there.
> ii **Jennie Lind Dudley** b. 29 Dec 1868, Wesley, Washington, Maine, m. (1) 10 Apr 1889, in Stacyville, Penobscot, Maine, **William Japhet Smith**, b. 10 May 1862, NB, m. (2) in Stacyville, Penobscot, Maine, **Guy Ansel Spinney**. Jennie died Lee, Penobscot, Maine.

305. iii **Emily Oretta Dudley** b. 19 Mar 1871.
306. iv **Mark Leroy Dudley** b. 4 Jun 1873.
307. v **Berthana Florilla Dudley** b. 21 May 1875.
> vi **Arthur Laverne Dudley** b. 29 Sep 1877, Princeton, Washington, Maine, occupation: carpenter, m. 5 Dec 1908, in Stacyville, Penobscot, Maine, **Carrie Bragg**. Arthur died 20 Oct 1920, Bangor, Penobscot, Maine.
> **Carrie**: The Day Genealogy has her given name as "Clara Belle."
> vii **Annie Philena Dudley** b. 31 Aug 1879, Princeton, Washington, Maine, m. 31 May 1900, in Stacyville, Penobscot, Maine, **Marvin Allen**. Annie died 9 Feb 1904, Stacyville, Penobscot, Maine. Annie died of smallpox.
> viii **Bertha Silence Dudley** b. 3 Mar 1881, Stacyville, Penobscot, Maine, d. 5 Apr 1881, Stacyville, Penobscot, Maine.
> ix **Hattie Belle Dudley** b. 11 May 1882, Stacyville, Penobscot, Maine, m. 16 Feb 1899, in Stacyville, Penobscot, Maine, **Charles Brackett**, b. 29 Sep 1860, Sherman, Penobscot, ME, (son of **Elijah Brackett** and **Cynthia Cummings**). Hattie died 3 Feb 1965, Millinocket, Penobscot, Maine, buried: Stacyville Cemetery, Stacyville, Maine. She was of Plt 2nd Range 6, when married.
> **Charles**: He was of Stacyville, ME when he married.
> x **Alvin Oscar Dudley** b. 4 Sep 1884, Stacyville, Penobscot, Maine, occupation: Maine guide, d. 25 Nov 1911, Stacyville, Penobscot, Maine. He froze to death a

short distance from his home while returning from a hunting trip.

    xi **John Stillman Dudley** b. 11 Sep 1886, Stacyville, Penobscot, Maine.

256. **Bethiah Dudley** (160.Rowland[6], 88.James[5], 43.Francis[4], 14.John[3], 4.John[2], 1.Francis[1]) b. ABT 1847, Maine, m. 1 Jan 1867, in Princeton, Washington, Maine, **Orris Moore Wellman**, b. 1 Nov 1836, Searsmont, Washington, ME, d. 29 Feb 1912, Calais, Washington, Maine. Bethiah died ABT 1871, Maine.

Orris: He married (3) Joan Fisher b 17 Apr 1862, Perry, ME. Yes, he married Dudley sisters.

    Children:

    i **Henry Orris Wellman** b. 5 May 1868, Garland, Washington, Maine, d. AFT 1918. Living in 1918. No issue [Wellman Genealogy].

    ii **Mary Wellman** b. 1871, Princeton, Washington, Maine, d. 1871, Princeton, Washington, Maine.

257. **John T. Dudley** (162.James[6], 88.James[5], 43.Francis[4], 14.John[3], 4.John[2], 1.Francis[1]) b. 26 Jun 1845, Lincoln, Penobscot, Maine, m. INT 9 APR 1870, in Lincoln, Penobscot, Maine, **Luzetta Nute**. John died AFT 1896. A 1905 Penobscot County deed indicates that John T. and Lusette Dudley had removed to Cumberland county, Maine by 1905.

Luzetta: Marriage intention: she was "of Lincoln, ME"

    Children:

    i **Ruth G. Dudley** b. ABT Jan 1876, Lincoln, Penobscot, Maine, d. 12 May 1876, Lincoln, Penobscot, Maine, buried: South Lincoln Cemetery, Lincoln, ME.

    ii **John Dudley** b. 20 Jan 1879, Lincoln, Penobscot, Maine, d. 7 Mar 1879, Lincoln, Penobscot, Maine, buried: South Lincoln Cemetery, Lincoln, ME.

258. **Silence H. Dudley** (163.Charles[6], 88.James[5], 43.Francis[4], 14.John[3], 4.John[2], 1.Francis[1]) b. ABT 1841, Mattawamkeag, Penobscot, ME, m. (1) 26 Nov 1861, in Mattawamkeag, Penobscot, ME, **Charles H. Dill**, b. 16 Jul 1830, Maine, (son of **John Dill** and **Rebecca W. Hinckley**) d. 18 Oct 1878, Sherman Mills, Aroostook, ME, m. (2) **Fred Hunt**. Silence died 25 May 1916, Sherman Mills, Aroostook, ME, buried: Sherman Corner Cemetery, Sherman, ME. The marriage intention was filed 18 Nov 1861 in Mattawamkeag, Maine.

    Children by Charles H. Dill:

308.   i **Ira B. Dill** b. 12 May 1862.

    ii **William A. Dill** b. ABT 1866, Maine.

    iii **Rosa E. Dill** b. 19 Apr 1868, Sherman, Aroostook, ME, m. 11 Apr 1885, in Sherman, Aroostook, ME, **Clarence R. Peavy**.

    iv **Sylance B. Dill** b. 6 Jul 1872, Sherman, Aroostook, ME.

    v **Charles Dill** b. ABT 1875.

259. **Mary E. Dudley** (163.Charles[6], 88.James[5], 43.Francis[4], 14.John[3], 4.John[2], 1.Francis[1]) b. ABT 1842, Maine, m. **Robert (?) Stacy**. After marrying Mr. Stacy, they removed to Stockton, California. Mary E. Stacy of Stockton, CA was informant for data on Ira Beane Dudley's death certificate, Merced, California

   Children:
   - i **Mary E. Stacy** b. ABT 1867.
   - ii **Albert Stacy** b. ABT 1869.

260. **Ira B. Dudley** (163.Charles[6], 88.James[5], 43.Francis[4], 14.John[3], 4.John[2], 1.Francis[1]) b. 10 Oct 1845, Mattawamkeag, Penobscot, ME, occupation: bricklayer, m. (1) 2 Apr 1868, in Sherman, Aroostook, ME, **Mary A. Davidson**, b. ABT 1846, Maine, m. (2) **Sophia _____**. Ira died 22 Dec 1916, Merced, Merced, CA, buried: IOOF Cemetery, Merced, CA. Ira moved to California about 1881. His death certificate noted he was a resident of California for 38 years and at current residence in Mercd for six years. Apparently he married twice, as "Sophia" is noted as his wife on his death certificate.
   Sophia: She is noted as wife on Ira's death certificate.

   Children by Mary A. Davidson:
   - i **infant son Dudley** b. 11 Jun 1869, Bangor, Penobscot, Maine, d. 14 Jul 1869, Bangor, Penobscot, Maine, buried: Mt. Hope Cemetery, Bangor, ME. Burial record Lot V-B:d Bangor, ME, age 1 mo, 3 da, son of Ira B & Mary Dudley

261. **James Hunter Dudley** (163.Charles[6], 88.James[5], 43.Francis[4], 14.John[3], 4.John[2], 1.Francis[1]) b. 29 Jan 1849, Mattawamkeag, Penobscot, ME, m. (1) 14 Dec 1864, in Bangor, Penobscot, Maine, **Elizabeth Ann "Annie" Roundy**, b. 25 Nov 1847, Bangor, Penobscot, Maine, (daughter of **Joshua (Rev.) P. Roundy** and **Elizabeth A. Sibley**) d. 25 Feb 1885, Passadumkeag, Penobscot, Maine, m. (2) 2 Oct 1886, in Passadumkeag, Penobscot, Maine, **Cora Annie Richardson**, b. 28 Jan 1872, Burlington, Penobscot, ME, d. 3 Jun 1956, Passadumkeag, Penobscot, Maine. James died 22 May 1909, Passadumkeag, Penobscot, Maine. Family tradition says that at least 2 additional children of his first marriage died in infancy. He died of pneumonia nad tuberculosis.
   Elizabeth: Died of diphtheria. -
   Cora: USC 1900 Passadumkeag, 20 Jun 1900, p. 141: b Jan 1872, age 28, m. 14 yrs, b ME. On gravestone: DUDLEY, Cora A June 3 1956 ae 84 yrs 4 m 6 dys.

   Children by Elizabeth Ann "Annie" Roundy:
   - i **infant dau** b. 14 Jun 1865, Bangor, Penobscot, Maine, d. 5 Jul 1865, Bangor, Penobscot, Maine, buried: 5 Jul 1865, Mt. Hope Cemetery, Bangor, ME.
   - ii **Lewis R. Dudley** b. 22 Feb 1868, Maine, d. 15 Sep 1884, Passadumkeag, Penobscot, Maine. Lewis died of diphtheria.
   - 309. iii **James E. Dudley** b. 13 Aug 1869.
   - iv **Charles H. Dudley** b. ABT Apr 1871, Bangor, Penobscot, Maine, d. 10 Mar

1872, Bangor, Penobscot, Maine, buried: 13 Mar 1872, Mt. Hope Cemetery, Bangor, ME.

    v   **Eliza Dudley** b. ABT 1875, Stacyville?, Penobscot, ME.

    vi **Annie E. Dudley** b. ABT 1877, Stacyville, Penobscot, Maine.

310.   vii **Emma Louise Dudley** b. 29 Jan 1881.

    viii **Lacey Dudley** b. 6 Jan 1884, Passadumkeag, Penobscot, Maine, d. 18 Jun 1904, West Enfield, Penobscot, ME. Lacey died by drowning.

Children by Cora Annie Richardson:

311.   ix **Bertha Edna Dudley** b. 10 Jun 1887.

312.   x   **Ira Beane Dudley** b. 21 Jan 1889.

313.   xi **Gertrude May Dudley** b. 9 Dec 1891.

    xii **Jessie Abigail Dudley** b. 25 Dec 1893, Passadumkeag, Penobscot, Maine, m. 22 Oct 1917, in Passadumkeag, Penobscot, Maine, **Levi Randall Day**, b. 14 Oct 1882, Mattawamkeag, Penobscot, ME, (son of **James Day** and **Miranda Kelley**) d. 1 Dec 1942, Passadumkeag, Penobscot, Maine, buried: Goulds Ridge Cemetery, Passadumkeag, ME. Jessie died 23 Dec 1970, Sunderland, Franklin, Mass., buried: Goulds Ridge Cemetery, Passadumkeag, ME. Jessie died of pneumonia and cancer. No issue.

           Levi: Drowned in Passadumkeag Stream, went through the ice, while tending his traps. He was a musician, and played the piano and violin.

314.   xiii **Meryl Everett Dudley** b. 2 Mar 1897.

315.   xiv **Cora Annie Dudley** b. 4 Apr 1900.

316.   xv **Lacey Harry Dudley** b. 20 Apr 1903.

262. Hannah H. Dudley (163.Charles[6], 88.James[5], 43.Francis[4], 14.John[3], 4.John[2], 1.Francis[1]) b. ABT 1850, East Indian Township, Penobscot, ME, m. **Elijah Brackett**.
    Children:

317.   i **Frederick A. Brackett** b. 1 Oct 1867.

263. Charles H. Dudley (163.Charles[6], 88.James[5], 43.Francis[4], 14.John[3], 4.John[2], 1.Francis[1]) b. 11 May 1852, Winn?, Penobscot, ME, occupation: lumberman, m. 10 Aug 1879, in Sherman, Aroostook, ME, **Ruth E. Darling**, b. 1859, d. 1947, Old Town, Penobscot, Maine, buried: Forest Hill Cemetery, Old Town, Maine. Charles died 13 Oct 1900, Old Town, Penobscot, Maine, buried: Forest Hill Cemetery, Old Town, Maine. Both he and wife were "of Stacyville, [Penobscot] ME" when married.
    Children:

    i **Harry B. Dudley** b. 1894, d. 1933, Old Town, Penobscot, ME?, buried: Forest Hill Cemetery, Old Town, Maine.

264. Abigail (Eliza?) Dudley (163.Charles[6], 88.James[5], 43.Francis[4], 14.John[3], 4.John[2], 1.Francis[1]) b. 20 Jul 1859, Mattawamkeag, Penobscot, ME, m. 27 Mar 1879, in

Sherman, Aroostook, ME, **Charles Elroy Morrill**, b. 17 Sep 1849, Howland, Penobscot, Maine, d. 17 Jul 1910, Stacyville, Penobscot, Maine, buried: Dudley Cemetery, Stacyville, ME. Abigail died 30 Jun 1916, Bangor, Penobscot, Maine, buried: Dudley Cemetery, Stacyville, ME. Abigail is "Eliza", age 1 in the 1860 census, but "Abigail", age 11 in the 1870 Census. She is "Abby F. Dudley" on her marriage record. I
Charles: He was of Passadumkeag, ME.

> *Children:*
>
> i **Grace Morrill** b. 1880, occupation: school teacher, d. 24 Sep 1901, Maine, buried: Dudley Cemetery, Stacyville, ME. Died of consumption.
> ii **Harriet Z. Morrill** b. ABT 1882, Stacyville, Penobscot, Maine, m. 30 Jul 1912, in Stacyville, Penobscot, Maine, **Durwood E. McGrath**.
> **Durwood**: Marriage record: of Stacyville, ME.
> iii **Myrtle Elaine Morrill** b. 26 Jul 1884, Maine.
> iv **Louis E. Morrill** b. 10 May 1888, Maine.
> v **Daffa Morrill** b. 15 May 1891, Maine.

265. **Lavina Dudley** (172.Asa⁶, 93.Stephen⁵, 45.Stephen⁴, 15.Samuel³, 6.Samuel², 1.Francis¹) m. **Norman Titus**, d. abt 1890. Lavina died 29 Mar 1881, Hannibal, N.Y.
Norman: Was from Hannibal, N.Y.

> *Children:*
>
> i **Celia Titus** m. **Robert Roges**. Had 2 children in Chicago.
> ii **Stephen Titus** m. **Irene Lezilere**.
> iii **Sadie Titus** m. **Dr. Boyd**.
> iv **Dudley Titus**. Died 12 years old.
> v **Robert Titus**. Died 13 years old.

266. **Caroline Dudley** (172.Asa⁶, 93.Stephen⁵, 45.Stephen⁴, 15.Samuel³, 6.Samuel², 1.Francis¹) m. (1) **Henry Moore**, m. (2) **Dr Rice**. Caroline died 1862. Caroline had no children by Henry.

> *Children by Dr Rice:*
>
> i **Jessie Rice**.
> ii **Carrie Rice**.
> iii **Frank Rice**. Died young.

267. **Elmina Dudley** (173.Sardis⁶, 93.Stephen⁵, 45.Stephen⁴, 15.Samuel³, 6.Samuel², 1.Francis¹) b. 23 Nov 1817, m. **Freedom Simons**. Elmina and Freedom had 5 children, but records on only the three.

> *Children:*
>
> i **Elma Dudley** b. Sauk Co., Wis. Was a missionary to "Burmah."
> ii **Anstis Dudley** b. Sauk Co., Wis.
> iii **Sardis Dudley** b. Sauk Co., Wis.

268. Isaac Vaughn Dudley (173.Sardis[6], 93.Stephen[5], 45.Stephen[4], 15.Samuel[3], 6.Samuel[2], 1.Francis[1]) b. Dec 1819, m. **Eliza Skelton**. The children were born at Knobnoster, Mo.

Children:

- i **Ellen Dudley** m. **Albert Kent**.
  Albert: Was from Wisconsin.
- ii **Edwin Dudley** m. **Miss Holster**. Lived in California.
- iii **Winter Dudley**. Had a large family in Knobnoster, Mo.
- iv **Belle Dudley**.
- v **Jay Dudley**.

269. Edwin Dudley (173.Sardis[6], 93.Stephen[5], 45.Stephen[4], 15.Samuel[3], 6.Samuel[2], 1.Francis[1]) b. Aug 1822, m. 5 Jun 1845, in Middlefield, Mass., **Caroline Smith**, b. ABT 1822, (daughter of **Asa Smith** and **Sally**). Edwin died 9 Nov 1871, Cato, Cayuga Co., N.Y. The five children were born at Cato, N.Y., but are listed as being from Meridian.

Caroline: The V.R. shows her age at 23 when she was married.

Children:

- i **Oakley Dudley** m. 4 May 1886, **Miss Dick**.
  Miss: Was from Meridian, N.Y.
- ii **Carol Dudley** m. 11 Feb 1885, **Libbie Stephens**. They have 3 children.
  Libbie: From Meridian, N.Y.
- iii **Emma Dudley** m. 24 May 1875, **Frank M. Pascoe**.
- iv **Lafton Dudley** occupation: Artist, m. 14 May 1878, **Cora Foote**.
- v **Stella Dudley** m. **Mr. Nourse**, occupation: Hospital Superintendent.
  Mr.: Worked in Philadelphia.

270. Anstis A. Dudley (173.Sardis[6], 93.Stephen[5], 45.Stephen[4], 15.Samuel[3], 6.Samuel[2], 1.Francis[1]) b. 1827, m. **Carter B. Hickok**.

Children:

- i **Grove Lawrence Hickok** b. 12 Jun 1847, Auburn, N.Y., m. 10 Jun 1878, in Syracuse, N.Y., **Helen Babcock**.
- ii **Eugene Hickok** b. 9 Apr 1849, Auburn, N.Y., m. 25 Mar 1875, in Meridian, N.Y., **Addie Simons**.
- iii **Herbert Hickok** b. 3 Aug 1852, Auburn, N.Y., m. 16 Mar 1877, **Nettie Ramsie**.
- iv **Eddie Hickok** b. 3 Aug 1852, Auburn, N.Y., m. **Alice Lamphire**.
- v **Emily Hickok** b. 1855, Auburn, N.Y. Unmarried.
- vi **Fanny Hickok** b. 18 Aug 1861, Auburn, N.Y., m. 3 Jan 1889, **Fred Miller**.

271. **Betsey A. Dudley** (173.Sardis[6], 93.Stephen[5], 45.Stephen[4], 15.Samuel[3], 6.Samuel[2], 1.Francis[1]) b. 10 Jun 1832, m. **W.H. Eddy**.
> *Children:*
> > i   **Mary Eddy** b. Auburn, N.Y.
> > ii **Carrie Eddy** b. Auburn, N.Y.
> > iii **Maud Eddy** b. Auburn, N.Y.
> > iv **Son Eddy** b. Auburn, N.Y.

272. **Lorenzo Dudley** (174.Lyman[6], 93.Stephen[5], 45.Stephen[4], 15.Samuel[3], 6.Samuel[2], 1.Francis[1]) b. abt 1817. Drowned in the Mississippi River at St. Louis.
> *Children:*
> > i   **Helen Dudley** m. **Wilson Dodge**.
> > **Wilson**: Was from Cleveland.

273. **Mary Ann Dudley** (176.Ira[6], 93.Stephen[5], 45.Stephen[4], 15.Samuel[3], 6.Samuel[2], 1.Francis[1]) b. 3 Jun 1823, m. 7 Oct 1841, **James B. Curtis**, occupation: Farmer.
> *Children:*
> > i   **Francis R. Curtis** b. 13 Feb 1848. Died young.
> > ii **Angie E. Curtis** b. 24 Jun 1849, d. 19 Feb 1874.
> > iii **Herbert A. Curtis**.
> > iv **James D. Curtis**.
> > v   **Carrie Curtis**.
> > vi **Willie L. Curtis**.

274. **Angeline A. Dudley** (176.Ira[6], 93.Stephen[5], 45.Stephen[4], 15.Samuel[3], 6.Samuel[2], 1.Francis[1]) b. 25 Feb 1825, m. 15 Aug 1844, **Robert Fullerton**, occupation: Merchant.
> *Children:*
> > i   **Walter Byron Fullerton** b. 11 Aug 1857.

275. **Emily Z. Dudley** (176.Ira[6], 93.Stephen[5], 45.Stephen[4], 15.Samuel[3], 6.Samuel[2], 1.Francis[1]) b. 23 Mar 1830, m. 18 Sep 1850, **L.M. Webb**.
> *Children:*
> > i   **Luella J. Webb**.
> > ii **Herbert J. Webb**.
> > iii **George A. Webb**.

276. **Judson H. Dudley** (176.Ira[6], 93.Stephen[5], 45.Stephen[4], 15.Samuel[3], 6.Samuel[2], 1.Francis[1]) b. 8 Apr 1832, m. 6 Jan 1857, **C.C. Bates**. Lived in St. Charles, N.Y.

Children:
    i **Lena S. Dudley.**
    ii **Bates Dudley** d. 1866, Oswego, N.Y.

277. **George P. Dudley** (176.Ira[6], 93.Stephen[5], 45.Stephen[4], 15.Samuel[3], 6.Samuel[2], 1.Francis[1]) b. 16 Apr 1838, m. 21 Mar 1861, **Emma J. Lawrence**. Moved to Garo, Park Co., Colorado.
        Children:
        i **Corinne Louise Dudley** b. 18 Sep 1862, m. 15 Jul 1880, **Louis Guiraud**. No children as of 1884.
318.   ii **Georgia Belle Dudley** b. 6 Jan 1864.
        iii **Son** b. 25 May 1869. Died in infancy.
        iv **Margaret Elizabeth Dudley** b. 1 May 1871.

278. **Myra A. Dudley** (178.Stephen[6], 93.Stephen[5], 45.Stephen[4], 15.Samuel[3], 6.Samuel[2], 1.Francis[1]) b. Oct 1828, Hannibal, N.Y., m. 1848, **J.D. Cooke**. Myra died 1862, California.
J.D.: Was from Sturgis, Mich.
        Children:
        i **J.F. Cooke.**
        ii **R.W. Cooke.**

279. **Jonathan Merritt Dudley** (178.Stephen[6], 93.Stephen[5], 45.Stephen[4], 15.Samuel[3], 6.Samuel[2], 1.Francis[1]) b. 7 Sep 1830, Hannibal, N.Y., occupation: Senator, m. 24 Nov 1857, in Dixon, California, **Elizabeth F. Dixon**. Jonathan died California. Twice elected to California Legislature and served in 1862 and 1863. Was a delegate to the constitutional convention that made the California Constitution. Was elected to state senate in 1883.
        Children:
        i **Lucy J. Dudley** b. 19 Aug 1858, Dixon, California, m. 2 Jul 1882, in Dixon, California, **James Campbell**. Lucy and James lived in Seattle.
           James: Was from Seattle, Washington.
319.   ii **Earl Delmar Dudley** b. 13 Jun 1860.
320.   iii **Frederick Merritt Dudley** b. 28 Oct 1861.
        iv **George D. Dudley** b. 1 Aug 1867, Dixon, California.
        v **Elizabeth Dudley** b. 26 Apr 1873, Dixon, California.

280. **Myron Samuel Dudley** (184.Stephen[6], 95.Peter[5], 45.Stephen[4], 15.Samuel[3], 6.Samuel[2], 1.Francis[1]) b. 20 Feb 1837, Peru, Bennington, Vt., occupation: Minister/Soldier, m. (1) 21 Aug 1873, **Martha Maria Hale**, (daughter of **Mordecai Hale** and **Jane Harvey**) d. 20 Jul 1876, m. (2) 26 Apr 1882, **Sarah Denman Todd**,

(daughter of **Rev John Todd** and **Mary Collins Brace**) d. 26 Oct 1884, m. (3) 14 Sep 1892, **Mary Elizabeth Marrett**, (daughter of **Avery Marrett** and **Elizabeth Bancroft Weston**). Myron died 17 Nov 1905, Newington, New Hampshire. Rose through the ranks to Captain in the Civil War. Wounded at the Battle of the Wilderness. At the end of the war went to Seminary and became a minister. After the death of his two wives, and no children, he never again married. He published a number of things, and was noted for his untiring efforts both in the ministry and in civil affairs. Myron was a member of the New Hampshire Genealogical Society.

Sarah: Sarah died of pneumonia

> *Children by Martha Maria Hale:*
>
> i **Daughter** b. Jul 1874, d. 1875.

281. **Edgar Swartwout Dudley** (187.James[6], 95.Peter[5], 45.Stephen[4], 15.Samuel[3], 6.Samuel[2], 1.Francis[1]) b. 14 Jun 1845, occupation: Soldier, m. 23 Jun 1870, **Mary Stewart**. Was a soldier since the Civil War, holding many positions. Was professor at the University of Nebraska, and organized the Military Science and Tactics, and the rest of the Military department there. Later rejoined his Artillery Battery, to which he was originally assigned. Later studied law, and was admitted to the N.Y. Bar. He was a Freemason, and was a Grand Commander of the Knights Templar for 1887/88 in Nebraska, and was a 33rd Degree.

> *Children:*
>
> i **Edgar Stewart Dudley** b. 17 Aug 1871.

282. **Edwin Augustus Dudley** (206.Jonathan[6], 104.Jonathan[5], 48.Jonathan[4], 18.Jonathan[3], 6.Samuel[2], 1.Francis[1]) b. 22 Jun 1827, Sutton, Worcester, Mass., m. 9 May 1849, **Elizabeth P. Howard**.

> *Children:*
>
> i **Ella Frances Dudley** b. 21 Dec 1852.
> ii **Emma Elizabeth Dudley** b. 6 Feb 1854.

283. **George Jason Dudley** (208.Jason[6], 104.Jonathan[5], 48.Jonathan[4], 18.Jonathan[3], 6.Samuel[2], 1.Francis[1]) b. 17 Feb 1849, Sutton, Worcester, Mass., m. **Jennie P Daniels**.

> *Children:*
>
> i **Frederick Albert Dudley** b. 5 Jan 1874.
> ii **Edith Louella Dudley** b. 2 May 1876.

284. **John Leonard Dudley** (211.James[6], 106.John[5], 49.John[4], 18.Jonathan[3], 6.Samuel[2], 1.Francis[1]) b. 20 Aug 1837, Wilkinsonville, Sutton, Mass., occupation: Merchant, m. **Frances E. Carpenter**, (daughter of **Cyrus Carpenter** and **Rebecca King**).

Children:
   i **Sarah Louisa Dudley** b. 22 Mar 1874.
   ii **John L. Dudley** b. 22 Oct 1881.

285. **Edward Dudley** (213.Silas[6], 107.Joseph[5], 49.John[4], 18.Jonathan[3], 6.Samuel[2],
   1.Francis[1]) b. 15 Dec 1829, Sutton, Worcester, Mass., m. 6 Jun 1854, **Mary M Ellis**, b.
   Mendon, Worcester, Mass.
      Children:
321.   i **Charlotte Armsby Dudley** b. 12 Jul 1855.
322.   ii **Silas Armsby Dudley** b. 5 Jul 1857.

286. **Henry Tyler Dudley** (216.David[6], 108.Pheobe[5], 50.Peter[4], 18.Jonathan[3],
   6.Samuel[2], 1.Francis[1]) b. 27 Apr 1841, Sutton, Worcester, Mass., m. **Lucina H
   Chace**, b. 7 Oct 1840, Millbury, Worcester, Mass., (daughter of **Silas Chace**) d. 30 Jun
   1890, buried: Wilkinsonville Cemetery, Sutton, Mass.
   Lucina: Name is also spelled CHASE.
      Children:
323.   i   **Nettie Dudley** b. 13 Feb 1859.
         ii **Beulah Dudley** b. ABT 1861, d. 9 Dec 1867. Wilkinsonville Cemetery
             inscription says "aged 6 yrs."
         iii **Lucy Gertrude Dudley** b. 14 Aug 1869.

287. **Anna Lauretta Dudley** (218.Joseph[6], 113.Amasa[5], 51.David[4], 21.Rogers[3],
   6.Samuel[2], 1.Francis[1]) b. 5 Jan 1844, m. 6 Apr 1869, in New York, N.Y., **Clarence
   Edgar Oakley**.
      Children:
         i   **Grace K. Oakley** b. 7 Nov 1870, Hudson City, N.J., d. 21 Oct 1871, New
             York, N.Y.
         ii **Egbert Simmons Oakley** b. 13 Oct 1872, New York, N.Y.
         iii **Frances Blair Oakley** b. 12 Nov 1875, Buffalo, Minn.
         iv **Walter Dudley Oakley** b. 13 Sep 1878, Buffalo, Minn.
         v   **Clara Lauretta Oakley** b. 12 Nov 1883, Buffalo, N.Y.

288. **Charles Virgil Dudley** (218.Joseph[6], 113.Amasa[5], 51.David[4], 21.Rogers[3],
   6.Samuel[2], 1.Francis[1]) b. 2 Sep 1852, Rome, NY, m. 19 Sep 1878, in Whitinsville,
   Worcester, Mass., **Eliza A. Pollock**.
      Children:
         i   **Frances Orleana Dudley** b. 10 Jul 1880, Northbridge, Worcester, Mass.
         ii **Eliza Pollock Dudley** b. 17 Jul 1883, Northbridge, Worcester, Mass.
         iii **Gladys Dudley** b. 18 Aug 1886, Northbridge, Worcester, Mass.

289. **William Blair Dudley** (218.Joseph[6], 113.Amasa[5], 51.David[4], 21.Rogers[3], 6.Samuel[2], 1.Francis[1]) b. 25 Nov 1857, Brooklyn, New York, m. 7 Oct 1884, in New York, N.Y., **Ellie Weeks Roberts**, d. 23 Dec 1890, New York, N.Y.
>> *Children:*
>> i **Virgil Roberts Dudley** b. 20 Jun 1887, New York, N.Y.

290. **Henry Merchant Dudley** (219.Paul[6], 113.Amasa[5], 51.David[4], 21.Rogers[3], 6.Samuel[2], 1.Francis[1]) b. 12 Aug 1846, Uxbridge, Worcester, Mass., occupation: Druggist, m. 6 May 1873, **Hattie L. Reed.** Graduated Yale Scientific School in 1868. Lived in Woonsocket, R.I.
>> *Children:*
>> i **Edith Dudley** b. 27 Oct 1875.
>> ii **Paul Whitin Dudley** b. 19 Jul 1877, d. 3 Oct 1877.
>> iii **Lena Weston Dudley** b. 11 Dec 1880.
>> iv **Carl Chester Dudley** b. 12 Jan 1886.

291. **Emma Dudley** (222.George[6], 116.David[5], 53.Paul[4], 23.William[3], 6.Samuel[2], 1.Francis[1]) b. 2 Jul 1846, Cincinnati, Ohio, m. 1 Jul 1873, **D.B. Miller**.
>> *Children:*
>> i **Dudley Breed Miller** b. 16 Jul 1874, Covington, Ky.
>> ii **Hugh Miller** b. 8 Mar 1876, Covington, Ky.
>> iii **Irving Miller** b. 16 Oct 1878, Covington, Ky.
>> iv **Mabel Miller** b. 23 Oct 1880, Covington, Ky., d. Mar 1883, Oxmoor, Ala.

292. **George Hiram Dudley** (222.George[6], 116.David[5], 53.Paul[4], 23.William[3], 6.Samuel[2], 1.Francis[1]) b. 29 Dec 1849, m. 24 Jun 1885, in Florence, Ala., **Sydenham O'Neil**.
>> *Children:*
>> i **Mary Olivia Dudley** b. Mar 1887, Montgomery, Alabama.

293. **Kate Dudley** (222.George[6], 116.David[5], 53.Paul[4], 23.William[3], 6.Samuel[2], 1.Francis[1]) b. 12 Nov 1851, Covington, Ky., m. 8 Jun 1880, in Covington, Ky., **Edward A. Bradley**.
>> *Children:*
>> i **Kate Dudley Bradley** b. 13 Oct 1883, Covington, Ky.
>> ii **Child** b. 4 Feb 1887, Covington, Ky., d. 4 Feb 1887.
>> iii **Edward Chase Bradley** b. 10 Aug 1888, Covington, Ky.

294. **Arthur James Dudley** (224.James[6], 117.John[5], 53.Paul[4], 23.William[3], 6.Samuel[2], 1.Francis[1]) b. 7 May 1839, Douglas, Worcester, Mass., m. 12 Nov 1861, **Christina Sarah Hill**, b. 28 Jun 1838, (daughter of **Aaron M. Hill**).

Children:
   i   **Walter John Hill Dudley** b. 23 Aug 1862.
   ii **Guilford Chauncey Dudley** b. 5 Mar 1864.
   iii **Robert Arthur Dudley** b. 23 Feb 1867.
   iv **L. Eliza Dudley** b. 7 Mar 1870.
   v   **Ralph Edward Dudley** b. 20 Apr 1876.

295. **William Aldrich Dudley** (226.Charles[6], 118.William[5], 53.Paul[4], 23.William[3], 6.Samuel[2], 1.Francis[1]) b. 7 Dec 1847, m. 19 Nov 1872, **Jennie L. Church.**
Graduated Amherst College.
      Children:
   i   **Charles E. Dudley** b. 30 Aug 1873, Providence, Rhode Island.
   ii   **Annie J. Dudley** b. 6 Feb 1875, Providence, Rhode Island.
   iii **William C. Dudley** b. 12 Jul 1876, Providence, Rhode Island.
   iv   **Frank C. Dudley** b. 29 Aug 1877, Providence, Rhode Island.
   v   **John A. Dudley** b. 12 Sep 1879, Providence, Rhode Island, d. 2 Nov 1879, Providence, Rhode Island.
   vi   **Clara L. Dudley** b. 16 Jan 1881, Providence, Rhode Island, d. 6 Feb 1884, Providence, Rhode Island.
   vii **Walter W. Dudley** b. 24 Mar 1885, Providence, Rhode Island.
   viii **Henry A. Dudley** b. 2 Oct 1886, Marlborough, Middlesex, Mass.

296. **Annie W. Dudley** (226.Charles[6], 118.William[5], 53.Paul[4], 23.William[3], 6.Samuel[2], 1.Francis[1]) b. 25 Sep 1849, m. 31 Oct 1883, **John E. Cummings.**
      Children:
   i   **Clara Dudley Cummings** b. 3 Dec 1886, Providence, Rhode Island.

297. **Gustavus Harrison Dudley** (229.William[6], 122.William[5], 54.Lemuel[4], 23.William[3], 6.Samuel[2], 1.Francis[1]) b. 29 Oct 1855, Douglas, Worcester, Mass., m. (1) 27 May 1879, **Adelle S White**, m. (2) 31 Mar 1887, in Douglas, Worcester, Mass., **Lucy Jane Dudley**, b. 22 Oct 1866, Douglas, Worcester, Mass., (daughter of **Silas P Dudley** and **Julie Ann White**) d. 4 Jul 1936, Douglas, Worcester, Mass., buried: Douglas Center Cemetery, Douglas, Mass. Gustavus died 19 Mar 1925, Douglas, Worcester, Mass., buried: Douglas Center Cemetery, Douglas, Mass. I originally had a death date of 1928, but his gravestone says "1855-1925."
Lucy: Gravestone records confirm dates.
      Children by Adelle S White:
   i   **Everett Justin Dudley** b. 3 Jul 1879, Mansfield, CT, d. 16 Mar 1885.
      Children by Lucy Jane Dudley:
   ii **Myrtice M. Leonard Dudley** b. 1885, d. 1889, Douglas, Worcester, Mass., buried: Douglas Center Cemetery, Douglas, Mass.

324. iii **William Harrison Dudley** b. 4 Aug 1888.

iv **Mabel M. Dudley** b. 1900, Douglas, Worcester, Mass., d. 1910, Douglas, Worcester, Mass., buried: Douglas Center Cemetery, Douglas, Mass.

298. **Charles Dudley** (230.Silas[6], 122.William[5], 54.Lemuel[4], 23.William[3], 6.Samuel[2], 1.Francis[1]) b. 19 Jun 1858, Douglas, Worcester, Mass., m. 5 Apr 1879, in Webster, Worcester, Mass., **Frances Leonard**, b. 2 May 1858, Sutton, Worcester, Mass., d. 3 Aug 1935, Oxford, Worcester, Mass. Charles died 9 May 1934, Webster, Worcester, Mass.

Children:

i **Roseltha Ann Dudley** b. 25 Sep 1880, Douglas, Worcester, Mass., m. 17 Oct 1900, **Lester Converse**. Roseltha died 8 Feb 1960.

ii **Lucy Jane Dudley** b. 12 Jul 1881, Douglas, Worcester, Mass., m. 16 Mar 1903, **John Hamilton**. Lucy died abt Feb 1962.

iii **Edith Emma Dudley** b. ABT. 1883, Douglas, Worcester, Mass., m. 4 May 1903, **Merrill Eccleston**, b. 21 Feb 1874, Southbridge, Worcester, Mass., d. 9 Mar 1946, Norwich, CT.

iv **Ralph H Dudley** b. ABT. 1885, Douglas, Worcester, Mass., m. **Mary Coker**.

325. v **Elmer E Dudley** b. 18 Oct 1887.

299. **Ida May Dudley** (230.Silas[6], 122.William[5], 54.Lemuel[4], 23.William[3], 6.Samuel[2], 1.Francis[1]) b. 15 Aug 1864, Douglas, Worcester, Mass., m. 17 Dec 1882, **Charles E Place**, b. 1863, d. 1915, Burrillville, RI. Ida died 9 May 1904, Burrillville, RI.

Children:

i **Nellis Place** b. 24 Aug 1896, m. **Fred Jones**.

ii **Florence Place**.

iii **Charles Henry Place** b. 25 Apr 1898, m. **Kathleen Agnes McDermott**. Charles died 27 Nov 1945.

300. **Lucy Jane Dudley** (230.Silas[6], 122.William[5], 54.Lemuel[4], 23.William[3], 6.Samuel[2], 1.Francis[1]) (See marriage to number 297.)

301. **Sarah Anne Dudley** (232.Hannah[6], 126.Persis[5], 60.Robert[4], 25.Douglassa[3], 6.Samuel[2], 1.Francis[1]) b. 7 Jun 1853, Webster, Worcester, Mass., m. **Fenner Thornton**, b. 1847. Sarah died 1878-1880, Webster, Worcester, Mass.

Children:

i **Florence Eden Madella Thornton** b. 14 Apr 1876, Webster, Worcester, Mass., m. 29 Nov 1893, in Webster, Worcester, Mass., **Clifford M Wilson**, b. 1870.

302. **Charles Eaton Dudley** (246.George[7], 151.William[6], 80.Ebenezer[5], 36.Ebenezer[4], 11.Benjamin[3], 3.Joseph[2], 1.Francis[1]) b. 11 Jul 1863, South Boston, Suffolk, Mass., m. **Lilla Ricker**, b. 1875.

> *Children:*

326.   i   **Lillian Ethel Dudley** b. 2 Jan 1897.

303. **Elbridge H. Dudley** (248.Aaron[7], 157.Aaron[6], 85.Nathan[5], 40.Peter[4], 14.John[3], 4.John[2], 1.Francis[1]) b. 26 Apr 1844, m. 20 Jul 1871, **Angie F. Heaton**.

> *Children:*

  i   **Elbridge C. Dudley** b. 29 Nov 1872.

304. **George S. Dudley** (249.Samuel[7], 157.Aaron[6], 85.Nathan[5], 40.Peter[4], 14.John[3], 4.John[2], 1.Francis[1]) b. 20 Jan 1839, Shutesbury, Franklin, Mass., m. 30 Mar 1863, **Jane E. Moore**, b. 4 Jan 1840, North Leverett, Hampshire, Mass.

> *Children:*

  i   **George S. Dudley**.
 ii   **James H. Dudley**.

305. **Emily Oretta Dudley** (255.Mark[7], 160.Rowland[6], 88.James[5], 43.Francis[4], 14.John[3], 4.John[2], 1.Francis[1]) b. 19 Mar 1871, Wesley, Washington, Maine, m. 15 Sep 1889, in Stacyville, Penobscot, Maine, **Frederick A. Brackett**, b. 1 Oct 1867, Stacyville, Penobscot, Maine, (son of **Elijah Brackett** and **Hannah H. Dudley**). Emily died 1922, Stacyville, Penobscot, Maine.

> *Children:*

  i   **Carrie Hannah Brackett** b. 11 Nov 1890, Stacyville, Penobscot, Maine, m. 17 Apr 1912, in Charlotte co, NB, **Clifton Winfield Fenlason**, b. 28 Oct 1889, Crawford, Washington, Maine, (son of **Winfield Sawyer Fenlason** and **Lillian Marita Allen**) d. 17 Jun 1963, Cumberland, Maine. Carrie died BEF 1960, Maine.

327. ii   **Rosemund Evelyn Brackett** b. 3 Mar 1893.

 iii   **Maurice Elmer Brackett** b. 3 Jun 1895, Stacyville, Penobscot, Maine, m. (1) 8 Aug 1920, in Howland, Penobscot, Maine, **Viola V. Madden**, m. (2) 2 Dec 1946, in Stacyville, Penobscot, Maine, **Violette L. Hayes**. Maurice died 19 Dec 1966, Island Falls, Aroostook, ME. He was of Howland, ME when married the 1st time; of Stacyville, ME the 2nd. His given name is also found as "Morris." **Violette**: marriage record: of Howland, ME.

  iv   **Edward "Eddie" Darcey Brackett** b. 3 Mar 1900, Stacyville, Penobscot, Maine, m. 20 Aug 1925, in Stacyville?, Penobscot, ME, **Beatrice Cullen**. Edward died Jul 1967. His marriage record lists him as Eddie Brackett.

Beatrice: In the marriage record: of Plt No 2, R6.

    v **Jenny Charlotte Brackett** b. 10 Oct 1903, Stacyville, Penobscot, Maine.

306. **Mark Leroy Dudley** (255.Mark[7], 160.Rowland[6], 88.James[5], 43.Francis[4], 14.John[3], 4.John[2], 1.Francis[1]) b. 4 Jun 1873, Wesley, Washington, Maine, m. (1) 5 Dec 1901, in Stacyville, Penobscot, Maine, divorced, **Bertha S. Dill**, b. ABT 1885, Penobscot County, Maine, (daughter of **Ira B. Dill** and **Martha S. Peavy**) m. (2) 29 Aug 1927, in Mount Peak, Mt. Katadin, Maine, **Abbie A. Curtis**. Mark died 14 Jun 1942, Stacyville, Penobscot, Maine. On his gravestone says "Katadin Storyteller."

    Children by Bertha S. Dill:

    i **Grace E. Dudley** b. 5 May 1903, Stacyville, Penobscot, Maine, m. 20 Feb 1919, in Stacyville, Penobscot, Maine, **Arthur Gilbert Seavey**, b. 18 Feb 1895, Stacyville, Penobscot, Maine, (son of **Andrew Johnson Seavey** and **Berthana Florilla Dudley**) d. 24 Feb 1984, Portland, Cumberland, Maine.

    ii **Violet H. Dudley** b. 12 Oct 1905, Stacyville, Penobscot, Maine, d. 23 Oct 1905, Lee, Penobscot, Maine.

    iii **Annie N. Dudley** b. 10 Feb 1906, Stacyville, Penobscot, Maine, m. 20 Oct 1921, in Stacyville, Penobscot, Maine, **Charles E. Curtis**, b. 11 Jul 1899, Maine, d. 8 Feb 1968, Island Falls, Aroostook, ME.

    iv **Leroy Gerald Dudley** b. 4 Jan 1908, Twp No 2, Range 6.

    v _____ **Dudley** b. 3 May 1913, Stacyville, Penobscot, Maine, d. 3 May 1913, Stacyville?, Penobscot, ME. Stillborn.

307. **Berthana Florilla Dudley** (255.Mark[7], 160.Rowland[6], 88.James[5], 43.Francis[4], 14.John[3], 4.John[2], 1.Francis[1]) b. 21 May 1875, Tomah Stream, Princeton, Washington, ME, m. 22 Apr 1894, in North Lincoln, Penobscot, ME, **Andrew Johnson Seavey**, b. 30 Jan 1866, Crawford, Washington, Maine, (son of **Luther Gilbert Seavey** and **Sarah B. ___**). Berthana died 25 May 1902, Montague, Enfield, Penobscot, Maine. Day Genealogy say m. "19 Apr." Marriage record: both of Lincoln, ME.

    Children:

    i **Arthur Gilbert Seavey** b. 18 Feb 1895, Stacyville, Penobscot, Maine, m. 20 Feb 1919, in Stacyville, Penobscot, Maine, **Grace E. Dudley**, b. 5 May 1903, Stacyville, Penobscot, Maine, (daughter of **Mark Leroy Dudley** and **Bertha S. Dill**). Arthur died 24 Feb 1984, Portland, Cumberland, Maine.

308. **Ira B. Dill** (258.Silence[7], 163.Charles[6], 88.James[5], 43.Francis[4], 14.John[3], 4.John[2], 1.Francis[1]) b. 12 May 1862, Sherman, Aroostook, ME, m. 15 Mar 1885, in Sherman, Aroostook, ME, **Martha S. Peavy**.

    Children:

328.   i **Bertha S. Dill** b. ABT 1885.

309. **James E. Dudley** (261.James⁷, 163.Charles⁶, 88.James⁵, 43.Francis⁴,
14.John³, 4.John², 1.Francis¹) b. 13 Aug 1869, Penobscot County, Maine, m. 24 Dec
1892, in Passadumkeag, Penobscot, Maine, **Sarah "Sadie" Sibley**. James died 28 Nov
1905, Passadumkeag, Penobscot, Maine.
Children:
  i **Lewis E. Dudley** b. 9 Oct 1893, Passadumkeag, Penobscot, Maine, d. 14 Jul
     1909, Passadumkeag, Penobscot, Maine. Died of tuberculosis
  ii **Everett Dudley** b. 25 Jan 1893, Passadumkeag, Penobscot, Maine, d. 1916,
     Passadumkeag, Penobscot, Maine. Died by falling into the waterwheel at the
     power house.
 iii **Donald David Dudley** b. 20 Jan 1900, Passadumkeag, Penobscot, Maine, d. 15
     Jun 1917, Passadumkeag, Penobscot, Maine. Died of diphtheria.
  iv **Cecil Earl Dudley** b. 1 Apr 1904, Passadumkeag, Penobscot, Maine.

310. **Emma Louise Dudley** (261.James⁷, 163.Charles⁶, 88.James⁵, 43.Francis⁴,
14.John³, 4.John², 1.Francis¹) b. 29 Jan 1881, Maine, m. 22 Jul 1899, in Milo,
Piscataquis, Maine, **Fred Albert Mayo**, b. 29 Aug 1880, Maine, d. 23 Nov 1957, Milo,
Piscataquis, Maine. Emma died 27 Apr 1946, Milo, Piscataquis, Maine.
Children:
  i **Blanch May Mayo** b. 4 Mar 1900, Milo, Piscataquis, Maine.
  ii **George R. Mayo** b. ABT Mar 1902, d. 4 Jul 1902, Milo, Piscataquis, Maine,
     buried: Evergreen Cemetery, Milo, ME. Grave record, Evergreen Cemetery,
     Milo, ME: d July 4 1902 4m
 iii **Fred Albert Mayo** b. 6 Mar 1903, Milo, Piscataquis, Maine.
  iv **Edward Mayo** b. 15 May 1905, Milo, Piscataquis, Maine.
   v **Gertrude Marion Mayo**.
  vi **Madelene Eleanor Mayo** m. 17 May 1945, in Milo, Piscataquis, Maine, **Carl
     F. Davis**.
 vii **Iris Evelyn Mayo** m. 25 Sep 1937, in Milo, Piscataquis, Maine, **Kenneth D.
     Davis**.
viii **Florence Mayo** b. 1 Jun 1906, Milo, Piscataquis, Maine. ? m. Stanley Bridges
     5/9/1926, she of Guilford, he of Sangerville.
  ix **Annie Emma Mayo** b. 25 Feb 1908, Milo, Piscataquis, Maine.
   x **Elizabeth Louise Mayo** b. 19 Feb 1914, Milo, Piscataquis, Maine, m. 21 Oct
     1932, in Milo, Piscataquis, Maine, **Edson Pineo**.

311. **Bertha Edna Dudley** (261.James⁷, 163.Charles⁶, 88.James⁵, 43.Francis⁴,
14.John³, 4.John², 1.Francis¹) b. 10 Jun 1887, Passadumkeag, Penobscot, Maine, m.
(1) 27 Nov 1909, in Passadumkeag?, Penobscot, ME, divorced, **Oscar Stanchfield**, m. (2)
17 Dec 1913, in Maine, **Ernest J. Roberts**, d. BEF 1931, m. (3) 8 May 1931, in Bar
Harbor, Hancock, ME, **Henry A. Soper**. Bertha died 26 May 1984, Bar Harbor, Hancock,

ME. USC 1900 Passadumkeag, ME. 20 Jun 1900, p. 141: b Jun 1886, age 13.

Ernest: Marriage record: of Bar Harbor, ME

Children by Oscar Stanchfield:

329.   i **Lacey Harry Dudley** b. 20 Apr 1903.

Children by Ernest J. Roberts:

    ii **Fred Leroy Roberts** b. 25 Nov 1914, Passadumkeag, Penobscot, Maine, m. 25 Aug 1934, in Bar Harbor, Hancock, ME, **Helen McFadden Haraden**, b. 20 May 1914, Bar Harbor, Hancock, ME, d. 14 Nov 1996, Bar Harbor, Hancock, ME. Fred died 23 Feb 1999, Bar Harbor, Hancock, ME.

312. **Ira Beane Dudley** (261.James[7], 163.Charles[6], 88.James[5], 43.Francis[4], 14.John[3], 4.John[2], 1.Francis[1]) b. 21 Jan 1889, Passadumkeag, Penobscot, Maine, m. 8 Jul 1922, in Penobscot County, Maine, **Margery R. Tozier**, b. 18 Aug 1884, Mattawamkeag, Penobscot, ME, d. 21 Apr 1937, West Enfield, Penobscot, ME, buried: West Enfield Cemetery, W. Enfield, ME. Ira died Nov 1949, Togus, Jefferson, Lincoln, ME, buried: West Enfield Cemetery, W. Enfield, ME.

Margery: She was of W. Enfield, ME when married.

Children:

    i **Ruth Tozier Dudley** b. 5 Oct 1925, West Enfield, Penobscot, ME, m. 22 Aug 1944, in Perth, Canada, **John Edward Barry**.

    ii **Phyllis Nina Dudley** b. 27 Jun 1927, Enfield, Penobscot, ME, m. (1) 9 Jul 1949, in Enfield, Penobscot, ME, **Richard Graham**, m. (2) **Maurice Perry**. Marriage record: Phyllis "M." Dudley, of Enfield, ME.

313. **Gertrude May Dudley** (261.James[7], 163.Charles[6], 88.James[5], 43.Francis[4], 14.John[3], 4.John[2], 1.Francis[1]) b. 9 Dec 1891, Passadumkeag, Penobscot, Maine, m. 27 Dec 1909, in Passadumkeag?, Penobscot, ME, **Jason Edward "Eddie" Raymond**. Gertrude died Oct 1917, Brewer, Penobscot, Maine.

Jason: In the marriage record: of Greenville, ME.

Children:

    i **Florence A. Raymond** b. 7 Apr 1910, Maine, m. 24 Sep 1937, in Hancock County, Maine, **George B. Scammon**, b. 1 Jun 1903, occupation: railroad worker, d. 13 Dec 1984, Passadumkeag, Penobscot, Maine. Florence died 7 Mar 1970, Bangor, Penobscot, Maine.

    ii **Victor D. Raymond** b. 24 Feb 1913, Maine, d. 27 Aug 1989, South Portland, Cumberland, ME.

    iii **Howard Raymond** m. **Mabel** _____.

    iv **James E. Raymond** m. 5 Dec 1936, in Penobscot County, Maine, **Gladys Runnells**. Marriage record: of Passadumkeag, Maine.

        Gladys: Marriage record: of Howland, Maine.

314. **Meryl Everett Dudley** (261.James[7], 163.Charles[6], 88.James[5], 43.Francis[4], 14.John[3], 4.John[2], 1.Francis[1]) b. 2 Mar 1897, Passadumkeag, Penobscot, Maine, m. **Mayme Estelle Tozier**, b. 17 Aug 1894, Passadumkeag, Penobscot, Maine, d. 6 May 1984, Enfield, Penobscot, ME, buried: West Enfield, Penobscot, ME. Meryl died 4 Nov 1985, Lincoln, Penobscot, Maine, buried: West Enfield, Penobscot, ME.
Mayme: gravestone: Mayme T Aug 12 1894 - May 6 1984 ME Archives death record: died age 89.

> *Children:*
> i **James T. Dudley** b. 13 Apr 1919, Maine, m. **Sylvia A. _____**, b. 1 Mar 1918, Maine, d. 30 Jan 1986, Bangor, Penobscot, Maine, buried: West Enfield, Penobscot, ME. James died 4 Apr 1996, Augusta, Kennebec, Maine, buried: West Enfield, Penobscot, ME.
> **Sylvia**: gravestone: Sylvia A. Mar 1 1918 - Jan 30 1986
> ii **Gilbert T. Dudley**.
> iii **Marjorie Tozier Dudley**.
> iv **Samuel T. Dudley** b. 8 Dec 1924.
> v **Frances M. Dudley** b. 1929.
> vi **Joy Eileen Dudley**.

315. **Cora Annie Dudley** (261.James[7], 163.Charles[6], 88.James[5], 43.Francis[4], 14.John[3], 4.John[2], 1.Francis[1]) b. 4 Apr 1900, Passadumkeag, Penobscot, Maine, m. 16 Oct 1919, in Bangor, Penobscot, Maine, **Fred Leroy Roberts**, (son of **Edgar Leroy Roberts** and **Susie M. Smith**). Cora died 24 Jan 1929, Bar Harbor, Hancock, ME. She is found in records as "Annie Doris" and "Cora Annie". She died in childbirth.
Fred: Marriage record: of Bar Harbor, Maine.

> *Children:*
> i **Charlotte Roberts**.

316. **Lacey Harry Dudley** (261.James[7], 163.Charles[6], 88.James[5], 43.Francis[4], 14.John[3], 4.John[2], 1.Francis[1]) b. 20 Apr 1903, Passadumkeag, Penobscot, Maine, occupation: various, m. 14 Feb 1925, in Howland, Penobscot, Maine, **Hazel Gertrude Hatch**, b. 28 Mar 1907, Lowell, Middlesex, Mass., (daughter of **Milan Rudolph Hatch** and **Emily Mildred Jones**). Occupation: barber, mill foreman, dairy owner. Adopted by James H. and C. Annie Dudley. Natural son of their daughter Bertha.
Hazel: Living.

> *Children:*
> i **infant son Dudley** d. 1926. stillborn child.
> 330. ii **Leland Pascal Dudley** b. 4 Apr 1928.
> 331. iii **Arlene Dudley** b. 14 Dec 1929.
> 332. iv **Marilyn Dudley** (details excluded).

317. **Frederick A. Brackett** (262.Hannah[7], 163.Charles[6], 88.James[5], 43.Francis[4], 14.John[3], 4.John[2], 1.Francis[1]) (See marriage to number 305.)

318. **Georgia Belle Dudley** (277.George[7], 176.Ira[6], 93.Stephen[5], 45.Stephen[4], 15.Samuel[3], 6.Samuel[2], 1.Francis[1]) b. 6 Jan 1864, m. 26 Mar 1885, **Harold Chalmers**. Georgia died 20 Jun 1886.
    Children:
    i **Belle Ellen Chalmers** b. 21 May 1886.

319. **Earl Delmar Dudley** (279.Jonathan[7], 178.Stephen[6], 93.Stephen[5], 45.Stephen[4], 15.Samuel[3], 6.Samuel[2], 1.Francis[1]) b. 13 Jun 1860, Dixon, California. It is unknown why his wife's name is not recorded.
    Children:
    i **Son** occupation: Farmer. This unnamed son was a farmer in Willows, Colusa County, California.

320. **Frederick Merritt Dudley** (279.Jonathan[7], 178.Stephen[6], 93.Stephen[5], 45.Stephen[4], 15.Samuel[3], 6.Samuel[2], 1.Francis[1]) b. 28 Oct 1861, Dixon, California.
    Children:
    i **Son** occupation: Lawyer. This unnamed son was a lawyer in St. Paul, Minn.

321. **Charlotte Armsby Dudley** (285.Edward[7], 213.Silas[6], 107.Joseph[5], 49.John[4], 18.Jonathan[3], 6.Samuel[2], 1.Francis[1]) b. 12 Jul 1855, m. 16 May 1876, **Erwin Augustus Snow**.
    Children:
    i **Florence Edith Snow** b. 19 Jan 1878, m. 27 Jun 1900, **Albert C Rhodes**.
    ii **Frederick Augustus Snow** b. 22 Sep 1883.
    iii **Rose Elizabeth Snow** b. 25 Jun 1887.
    iv **Mabel Dudley Snow** b. 16 Jul 1888.
    v **Charlotte Armsby Snow** b. 4 Jul 1892.

322. **Silas Armsby Dudley** (285.Edward[7], 213.Silas[6], 107.Joseph[5], 49.John[4], 18.Jonathan[3], 6.Samuel[2], 1.Francis[1]) b. 5 Jul 1857, m. (1) 15 Jul 1888, **Ella F Prentice**, d. 13 Feb 1892, m. (2) 28 Aug 1895, **Carrie Van Cott Jordan**.
    Children by Carrie Van Cott Jordan:
    i **Ruth Marguerite Dudley** b. 6 Oct 1898.
    ii **Edward Armsby Dudley** b. 22 Jun 1901.
    iii **Charlotte Dudley** b. 19 Dec 1906.

323. **Nettie Dudley** (286.Henry[7], 216.David[6], 108.Pheobe[5], 50.Peter[4], 18.Jonathan[3], 6.Samuel[2], 1.Francis[1]) b. 13 Feb 1859, Sutton, Worcester, Mass., m.

Charles Norcross, b. 13 Aug 1850, Derry, New Hampshire.
　　　　Children:
　　　i　**Annie Norcross** b. abt 1884, d. abt 1885.
　　　ii　**Edith D Norcross** b. ABT. 1885, d. 2 Jun 1892.

324.　**William Harrison Dudley** (297.Gustavus[7], 229.William[6], 122.William[5], 54.Lemuel[4], 23.William[3], 6.Samuel[2], 1.Francis[1]) b. 4 Aug 1888, Douglas, Worcester, Mass., m. (1) 29 Jan 1909, in Douglas, Worcester, Mass., **Clara Estelle Blake**, b. 5 Jun 1888, Burrillville, RI, d. 11 Sep 1963, Douglas, Worcester, Mass., m. (2) ABT. 1946, **Ruth McMahon**, b. 29 Jan 1903, d. ABT. 1970, Douglas, Worcester, Mass. William died 9 Jul 1979, Douglas, Worcester, Mass.
　　　　Children by Clara Estelle Blake:
333.　　i　**Evelyn Elizabeth Dudley** b. 29 Jul 1909.
334.　　ii　**Maud Frances Dudley** b. 7 Dec 1910.
335.　　iii　**Alice Doris Dudley** b. 29 Dec 1912.
336.　　iv　**Gustavus William Dudley** b. 7 Feb 1914.
337.　　v　**Lucy Jane Dudley** b. 12 Nov 1915.
338.　　vi　**Harold Prentice Dudley** b. 6 Feb 1917.
339.　　vii　**Beatrice Irene Dudley** b. 24 Apr 1922.
　　　　Children by Ruth McMahon:
340.　　viii　**Linda Ann Dudley** (details excluded).

325.　**Elmer E Dudley** (298.Charles[7], 230.Silas[6], 122.William[5], 54.Lemuel[4], 23.William[3], 6.Samuel[2], 1.Francis[1]) b. 18 Oct 1887, m. **Mertice Robbins**.
　　　　Children:
341.　　i　**Walter Ellsworth Dudley** b. 2 Mar 1911.
　　　ii　**Berl Irene Dudley** b. 3 Sep 1913.

326. **Lillian Ethel Dudley** (302.Charles[8], 246.George[7], 151.William[6], 80.Ebenezer[5], 36.Ebenezer[4], 11.Benjamin[3], 3.Joseph[2], 1.Francis[1]) b. 2 Jan 1897, Boston, Suffolk, Mass., m. 7 Nov 1914, in Boston, Suffolk, Mass., **Joseph William Curran**, b. 11 Mar 1892, England, occupation: Forman, d. 15 Jan 1969, Brockton, Plymouth, Mass. Lillian died 26 Oct 1971, Milton, Norfolk, Mass.

> *Children:*
> i **Daughter**. Died at birth.
> ii **Lillian Curran** b. 1916, Boston, Suffolk, Mass.
> iii **Edward James Curran** b. 25 Jan 1921, Boston, Suffolk, Mass., d. 28 Dec 1992, Brockton, Plymouth, Mass.
> iv **Eleanor Curran** b. 1924, Boston, Suffolk, Mass.
> v **Joseph Curran** b. 1930, d. Oct 1991, Florida.
> vi **Charles Paul Curran** (details excluded).
> vii **Jean M. Curran** b. 1936, Boston, Suffolk, Mass., d. 1937, Massachusetts.

327. **Rosemund Evelyn Brackett** (305.Emily[8], 255.Mark[7], 160.Rowland[6], 88.James[5], 43.Francis[4], 14.John[3], 4.John[2], 1.Francis[1]) b. 3 Mar 1893, Stacyville, Penobscot, Maine, m. 18 Mar 1911, in Stacyville, Penobscot, Maine, **Wesley Morey McDonough**, b. 20 Mar 1892, Waite, Washington, Maine, (son of **Henry Reuben McDonough** and **Della Olivia Neal**) d. 4 Mar 1975, Calais, Washington, Maine.

> *Children:*
> i **Darrell Frederick McDonough** b. 20 Oct 1912, Stacyville, Penobscot, Maine.

328. **Bertha S. Dill** (308.Ira[8], 258.Silence[7], 163.Charles[6], 88.James[5], 43.Francis[4], 14.John[3], 4.John[2], 1.Francis[1]) (See marriage to number 306.)

329. **Lacey Harry Dudley** (261.James[8], 163.Charles[7], 88.James[6], 43.Francis[5], 14.John[4], 4.John[3], 1.Francis[1]) (See marriage to number 316.)

330. **Leland Pascal Dudley** (329.Lacey[8], 261.James[7], 163.Charles[6], 88.James[5], 43.Francis[4], 14.John[3], 4.John[2], 1.Francis[1]) b. 4 Apr 1928, Howland, Penobscot, Maine, occupation: auto dealer, m. (1) 20 Nov 1949, in Penobscot County, Maine, divorced, **Myrtie Gail York**, b. 15 May 1928, Bangor, Penobscot, Maine, occupation: teacher, m. (2) **Joyce Foster**, (details excluded).

> *Children by Myrtie Gail York:*
> i **Joline Joyce Dudley** (details excluded), m. **David Godfrey**.
> 342. ii **Lee Brent Dudley** (details excluded).
> 343. iii **Leon Kevin Dudley** (details excluded).

331. **Arlene Dudley** (329.Lacey[8], 261.James[7], 163.Charles[6], 88.James[5], 43.Francis[4], 14.John[3], 4.John[2], 1.Francis[1]) b. 14 Dec 1929, Howland, Penobscot, Maine, m. **Willard Stanley Parker**, b. 31 Jan 1927, Providence, RI, (son of **William Parker** and **Florence Foote**).

Children:
- i **Wayne Parker** b. 15 Feb 1953, d. 15 Feb 1953. Stillborn.
- ii **Debra Ann Parker** (details excluded).
- iii **Sheila Ann Parker** (details excluded).
- iv **Michael David Parker** b. 5 Jan 1960, d. 5 Apr 1980. Died in auto accident.

332. **Marilyn Dudley** (329.Lacey[8], 261.James[7], 163.Charles[6], 88.James[5], 43.Francis[4], 14.John[3], 4.John[2], 1.Francis[1]) (details excluded), m. **Orin Delamr Fogg**, b. 13 Jan 1927, South Portland, Cumberland, ME, (son of **Elton Fogg** and **Lulu Campbell**).

Children:
- i **Lisa Fogg** (details excluded).
- ii **Gary Alan Fogg** (details excluded).

333. **Evelyn Elizabeth Dudley** (324.William[8], 297.Gustavus[7], 229.William[6], 122.William[5], 54.Lemuel[4], 23.William[3], 6.Samuel[2], 1.Francis[1]) b. 29 Jul 1909, Douglas, Worcester, Mass., m. 22 Feb 1928, **Valmore Favreau**, b. ABT. 1905, d. ABT. 1957. Evelyn died Oct 1985, Virginia.

Children:
- i **Roger W Favreau** b. 24 Aug 1928, m. **Maybelle Caplet**, (details excluded).
- ii **Eleanor L Favreau** b. 12 Jan 1930, m. 27 Aug 1949, in Douglas, Worcester, Mass., **Paul A Cupka**, b. ABT. 1928.
- iii **Robert D Favreau** b. 23 Apr 1933, m. 1960, **Helen Petrie**. Robert died 1975.
- iv **Deborah E Favreau** (details excluded), m. **Hubert Bentley**, b. 1931, d. 1990.

334. **Maud Frances Dudley** (324.William[8], 297.Gustavus[7], 229.William[6], 122.William[5], 54.Lemuel[4], 23.William[3], 6.Samuel[2], 1.Francis[1]) b. 7 Dec 1910, Douglas, Worcester, Mass., m. 8 Oct 1927, in Douglas, Worcester, Mass., **Earl Ballou**, b. 7 Mar 1905, Douglas, Worcester, Mass., d. 26 Aug 1975, Douglas, Worcester, Mass.

Children:
- i **Edward Ballou** (details excluded).
- ii **Howard Earl Ballou** (details excluded).
- iii **Gary Douglas Ballou** (details excluded), m. **Diane Gaudere**.

335. **Alice Doris Dudley** (324.William[8], 297.Gustavus[7], 229.William[6],

122.William[5], 54.Lemuel[4], 23.William[3], 6.Samuel[2], 1.Francis[1]) b. 29 Dec 1912, Douglas, Worcester, Mass., m. 7 Jan 1933, **Newell Paige Sherman**, b. 26 Apr 1909, Sutton, Worcester, Mass., d. 4 Aug 1936. Alice died 20 Jul 1935, Sutton, Worcester, Mass.

Children:
- i **Janice Mae Sherman** (details excluded).
- ii **Dudley Paige Sherman** (details excluded), m. **Alice Wikinin**.

336. **Gustavus William Dudley** (324.William[8], 297.Gustavus[7], 229.William[6], 122.William[5], 54.Lemuel[4], 23.William[3], 6.Samuel[2], 1.Francis[1]) b. 7 Feb 1914, Douglas, Worcester, Mass., m. **Anna Joyce McCullum**, b. 7 Aug 1911, d. 15 Oct 1997, Holiday, FL.

Children:
- 344.   i **Ronald Wilbur Dudley** (details excluded).
-   ii **Dana Dudley** b. ABT. Apr 1937, Douglas, Worcester, Mass., d. 10 Oct 1937, Douglas, Worcester, Mass.
-   iii **David William Dudley** (details excluded).
- 345.   iv **Marilyn Dudley** (details excluded).

337. **Lucy Jane Dudley** (324.William[8], 297.Gustavus[7], 229.William[6], 122.William[5], 54.Lemuel[4], 23.William[3], 6.Samuel[2], 1.Francis[1]) b. 12 Nov 1915, Douglas, Worcester, Mass., m. 25 Jun 1938, **George Jones**. Lucy died 22 Apr 1997.

Children:
- i **Marcia Mae Jones** (details excluded).
- ii **Peggy Ann Jones** (details excluded).
- iii **Jonathan Jones** (details excluded).

338. **Harold Prentice Dudley** (324.William[8], 297.Gustavus[7], 229.William[6], 122.William[5], 54.Lemuel[4], 23.William[3], 6.Samuel[2], 1.Francis[1]) b. 6 Feb 1917, Douglas, Worcester, Mass., m. 15 Oct 1938, in Berwick, Mass., **Mary Jeannette Zehrer**, b. 21 Nov 1919, New Britain, Ct, d. 5 Dec 1996, Douglas, Worcester, Mass.

Children:
- 346.   i **Patricia Ellen Dudley** (details excluded).
- 347.   ii **Karen Jeannette Dudley** (details excluded).
-   iii **Dan Ellis Dudley** (details excluded).

339. **Beatrice Irene Dudley** (324.William[8], 297.Gustavus[7], 229.William[6], 122.William[5], 54.Lemuel[4], 23.William[3], 6.Samuel[2], 1.Francis[1]) b. 24 Apr 1922, Douglas, Worcester, Mass., m. 22 Jun 1936, in Douglas, Worcester, Mass., **Duty Caswell**. Beatrice died 4 Apr 1984, Florida.

Children:
- i **Duty Caswell** (details excluded), m. **Shirley Benson**, (details excluded).

ii   Sue Ellen Caswell (details excluded), m. Ronald Reardon.

340. **Linda Ann Dudley** (324.William[8], 297.Gustavus[7], 229.William[6], 122.William[5], 54.Lemuel[4], 23.William[3], 6.Samuel[2], 1.Francis[1]) (details excluded), m. **John C O'Neill**, (details excluded).
> *Children:*
> i   **Patricia Ann O'Neill**.
> ii   **Sean O'Neill**.
> iii   **Michael O'Neill**.

341. **Walter Ellsworth Dudley** (325.Elmer[8], 298.Charles[7], 230.Silas[6], 122.William[5], 54.Lemuel[4], 23.William[3], 6.Samuel[2], 1.Francis[1]) b. 2 Mar 1911, m. 1 Oct 1932, **Simone Lefebve**.
> *Children:*
> i   **Walter Elsworth Dudley** (details excluded).

342. **Lee Brent Dudley** (330.Leland[9], 329.Lacey[8], 261.James[7], 163.Charles[6], 88.James[5], 43.Francis[4], 14.John[3], 4.John[2], 1.Francis[1]) (details excluded), m. **Deborah Dunn**, (details excluded).
> *Children:*
> i **Lee Kristopher Dudley** (details excluded).
> ii **Kari Lynn Dudley** (details excluded).

343. **Leon Kevin Dudley** (330.Leland[9], 329.Lacey[8], 261.James[7], 163.Charles[6], 88.James[5], 43.Francis[4], 14.John[3], 4.John[2], 1.Francis[1]) (details excluded), m. (1) **Kathy Tucker**, m. (2) **Ethel Dawn Daniels**.
> *Children by Kathy Tucker:*
> i **Meghan Nicole Dudley**.
> *Children by Ethel Dawn Daniels:*
> ii **Brooke Dudley**.
> iii **Jessica Dudley**.

344. **Ronald Wilbur Dudley** (336.Gustavus[9], 324.William[8], 297.Gustavus[7], 229.William[6], 122.William[5], 54.Lemuel[4], 23.William[3], 6.Samuel[2], 1.Francis[1]) (details excluded), m. **Constance Ann Rawson**, (details excluded).
> *Children:*
> 348.   i **Dan Robert Dudley** (details excluded).
> 349.   ii **Rhonda Ellen Dudley** (details excluded).
> 350.   iii **Natalie Joy Dudley** (details excluded).
>   iv **Mark Nelson Dudley** (details excluded), m. **Betty Lou Ellis**, (details excluded).
> 351.   v **Beth Dudley** (details excluded).
>   vi **Ronald Cory Dudley** (details excluded).

345. **Marilyn Dudley** (336.Gustavus[9], 324.William[8], 297.Gustavus[7], 229.William[6], 122.William[5], 54.Lemuel[4], 23.William[3], 6.Samuel[2], 1.Francis[1]) (details excluded), m. **Lawrence Holland**.
> *Children:*
> i **Lauren Holland**.
> ii **Todd Holland**.

346. **Patricia Ellen Dudley** (338.Harold[9], 324.William[8], 297.Gustavus[7], 229.William[6], 122.William[5], 54.Lemuel[4], 23.William[3], 6.Samuel[2], 1.Francis[1]) (details excluded), m. **Robert Duane Reprecht**.
> *Children:*

    i   **John William Reprecht** (details excluded).

    ii **James Robert Reprecht** (details excluded).

    iii **Keith Allen Reprecht** (details excluded).

347. **Karen Jeannette Dudley** (338.Harold[9], 324.William[8], 297.Gustavus[7], 229.William[6], 122.William[5], 54.Lemuel[4], 23.William[3], 6.Samuel[2], 1.Francis[1]) (details excluded), m. **Jerome Waldo Howard**, (details excluded).

        Children:

    i   **Judith Ann Howard** (details excluded), m. **Alan Richard Lessard**, (details excluded).

348. **Dan Robert Dudley** (344.Ronald[10], 336.Gustavus[9], 324.William[8], 297.Gustavus[7], 229.William[6], 122.William[5], 54.Lemuel[4], 23.William[3], 6.Samuel[2], 1.Francis[1]) (details excluded), m. **Brenda Elaine Pirkle**, (details excluded).

    Children:
- i **Amy Marie Dudley** b. 8 Feb 1983, Atlanta, Ga., d. 28 May 1994, Atlanta, Ga.
- ii **James Benjamin Dudley** (details excluded).
- iii **Hannah Elizabeth Dudley** (details excluded).
- iv **Laura Ruth Dudley** (details excluded).

349. **Rhonda Ellen Dudley** (344.Ronald[10], 336.Gustavus[9], 324.William[8], 297.Gustavus[7], 229.William[6], 122.William[5], 54.Lemuel[4], 23.William[3], 6.Samuel[2], 1.Francis[1]) (details excluded), m. **George Michael Springhart**, (details excluded).

    Children:
- i **Michael Brandon Springhart** (details excluded).
- ii **Elica Suzanne Springhart** (details excluded).
- iii **Nathan Zachary Springhart** (details excluded).
- iv **Aaron Gregory Springhart** (details excluded).
- v **Kyle Marcus Springhart** (details excluded).

350. **Natalie Joy Dudley** (344.Ronald[10], 336.Gustavus[9], 324.William[8], 297.Gustavus[7], 229.William[6], 122.William[5], 54.Lemuel[4], 23.William[3], 6.Samuel[2], 1.Francis[1]) (details excluded), m. **Scott Willard Hilt**, (details excluded).

    Children:
- i **Kimberly Renee Hilt** (details excluded).
- ii **Kristin Breanna Hilt** (details excluded).
- iii **Karise Davita Hilt** (details excluded).
- iv **Kayla Michelle Hilt** (details excluded).
- v **Kiersti Amara Hilt** (details excluded).

351. **Beth Dudley** (344.Ronald[10], 336.Gustavus[9], 324.William[8], 297.Gustavus[7], 229.William[6], 122.William[5], 54.Lemuel[4], 23.William[3], 6.Samuel[2], 1.Francis[1]) (details excluded), m. **Roger Edward Stembridge**, (details excluded).

    Children:
- i **Chad Patrick Stembridge** (details excluded).
- ii **Tyler Gregory Stembridge** (details excluded).

Index

Index

Index

Index

Index

Index

Index

Index

Index

Index

Index

Index

Index

Index

Index

Index

Index

Index

Index

Index

Index

Index

Index

Index

Index

Index

Index

Index

Index

Bibliography

Town Vital Records

Vital records of Acton, Massachusetts to the year 1850. Boston, MA : New England Historic Genealogical Society, 1923.

Vital Records of Alexander, Washington County, Maine. Sharon D. Howland, compiler. Rockport, ME: Picton Press. 1999.

Vital records of Bedford, Massachusetts to the year 1850. Boston, MA : New England Historic Genealogical Society, 1903

Vital records of Beverly, Massachusetts to the end of the year 1849. Topsfield, MA : Topsfield Historical Society, 1906-1907

Vital records of Billerica, Massachusetts to the year 1850. Boston, MA : New England Historic Genealogical Society, 1908

Vital records of Bolton, Massachusetts to the end of the year 1849. Worcester, MA : Franklin P. Rice, 1910

Vital records of Chelmsford, Massachusetts to the end of the year 1849. Salem, MA : Essex Institute, 1914

Concord, Massachusetts births, marriages and deaths, 1635 - 1850. Concord, MA : Printed by the Town, [1891?]

Vital records of Danvers, Massachusetts to the end of the year 1849. 2 vol. Salem, MA : Essex Institute, 1909-1910

Vital records of Douglas, Massachusetts to the end of the year 1849. Worcester, MA : Franklin P. Rice, 1906

Vital records of Dudley, Massachusetts to the end of the year 1849. Worcester, MA : Franklin P. Rice, 1908.

Vital records of Framingham, Massachusetts to the year 1850. Thomas W. Baldwin, comp. Boston : Wright & Potter Printing Company, 1911.

Vital records of Groton, Massachusetts to the end of the year 1849. Salem, MA : Essex Institute, 1926-1927.

Vital records of Hallowell, Maine to the year 1892. Mabel Goodwin Hall, editor. Auburn, ME : Merrill & Webber Co. for the Maine Historical Society, 1924-1929.

Vital records of Hamilton, Massachusetts to the end of the year 1849. Salem, MA : Essex Institute, 1908.

Vital records of Harvard, Massachusetts to the year 1850. Thomas W. Baldwin, comp. Boston : Wright & Potter Printing Company, 1917

Vital records of Hopkinton, Massachusetts to the year 1850. Boston, MA : New England Historic Genealogical Society, 1911.

The birth, marriage and death register, church records and epitaphs of Lancaster, Massachusetts, 1643 - 1850 / edited by Henry S. Nourse. Clinton, MA: W. J. Coulter, printer, 1890.

Vital records of Leicester, Massachusetts to the end of the year 1849. Worcester, MA: Franklin P. Rice, 1903.

Lexington, Mass. record of births, marriages and deaths to January 1, 1898. Boston: Wright & Potter Printing Company, 1898

Vital records of Lincoln, Massachusetts to the year 1850. Boston, MA : New England Historic Genealogical Society, 1908

Records of Littleton, Massachusetts.. Concord, MA : Patriot Press, 1900.

Vital records of Lynn, Massachusetts to the year 1849, Vol 2, Marriages and Deaths. The Essex Institute, publishers, Newcomb and Gaus, printers. 1906.

Vital records of Marlborough, Massachusetts to the end of the year 1849. Worcester, MA : Franklin P. Rice, 1908.

Vital records of Mendon, Massachusetts to the year 1850. Boston, MA: Wright & Potter Printing Company, 1920.

Vital records of Millbury, Massachusetts to the end of the year 1849. Worcester, MA : Franklin P. Rice, 1903.

Vital records of Natick, Massachusetts to the year 1850 / compiled by Thomas W. Baldwin. Bowie, MD : Heritage Books, 1991.

Vital records of Oxford, Massachusetts to the end of the year 1849. Worcester, MA : Franklin P. Rice, 1905

Vital records of Petersham, Massachusetts to the end of the year 1849. Worcester, MA : Franklin P. Rice, 1904

Vital records of Roxbury, Massachusetts to the end of the year 1849 2 vol. Salem, MA : Essex Institute, 1925-1926

Vital records of Royalston, Massachusetts to the end of the year 1849. Worcester, MA : Franklin P. Rice, 1906.

Scarborough, Maine Vital Records from Town Reports 1892-1944. Thomas Henley, comp. Maine : T.S. Henley and S.J. Bentley, 1999.

Vital records of Sherborn, Massachusetts to the year 1850. Thomas W. Baldwin, comp. Boston, MA : Stanhope Press, F.H. Gilson Company, 1911.

Vital records of Shrewsbury, Massachusetts to the end of the year 1849. Worcester, MA : Franklin P. Rice, 1904.

Vital records of Southborough, Massachusetts to the end of the year 1849. Worcester, MA : Franklin P. Rice, 1903

Vital records of Sudbury, Massachusetts to the year 1850. Boston, MA : New England Historic Genealogical Society, 1903

Vital records of Sutton, Massachusetts to the end of the year 1849. Worcester, MA : Franklin P. Rice, 1907

Watertown Records, comprising the Third Book of Town Proceedings and the Second Book of Births, Marriages and Deaths to the End of 1737. Vol. 2. Watertown, Mass.: Press of Fred G. Barker.

Vital records of Wayland, Massachusetts to the year 1850. Boston, MA : New England Historic Genealogical Society, 1910.

Vital Records of Wenham, Massachusetts to the end of the year 1849. Salem, MA:Essex Institute. 1904.

Vital records of Westborough, Massachusetts to the end of the year 1849. Worcester, MA : Franklin P. Rice, 1903.

Vital records of Westford, Massachusetts to the end of the year 1849. Salem, MA : Essex

Institute, 1915.

Town of Weston : births, deaths and marriages, 1707 - 1850; 1703, gravestones, 1900; church records, 1709 - 1825. Boston:McIndoe Bros., 1901.

Vital Records of Winslow, Maine to the year 1892: births, marriages and deaths. Sara Drummund Lang, editor. Auburn : Merrill & Webber Co. for Maine Historical Society, 1937.

Miscellaneous Books

Annals of Oxford, Maine. King, Marquis Fayette. Portland, ME : Marquis Fayette King, 1903.

Ashes to Ashes, Dust to Dust : the cemetery and burial records of the past and present in the town of Westmoreland, New Hampshire. Cemeteries committee of the Westmoreland Historical Society. Westmoreland, NH : Cemeteries Committee of the Westmoreland Historical Society, 1989.

Boston Births, Baptisms, Marriages, and Deaths 1630-1699, and Boston Births 1700-1800 William S. Appleton, ed., Genealogical Publishing Co.,1978,

Colonial Gravestone Inscriptions in the State of New Hampshire.

Dudley, Dean, The History of the Dudley Family, 12 Vols, 1894 Higgenson Books reprint 1992.

---, Supplement to the History of the Dudley Family, 1898 Higgenson Books reprint 1992.

Day Genealogy. Day Family Genealogical Committee, compilers. Boston, Mass: The Warren Press, 1916

Earliest Records of Machias, Maine 1767-1827, pub by Mrs. Beulah Jackson, Concord, NH, no date.

Early Connecticut Marriages, Bailey, Frederick W. ed. Genealogical Publishing Co., Inc, Baltimore MD, 1968

History of the Town of Exeter, New Hampshire. Bell, Charles H. First published at Exeter, Heritage Books Reprint 1990.

History of Paris, Maine Lapham, William Berry and Silas P. Maxim. Paris, ME : [s.n.], 1884.

History of Waterford, Oxford County, Maine. Warren, Henry P., Rev. William Warren and

Samuel Warren. Portland : Hoyt, Fogg & Donham. 1879.

History of the Kimball Family in America. Morrison, Leonard A. & Stephen A. Sharples. Boston: Damrell & Upham. 1897.

History of Westmoreland (Great Meadow), New Hampshire 1741-1970: and genealogical data. Published by the Westmoreland History Committee. Westmoreland History Committee.1976.

History of Woodstock, with family sketches; and an appendix. Lapham, William Berry. Portland : Stephen Berry, 1882.

Marriage Returns of Oxford County, Maine prior to 1892. Rev.Donald McAllister and Lucille Naas, editors. Maine Genealogical SocietySpecial Pub No 16. 1993

Massachusetts Soldiers and Sailors of the Revolutionary War. A compilation from the archives, prepared and published by the Secretary of the Commonwealth in accordance with chapter 100, resolves of 1891. Boston, Wright and Potter Printing Co., State Printers, 1896-1908.

Our Town, Our People. Horne, Hope Braley. Winslow, H. B. Horne: Decorah, Iowa : Anundsen Publishing Co.1991.

Vassalboro Cemetery Records, Vassalboro, Maine compiled 1957/58, verified 1994 by J. Rowe, R. Smith & B. Taylor. Bound typescript on file at Maine State Library. No date.

Descendants of Thomas Wellman of Lynn, Massachusetts, Wellman, Rev. Joshua W., Boston, Mass.: Arthur Holbrook Wellman. 1918

www.ingramcontent.com/pod-product-compliance
Lightning Source LLC
Chambersburg PA
CBHW080613270326
41928CB00016B/3040